Newton Bromshold

WELLINGBOROUGH
RUSHDEN • Irchester
• Gt Doddington • Wollaston
• Wilby • Strixton
Mears • Ashby • Bozeat
Ashby • Grendon • Easton Maudit
• Earls Barton • Cogenhoe Castle
Whiston • Brafield-on-the-Green
• Overstone • Denton • Yardley Hastings
• Sywell • Weston Favell • Hackleton
• Pitsford Gt • Ecton • Piddington
Moulton • Billing • Quinton
• Boughton Kingsthorpe
• Harlestone NORTHAMPTON Hardingstone
• Church Brampton Lit Houghton • Hartwell
• Holdenby Dallington • Wootton • Grafton Regis
Brockhall Nobottle • Duston Gt Houghton • Collingtree • Yardley Gobion
• Muscott Harpole Upton • Milton • Roade • Furtho
• Whilton Upper • Rothersthorpe • Blisworth Stoke • Ashton • Potterspury • Cosgrove
Heyford • Gayton Bruerne • Old Stratford
Brixworth Nether Heyford Tiffield • Easton Neston • Alderton Deanshanger
• Holcot Stowe • Bugbrooke Greens • Grafton Regis Paulerspury • Wicken
Hollowell Nine Churches Norton • TOWCESTER • Whittlebury
Creaton Farthingstone Cold • Blakesley Woodend • Silverstone R Ouse
• Coton • Spratton Litchborough Higham Slapton • Abthorpe • Syresham
Ravensthorpe • Everdon Maidford Adstone • Bradden Wappenham • Whitfield
E Haddon • Preston Capes Canons • Weedon Helmdon
• Long Buckby Althorp Woodford Ashby Lois • Sulgrave Whittlebury
West Haddon Flore • Fawsley Morton • Greatworth Radstone
Crick Norton Weedon Bec Pinkney • Culworth • Thanford • Brackley
• Kilsby Welton DAVENTRY Eydon • Chipping Warden • Evenley
Barby Dodford Newnham • Aston le Walls Westhorpe • Charlton
Ashby St Ledgers Badby Byfield Hinton • Edgcote Middleton Hinton-in-the-Hedges • Croughton
Braunston Woodford Halse Thorpe Mandeville Cheney • Newbottle • Aynho
Staverton • Hinton Upper Boddington Chacombe • Warkworth • King's Sutton
Catesby • Fawsley Lower Boddington Overthorpe • Farthinghoe • Charlton
Hellidon • Charwelton • Steane

Grand Union Canal

R Ouse

N

0 5 10
Miles

THE MAKING OF THE ENGLISH LANDSCAPE

THE NORTHAMPTONSHIRE LANDSCAPE

THE MAKING OF THE ENGLISH LANDSCAPE
Edited by W. G. Hoskins

The Northamptonshire Landscape

Northamptonshire and the
Soke of Peterborough

by

JOHN STEANE

HODDER AND STOUGHTON
LONDON SYDNEY AUCKLAND TORONTO

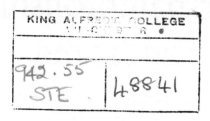

To Nina, without whom this book
would never have been written

Preface

MY FIRST GLIMMERINGS of an interest in the history of the landscape came from the friendship shown to my brother and me by the Rev. D. H. Poole, F.S.A., in the 1940s; he encouraged us to accumulate records of medieval churches in the Home Counties. This was powerfully reinforced in my case by participation in W. G. Hoskins' 1952 Oxford seminar in landscape history, given while he was Reader in Economic History at All Souls. His gentle urging of my generation of undergraduates studying history to put on our boots and tramp the fields and hedgerows (after due preparation in the libraries!) to search out the origins of the landscape, made an ineffaceable impression on me. I owe much to successive generations of boys at Alsop High School, Liverpool, King George V School, Southport, and at Kettering Grammar School, who have shared with me a zest for fieldwork and archaeological excavation. In particular I should like to thank Robert Carr, Brian Dix, Roger Walker, Peter Crane and Robert Croft, successive boy Chairmen of the Kettering Grammar School Local History and Archaeological Society, who have shown unflagging interest in many of the subjects covered in this book. The field observations and excavations undertaken by their Society have made a valuable contribution to the recording of the county's fast-vanishing legacy of archaeological sites.

My debt to three of the more ancient of the county's historians will become apparent. John Morton's *Natural History of Northamptonshire* published in 1712 is full of interest for the historical topographer. John Bridges started collecting material for his projected *History* in 1719: he died in 1724. His material was edited and published in 1791 by the Rev. Peter Whalley (see *Northants, Past and*

7

Present, Vol. IV, 5, 1970/1, pp. 287–91). G. T. Baker's
History (2 vols, 1822–41) covered the south of the county.

The *Victoria County History* (4 vols., 1902–37) has so far
dealt with the north-east part of the county from a line
south of Northampton to the Soke of Peterborough. The
Northamptonshire Record Society by publishing a series of
texts relating to the history of the county and an annual and
very readable journal, *Northamptonshire Past and Present,* has
contributed notably. Since 1965 the annual *Bulletin of the
Federation of Northamptonshire Archaeological Societies* has kept
abreast with current excavations and fieldwork.

I have been treated with patience and courtesy by farmers,
farmworkers and landowners and in particular have
benefited from valuable conversations with Earl Spencer of
Althorp, Mr E. J. Acott of Greens Norton, Mr and Mrs R.
Brassington of Lowick, Mr and Mrs J. Eady of Pytchley,
Mr C. T. L. Hakewill of Braybrooke, Mr J. Harker of Little
Oakley, Mr and Mrs J. C. E. Bevin of Welford, Mr J. K.
Royston, Agent to the Buccleuch estates, Mr V. Vinson,
Agent to the Gloucester estates, and Dr Max Hooper of the
Monks Wood Nature Conservancy Station. The area round
Blisworth has become familiar to me through several
unforgettable walks in the company of George Freeston.
Mr J. M. Greaves provided valuable information on sand
and gravel extraction.

A number of friends have been kind enough to read
various chapters in typescript and in particular Tony Brown
of the University of Leicester, Brian Dix of London
University Institute of Archaeology, Dr Edmund King of
Sheffield University, Patrick King, County Archivist, Sir
Gyles Isham of Lamport and David Woodhall, County
Planning Officer, have all helped in this way. I owe much to
the doyen of Northampton historians, Victor A. Hatley; I
have benefited from his observant eye and meticulous
scholarship, I have enjoyed the generous loan of books and
papers from his capacious library and I have learned much

from his unsurpassed knowledge of the town of Northampton in the later centuries.

I should like to record my gratitude to the staffs of the libraries of the Borough of Northampton (particularly the local collection), the Bodleian, Cambridge University, and the Society of Antiquaries. I have received much help from the records in the Archaeological Office of the Ordnance Survey, Southampton, and from the Borough Museum, Northampton. I am particularly indebted to Mr P. I. King and his staff at the Northamptonshire County Record Office and to Mr J. S. Burden, Librarian of Kettering, for making books so readily available and for treating my frequent demands with forbearance and efficiency.

Next I should like to thank Mrs J. H. Izod for typing the manuscript, Mrs C. J. Phillips and Mrs C. T. H. Perkins for helping to type the final revisions, my mother who accompanied me on expeditions in search of archaeological data at the Ordnance Survey Office, Southampton, and who read the proofs, my daughter Catherine who helped with the maps and indexing, and my wife, Nina, who has suffered the deluge of papers, books, boys, maps and mud with unfailing patience over the years.

Finally my thanks are due to the general editor, William G. Hoskins, the progenitor of the subject, whose wisdom, good judgment, kindness and constant encouragement have made the writing of this book a pleasure.

Kettering   J. M. STEANE
Northamptonshire

Contents

Contents

List of plates

List of plates

14

ACKNOWLEDGMENTS

The author wishes to thank the following for permission to use their photographs:

The Committee for Aerial Photography, Cambridge: Plates 1, 4, 9, 11, 16, 17, 19, 20, 21, 30 (Photographs by J. K. St Joseph, Cambridge University Collection, copyright reserved)

The Trustees of the British Museum: Plates 2, 8, 22, 23, 24, 25, 26, 27

D. A. Jackson: Plate 3

The National Monuments Record: Plates 5, 7, 13, 15, 32, 34, 35, 38, 44

The Ministry of Defence (Air Force Department): Plates 6, 39, 46 (Crown Copyright reserved)

D. N. Hall: Plate 10

J. Marshall: Plate 12, which is taken from G. T. Baker's *History and Antiquities*, 1825–41; Plates 28 and 29, which are taken by kind permission of His Grace the Duke of Buccleuch from original maps in his collection at Boughton House; and Plates 40 and 41 which are taken from J. C. Bourne's *Drawings of the London–Birmingham Railway*, 1839

M. Barley: Plate 14

Aerofilms Limited: Plate 18

The Architects' Journal: Plate 36

Northampton Reference Library: Plate 37

Northampton Chronicle and Echo: Plate 48 (Photographer, Bob Price)

Plates 31, 33, 42, 43, 45 and 47 are by the author

List of maps and plans

THE HISTORIC BOUNDARIES of Northamptonshire are shown as they were in 1965 before the Soke of Peterborough was removed from the county and handed over to the county of Huntingdon and Peterborough. There are several good historical reasons for continuing to consider the Soke and the City of Peterborough as one with the county of North-amptonshire for a book such as this. It was an integral part of the county in the first thousand years of the shire organisation of the Midlands; Peterborough Abbey was one of the major landowners in the county until the Dissolution; the rivers Nene and Welland which encompass the Soke to the south and north were main routeways into the county from the sixth century to the nineteenth.

List of maps and plans

Editor's Introduction

SOME SIXTEEN YEARS ago I wrote: "Despite the multitude of books about English landscape and scenery, and the flood of topographical books in general, there is not one book which deals with the historical evolution of the landscape as we know it. At the most we may be told that the English landscape is the man-made creation of the seventeenth and eighteenth centuries, which is not even a quarter-truth, for it refers only to country houses and their parks and to the parliamentary enclosures that gave us a good deal of our modern pattern of fields, hedges, and by-roads. It ignores the fact that more than a half of England never underwent this kind of enclosure, but evolved in an entirely different way, and that in some regions the landscape had been virtually completed by the eve of the Black Death. No book exists to describe the manner in which the various landscapes of this country came to assume the shape and appearance they now have, why the hedgebanks and lanes of Devon should be so totally different from those of the Midlands, why there are so many ruined churches in Norfolk or so many lost villages in Lincolnshire, or what history lies behind the winding ditches of the Somerset marshlands, the remote granite farmsteads of Cornwall, and the lonely pastures of upland Northamptonshire.

"There are indeed some good books on the geology that lies behind the English landscape, and these represent perhaps the best kind of writing on the subject we have yet had, for they deal with facts and are not given to the sentimental and formless slush which afflicts so many books concerned only with superficial appearances. But the geologist, good though he may be, is concerned with only one aspect of the subject, and beyond a certain point he is obliged to leave the historian and geographer to continue

and complete it. He explains to us the bones of the landscape, the fundamental structure that gives form and colour
to the scene and produces a certain kind of topography and
natural vegetation. But the flesh that covers the bones, and
the details of the features, are the concern of the historical
geographer, whose task it is to show how man has clothed
the geological skeleton during the comparatively past—
mostly within the last fifteen centuries, though in some
regions much longer than this."

In 1955 I published *The Making of the English Landscape*.
There I claimed that it was a pioneer study, and if only for
that reason it could not supply the answer to every question.
Four books, in a series published between 1954 and 1957,
filled in more detail for the counties of Cornwall, Lancashire,
Gloucestershire, and Leicestershire.

Much has been achieved since I wrote the words I have
quoted. Landscape-history is now taught in some univer-
sities, and has been studied for many parts of England and
Wales in university theses. Numerous articles have been
written and a few books published, such as Alan Harris's
The Rural Landscape of the East Riding 1700–1850 (1961) and
more recently Dorothy Sylvester's *The Rural Landscape of
the Welsh Borderland* (1969).

Special mention should perhaps be made of a number of
landscape-studies in the series of Occasional Papers published by the Department of English Local History at the
University of Leicester. Above all in this series one might
draw attention to *Laughton: a study in the Evolution of the
Wealden Landscape* (1965) as a good example of a microscopic
scrutiny of a single parish, and Margaret Spufford's *A
Cambridgeshire Community* (*Chippenham*) published in the
same year. Another masterly study of a single parish which
should be cited particularly is Harry Thorpe's monograph
entitled *The Lord and the Landscape*, dealing with the Warwickshire Parish of Wormleighton, which also appeared in 1965[1].

[1] *Transactions of the Birmingham Archaeological Society,* Vol. 80, 1965.

Geographers were quicker off the mark than historians in this new field, for it lies on the frontiers of both disciplines. And now botany has been recruited into the field, with the recent development of theories about the dating of hedges from an analysis of their vegetation.

But a vast amount still remains to be discovered about the man-made landscape. Some questions are answered, but new questions continually arise which can only be answered by a microscopic examination of small areas even within a county. My own perspective has enlarged greatly since I published my first book on the subject. I now believe that some features in our landscape today owe their origin to a much more distant past than I had formerly thought possible. I think it highly likely that in some favoured parts of England farming has gone on in an unbroken continuity since the Iron Age, perhaps even since the Bronze Age; and that many of our villages were first settled at the same time. In other words, that underneath our old villages, and underneath the older parts of these villages, there may well be evidence of habitation going back for some two or three thousand years. Conquests only meant in most places a change of landlord for better or for worse, but the farming life went on unbroken, for even conquerors would have starved without its continuous activity. We have so far failed to find this continuity of habitation because sites have been built upon over and over again and have never been wholly cleared and examined by trained archaeologists.

At the other end of the time-scale the field of industrial archaeology has come into being in the last few years, though I touched upon it years ago under the heading of Industrial Landscapes. Still, a vast amount more could now be said about this kind of landscape.

Purists might say that the county is not the proper unit for the study of landscape-history. They would say perhaps that we ought to choose individual and unified regions for such an exercise; but since all counties, however small, contain a wonderful diversity of landscape, each with its own special history, we get, I am sure, a far more appealing book than if we adopted the geographical region as our basis.

The authors of these books are concerned with the ways in which men have cleared the natural woodlands, reclaimed marshland, fen, and moor, created fields out of a wilderness, made lanes, roads, and footpaths, laid out towns, built villages, hamlets, farmhouses, and cottages, created country houses and their parks, dug mines and made canals and railways, in short with everything that has altered the natural landscape. One cannot understand the English landscape and enjoy it to the full, apprehend all its wonderful variety from region to region (often within the space of a few miles), without going back to the history that lies behind it. A commonplace ditch may be the thousand-year-old boundary of a royal manor; a certain hedge-bank may be even more ancient, the boundary of a Celtic estate; a certain deep and winding lane may be the work of twelfth-century peasants, some of whose names may be made known to us if we search diligently enough. To discover these things, we have to go to the documents that are the historian's raw material, and find out what happened to produce these results and when, and precisely how they came about.

But it is not only the documents that are the historian's guide. One cannot write books like these by reading someone else's books, or even by studying records in a muniment room. The English landscape itself, to those who know how to read it aright, is the richest historical record we possess. There are discoveries to be made in it for which no written documents exist, or have ever existed. To write the history of the English landscape requires a combination of documentary research and of fieldwork, of laborious scrambling on foot wherever the trail may lead. The result is a new kind of history which it is hoped will appeal to all those who like to travel intelligently, to get away from the guide-book show-pieces now and then, and to know the reasons behind what they are looking at. There is no part of England, however unpromising it may appear at first sight, that is not full of questions for those who have a sense of the past. So much of England is still unknown and unexplored. Fuller enjoined us nearly three centuries ago:

"Know most of the rooms of thy native country
before thou goest over the threshold thereof.
Especially seeing England presents thee with
so many observables."

These books on The Making of the English Landscape are concerned with the observables of England, and the secret history that lies behind them.

Exeter, 1970   W. G. HOSKINS

1. Prehistoric and Roman landscapes

The natural background. The prehistoric landscape. Roman Northamptonshire

The natural background

CHRISTOPHER SAXTON, the Tudor cartographer, published the first map of the county in 1576. His survey, though mildly inaccurate in some ways, brings out the fundamental physical contrast between the hills of the high country in the west, and the Nene valley in the centre and north-east. He shows a series of pudding-like shapes which represent the uplands and these diminish when the wriggling line which marks the course of the Nene is reached.

Most of these uplands lie over 400 feet above sea level and they stretch from Daventry in a north-east direction, ending near Stamford in Lincolnshire where the river Welland has worn a valley through. The traveller along the M1 motorway is hardly conscious that he is passing across the main watershed of Midland England; perhaps all he notices is a long gradual uphill gradient to the Watford gap. This is not surprising, because the surface of these Northamptonshire uplands is rounded and undulating; the principal underlying strata are the intractable, but not unduly hard, heavy clays of the Middle and Upper Lias, often blanketed by a thick mantle of Boulder Clay. All the sharper features have been smoothed away by the long process of denudation. The landscape is predominantly green, since there is a good deal of permanent pasture, and it is not wildly exciting. The long, level views are criss-crossed by a web of hedgerows with trees, mostly ash, punctuating the field boundaries at intervals. Innumerable spinneys give the wrong impression that the country is well wooded. They are simply the vestigial scraps of a once thick and almost total forest cover. There are few considerable views to be gained because the vantage points are scarce. The highest points are Arbury hill, about 800 feet, Charwelton hill, over 700 feet, and Naseby, over 600 feet. These uplands do not strike the observer as a formidable barrier but from the watershed spring the sources of the Welland, Nene and Ouse whose waters flow ever more slowly and circuitously over the level fen and silt lands to the Wash. In the south the Cherwell rises near Charwelton; its willow-lined course forms the boundary of the shire in its extreme south-west corner as it goes south into Oxfordshire on its way to the Thames. The source of the Avon is found in the uplands near Naseby, on the north-west side of the hill; it trickles west and then flows south-west out into Warwickshire and eventually joins the Severn.

As one drives south of Daventry, and even more notice-ably if one bicycles or walks, one is conscious of being in a much hillier region. Between Daventry and Brackley is the area which might be called 'The Wolds'. Much of the land is again above 400 feet, but here the undulations are sharper and more frequent. The light soils of the Oolite Series, the Upper and Middle Lias predominate, and there is less Boulder Clay. The smaller fields, the network of winding roads and the fact that the villages are spaced at closer intervals, all suggest that the comparatively favourable conditions for cultivation produced a denser settlement pattern already in early medieval times.

The Nene valley occupies the centre of this laurel-leaf-shaped shire and provides its most distinctive feature. Whenever you journey across the county you are never far from the Nene. The name of the river seems to be connected

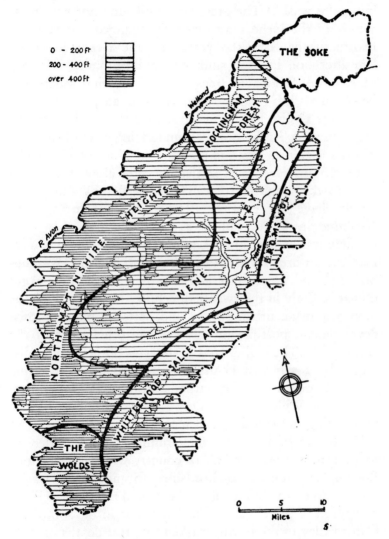

Fig. 1. Northamptonshire: natural regions

with Old English words meaning 'it snows' or 'it rains' or perhaps 'to be brilliant'. Another possibility is that the name means 'to wash'.[1] The grey, rather oily and not very rapid waters of the Nene have evidently changed somewhat in nature in the last 1500 years, but the river seen on a late afternoon in high summer, bank-brimming with the reflection of full-leaved trees in its shimmering waters, can be of surpassing beauty. It has cut a broad valley through the Great Oolite Limestone, the Estuarine Series and the Northampton Sands with their underlying clays of the Lias. These rocks form low and unimpressive hills on either side but they provided ideal settlement sites along the spring lines to the Anglo-Saxons. The alluvial soils and gravel terraces have been continuously occupied and farmed since Neolithic times. The valley was for long a main channel of communication and the occasional bridging points were magnets for urban trade at Peterborough, Oundle, Wellingborough and Northampton from the early Middle Ages onwards. Only in the twentieth century has the ubiquitous motorcar made urban sprawl and, latterly, planned-town development, possible on any scale in other parts of the countryside. The higher land to the west of the Nene is dissected by a series of gentle tributary-valleys such as the Stowe Brook, the Ise, the Harper's Brook, and, past Fotheringhay, the Willow Brook. Between these are spurs of low hills jutting out eastwards.

To the east of the Nene valley, running from Whittlebury to Lutton, is a narrow belt of country which spreads into Buckinghamshire and Bedfordshire, forming a low watershed between the basins of the Nene and the Ouse. This is composed of the Great Oolite Limestone in the south and Oxford Clay in the north, masked by great depths of drift Boulder Clay left by the glaciers of the last Ice Age. It has produced a flattish, rather dull landscape. Here were great tracts of woodland in early historic times; Whittlewood and

[1] E. Ekwall, *English River Names* (Oxford, 1928), pp. 299–300.

Salcey forests on the cold clays about 400 feet above sea level, Yardley Chase and the western part of the forest of Bromswold. Some of the dotard oaks surviving in Salcey date back to Elizabeth I's reign. Salcey forest in the autumn is Northamptonshire's nearest equivalent to the New England Fall. The whole tree-scape glows with fiery reds and oranges for a few weeks in late September and October. Only in one place is there a marked physical division; this is where the river Tove cuts a winding tributary course south-eastwards to the Ouse, and here the Upper Lias Clays are exposed.

North of the Nene lies Rockingham forest. This covered an extensive area from Kettering to Stamford and between Nene and Welland in the early Middle Ages. Settlement was sparse here and agricultural development came late. The complex of Jurassic Limestones and Cornbrash, covered on the higher ground by drift Boulder Clay, produced a heavily wooded region, famous for hunting, and later for timber. Despite the heavy exploitation by open-cast mining of the underlying Northampton ferruginous sandstone, the modern Ordnance Survey maps still record large green patches in this area, indicating a great extent of tree cover.

Farther north again and forming the county boundary with Leicestershire and Rutland between Market Harborough and Stamford is the river Welland. The valley side is more steeply scarped than the Nene, and the heights over-looking it, notably at Rockingham and Gretton, provide some of the few extensive panoramic views which the county has to offer over the watermeadows of the Welland to the green patchwork of fields of Leicestershire.

Turning north-east and going out of the modern administrative area of Northamptonshire into the Soke of Peterborough, the lower Nene valley broadens out as it reaches the fens into a flat, low-lying region. Tremendous sky-scapes only serve to emphasise the monotony of the landscape here:

huge black fields broken by drainage channels, unending grass embankments, long causewayed roads, shelter belts of trees and occasional groups of buildings. Although some fifteen miles away, the long low bulk of Peterborough Cathedral can be seen with a forest of brickwork chimneys etching the horizon of a gun-metal sky to the south.

The prehistoric landscape

It is easy to underestimate the contribution of prehistoric man to the landscape. The total lack of documentary evidence, and the tendency of subsequent occupation to erase most of the physical signs, tend to make the historian of landscape hurry over and belittle in the process the beginnings of man's attempts to control his natural environment. The available archaeological data, often in the form of artifacts found at random and unrelated to occupation sites, such as those mapped religiously by the compilers of the Victoria County History, has recently been splendidly supplemented by the aerial photography of Dr J. K. St Joseph of Cambridge and by a remarkable series taken in recent years by Mr R. Hollowell of Cogenhoe. Controlled excavation has also produced information on burial and occupation sites.

Some hints of the nature of the landscape in Palaeolithic times, at any rate in the Nene valley around Great Billing, have come from an examination of organic silts embedded with the gravels which have yielded the bones of horse, woolly rhinoceros and mammoth. The fossil fauna and flora indicate that the area had small pools colonised by aquatic mosses, sedges and rushes. In the better-drained part of the sand and gravel the vegetation consisted of shrubs, such as dwarf birch and willow, together with various kinds of low-growing perennials. The insect fauna indicated arctic tundra-like conditions with an average annual temperature below 0°Centigrade. A few flint flakes indicated that man was present in these barren conditions.[2] It is unlikely that Palaeolithic man, probably to be numbered in his dozens, made any lasting impression on the landscape. His pear-shaped hand axes, picked up from the Nene gravels, were meant for cutting up animals, not cutting down trees. The geographical distribution of the thirty to forty Neolithic polished stone axes found in Northampton-shire indicates that their owners, settlers whose basic way of life was mixed farming, did not restrict themselves to the uplands, for the find spots occur equally in the valleys of the Nene, the Tove and the fen round Peterborough. Much natural scrub and woodland was cleared by burning and cutting with these efficient axes. Probably the most potent instruments of clearance, however, were the teeth of goats, sheep and cattle; seedlings and saplings chewed by domesti-cated animals inhibited natural regeneration.

The use by Neolithic men of a river-valley site as the focus of religious activities has been shown by recent excavations of a mortuary enclosure at Aldwinkle. The circular ditched site, a quarter-mile to the north of the village of Thornhaugh by Manor Farm, which has a low bank flanked by two ditches, maximum diameter being 275 feet, may be a diminutive version of a henge or sanctuary monument. A possible Neolithic long barrow is on Lymans hill about 100 yards up the lane to the village of Pitsford off the main Northampton road. So far there are few traces of settlement apart from a scatter of flints of varying types in Upton parish near Northampton and the considerable remains in the Nene gravels of the Peterborough area. The discoveries in the Fengate have given the name 'Peter-borough' to one of the main components of the British Neolithic Age. Here commercial excavation for sand and gravel has produced a profuse number of finds in extremely diffuse order on the surface in pits of various shapes and

[2] *Bulletin of the Northants. Federation of Archaeological Societies*, 3 (April 1969), p. 5. (Hereinafter *B.N.F.A.S.*)

31

sizes and by 'cooking holes'. Similarly, west of Orton Longueville park, sherds have come from 'hut sites' which are more likely to be storage pits—found during gravel working before 1932.

This does not amount to much but it does emphasise the attraction that gravels seem to have had for prehistoric man, and it is on the Welland and the Nene gravels that aerial photography has made its most remarkable contributions to our understanding of the prehistoric landscape.[3] The river Welland east of Stamford flows for six miles through a broad spread of gravel which was originally laid down in the form of a great delta in post-glacial times. In the Northamptonshire parishes of Bainton, Barnack, Helpston, Maxey and Northborough are a complex of criss-crossing earthworks, ditches and enclosures. Without extensive excavation it is difficult to disentangle their chronological sequence but it is obvious that we have here a great religious centre, of the late Neolithic and Bronze Age, a sanctuary and cemetery combined. There are two cursuses, those enigmatic earthworks with long parallel banks and ditches which may have been processional ways or may equally have been used for racing or funeral games. The smaller, north of Barnack, has the typical squared end. The Maxey cursus began near the river and thence its straight, narrow, parallel ditches, generally about 200 feet apart, can be traced for 2800 feet to the south-east and then for a further 3000 feet after a slight change of direction. Both cursuses are surrounded by circles, ten at Barnack and over fifty at Maxey. It is likely that these indicate the ditches of a vanished cemetery of Beaker and Bronze Age burial mounds. There is no trace above ground of these structures; their ditches and pits show up as dark organic soil fill against the lighter brown plough soil and, in summer, as crop-marks of darker lusher grass or corn.

[3] Royal Commission on Historical Monuments, *A Matter of Time*, An Archaeological Survey (London, 1961).

The memories of sanctity lingered long: the Norman church of Maxey stands a mile to the west of the present village, solitary on a sacred prehistoric mound; the churchyard in an eighteenth-century watercolour shows up as quite circular. The wind ripples the barley over the huge, unfenced fields lined with the long, grey, squalid sheds of poultry battery farms where 4000 years ago there echoed the cries of Bronze Age mourners.

Northamptonshire is in an area traditionally considered to be devoid of barrows and only about seventy are recorded in the county as compared with over 2000 in Wiltshire. They are usually found on hilltops in other parts of the country but the air-photographs of Mr R. Hollowell show that we should perhaps look for valley-bottom sites for the settlements and burial places of people of the Bronze Age in this area.[4] The recent excavation of two Beaker barrows and a bell barrow of the Wessex culture, found on the flood plain of the river Nene at Earls Barton, backs this up.[5] The whole of the middle and upper Nene valleys are thick with circular-ditched enclosures, many of which are undoubtedly ploughed-flat barrows. The composition of the Earls Barton barrow throws an interesting sidelight on the landscape of the Nene valley at this time, *c.* 1700 B.C. The bell-shaped mound was built of a fine loam soil, contrasting markedly with the thick band of alluvial clay which now covers the underlying gravels of the surrounding flood plain. It is possible that we have a glimpse here of the natural ecology of the Nene valley in the early Bronze Age when it was fertile, well drained and therefore attractive to early farmers. The subsequent climatic deterioration, combined with man's interference with the drainage, produced conditions favouring the deposition of these recent alluvial clays. In recent gravel-quarrying at Aldwinkle near Thrapston, I have seen

[4] R. Hollowell, 'Aerial Photographs and Fieldwork in the Upper Nene Valley', *B.N.F.A.S.*, 6 (1971).
[5] 'The Earls Barton Barrow', *Current Archaeology*, 32 (May 1972), pp. 238–41.

whole trees, blackened and sodden, but perfectly preserved, dating from the Neolithic by association with pottery-filled pits and overlain by six feet of clays and gravels.

Round about 700 B.C. we move into the Pre-Roman Iron Age: a fresh migration of farmers from the continent introduced the so-called *Hallstatt* Iron Age culture into eastern Britain. On the edge of the fenland basin which, owing to a deterioration of the climate causing a rise in sea level, had been made uninhabitable, a gravel spit on the north bank of the river Nene was the site of a farming settlement. Numerous grain-storage pits have been found—many containing Iron Age pottery—and a swan's-neck iron pin and *situla*-shaped pots based on metal prototypes point to an origin for these strangers in the Low Countries.

Approximately two centuries later, *c.* 400 B.C., the iron-using peoples had penetrated into the uplands of the midland region, and Northamptonshire has three examples of the earthworks known as hill forts which still make an important contribution to the landscape. The term 'hill fort' is rather a grandiose term for the oval enclosure of four acres at the highest point of the gently rounded Hunsbury hill overlooking the Nene valley crossing a mile to the south of Northampton. Surrounded by a ditch and rampart, overgrown with eighteenth-century tree plantings, but still a formidable barrier, it was the Iron Age equivalent of a medieval fortified manor house, the home of a petty chieftain or squire, and in the opinion of its recent excavator it never contained more than half a dozen circular dwellings.[6] Even its 300 pits, whose contents were indiscriminately plundered by the iron-ore quarriers of the 1870s and 1880s who stripped out the centre of Hunsbury hill, represent the successive underground storage spaces of no more than fifteen to twenty people over a period of two to three centuries.

[6] Professor R. J. C. Atkinson in 'Hunsbury Hill', a lecture delivered to the Northampton Civic Society, 1968.

Rainsborough camp (Plate 2), a mile south of Charlton, lies higher (480 feet) and is slightly larger—6·25 acres; its double rampart and ditch have suffered somewhat from landscape gardening, the work of Mr Gilkes, *c.* 1772, but recent excavations have shown that it had a long and complex history.[7] At its most impressive stage, in the fifth century B.C., it had an inner rampart of three-tiered wall construction, and this was pierced by an inner entrance with two stone-lined guardhouses set at the end of a sixty-foot wood-lined passageway closed by double gates and a bridge structure over the gates. Despite the fact that its plateau position barely dominates the Cherwell valley and the surrounding area, Rainsborough must in its time and for hundreds of years have been the greatest single change wrought by prehistoric man in the landscape.

Borough hill near Daventry has been even more tampered with; golf balls skim over the turf of its now gently undulating earthworks; its commanding position has been exploited by a forest of television masts and aerials. The north end of the hill is fortified on two sides of the triangle by two ditches and ramparts and on the south side by three. A larger enclosure roughly follows the 600-foot contour and this second addition enclosed an additional sixteen acres.

These three hill forts are all situated near an important prehistoric routeway connecting the north-east and the south-west of Britain; archaeologists refer to this as the 'Jurassic Way'[8] (Fig. 2). It entered the county in the neighbourhood of the bridge at Stamford and probably passed Wakerley, Duddington and Harringworth, keeping to the middle of the slope above the Welland with its favourable drainage conditions. Beyond Gretton it followed the

[7] M. Avery, J. E. G. Sutton, J. W. Banks, 'Rainsborough, Northants., England. Excavations 1961–5', *Proceedings of the Prehistoric Society*, N.S, XXXIII (1967), pp. 207–307.

[8] For the next paragraph see W. F. Grimes on 'The Jurassic Way' in *Aspects of Archaeology in Britain and Beyond*, Essays presented to O. G. S. Crawford, 1951.

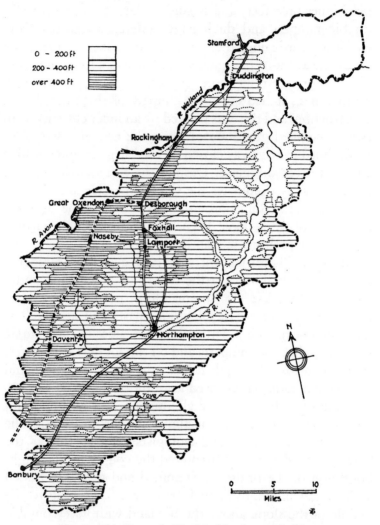

Fig. 2. The 'Jurassic Way' in Northamptonshire

With acknowledgments to W. F. Grimes's map in *Aspects of Archaeology in Britain and Beyond*, Essays presented to O. G. S. Crawford, 1951.

uplands running south-west from Rockingham between the Welland and the Ise. Here the ridge is about 450–500 feet above sea level and the route takes a direct line along the high ground to a mile north of Desborough, where an Iron Age site has yielded one of the finest bronze mirrors in Britain. There are two likely alternatives for the course here; one went through Great Oxendon, Naseby and West Haddon to Daventry, keeping to the high ground; the other crossed the Ise at Newbottle bridge and continued past the Iron Age site at Draughton. Thence there were two routes south. The eastern curved round, avoiding Faxton stream and became the wide, grass-verged, hedge-lined road now beloved of gipsies. Its great age is suggested by the fact that it serves as parish boundaries here for ten miles. It goes across Broughton common, a disused lane choked with vegetation, and strikes the Kettering–Northampton road which was turnpiked in the early nineteenth century. Thence to the Nene crossing where it swings south-west to Hunsbury hill. The other alternative route is through Lamport where it becomes the main Northampton–Market Harborough road through Brixworth. From Hunsbury it covers the twenty-two miles to Banbury keeping to the high ground and thus maintaining commanding views all the way. It then pursues its course south to the Cotswolds and ultimately reaches Somerset.

This routeway went through a landscape already dotted in the Pre-Roman Iron Age with isolated farms found sited on the slopes of ridges and making use of the better-drained soils of the Great Oolite Limestone and the Northampton Sandstone. Such are those recently excavated at Warkton Lane, Kettering, Overstone and Moulton. The stripping of overburden prior to ironstone-quarrying north of the village of Twywell between Kettering and Thrapston revealed an enclosure 138 feet long and 50 feet wide.[9] This was

---

[9] *B.N.F.A.S.*, 4 (1970), pp. 43–44, and a lecture by D. A. Jackson to the Friends of the Kettering Museum and Art Gallery.

presumably a stockyard because the remains of three circular huts were found outside it, but evidently there had been occupation at an earlier stage since both the area enclosed and that outside were riddled with pits. These contained ample evidence of agriculture; bones of dogs and pigs and, most interesting, one was filled with carbonised grain in three layers, one wheat and two barley, representing three seasons of cropping. Doubtless the presence of surface ironstone influenced the choice of site. Much of the country round here has been quarried for ironstone; the fields are now levelled and restored to agriculture, but their slightly sunken surface below the hedgelines bordering the roads and the thorn-filled gullies of the quarry faces betray the fact that fifty feet below the surface the ironstone has been ripped out.

Another small settlement of three circular huts enclosed in a circular ditch was found on an airfield during the 1939–45 war, at Draughton.[10] The huts were surrounded by roof water gullies three feet deep and each had an overflow outlet. Such evidence as ditches and drainage gullies which characterise Pre-Roman Iron Age farmstead sites in the East Midlands point towards a deterioration of the climate as the cool and wet sub-Atlantic phase came in *c.* 600 B.C.

Probably the greatest changes in the landscape in Northamptonshire during the Pre-Roman Iron Age were taking place in the valleys of the Welland and the Nene. On the Welland gravels the process of clearing primeval woodland must have advanced far by the first century B.C. because pollen analysis of the contents of a pit at Tallington five miles east of Stamford has demonstrated the importance of arable agriculture and the consequent open appearance of the countryside. Tree and shrub pollens represented only seven per cent of the total count, grass pollens were nearly

---

[10] W. F. Grimes, 'Some Smaller Settlements, a Symposium', pp. 17–29, in *Problems of the Iron Age in Southern Britain* (no date).

half, forty-seven per cent, and pollens of cereals and weeds of cultivation were relatively high.[11]

In places like Maxey, Lynch Farm, Alwalton, North-borough and Helpston, the complex of intersecting lines of ditches, irregular rounded and rectilinear or trapezoidal enclosures, and boundary works of various kinds, must represent long-established settlements with generations of occupation extending into the Roman period. The most irregular enclosures associated with clustered storage pits date from the Iron Age A settlement. As the Iron Age proceeded the ditch patterns tend to become more rectilinear as farmyard enclosures and paddock boundaries were recut. Long rows of pit alignments show that the density of settlements required clear systems of land division. The pits themselves seem to have been quarries to provide material for a continuous bank. Often they seem to stop for no reason out in the middle of a field but it may well be that this was the limit of cultivation at the time and thence the untamed forest or fen took over. Possibly the boundary continued in the form of a hedge or a bank which would leave no trace as a crop-mark. There are relatively few signs of fields but it cannot be assumed that there were never any considerable groups of 'Celtic' fields in the river gravels. If they were not individually surrounded by ditches their remains are likely to have been utterly obliterated by subsequent intensive agriculture.

Although less archaeological excavation has taken place in the Nene valley, air-photography suggests that settlement was at least as dense in the middle and lower stretches as in the valley of the Welland. Again the pattern of crop-marks suggests a series of isolated farms with enclosures, trackways, grain storage pits and pit alignments. On the northern side of the Nene valley, 300 feet above sea level, at Black-thorn Farm within the Northampton Development area,

[11] C. Thomas (ed.), *Rural Settlement in Roman Britain*, C.B.A. Research Report (London, 1966), Fig. 4, p. 20.

excavations in 1972 revealed concentric ditch systems surrounding a quarter-acre site of a farmstead, possibly the
home of a petty chieftain midway up the scale of the highly
stratified society of the Pre-Roman Iron Age.

By the time that the Romans appeared in the area, in the
middle of the first century A.D., the landscape of Northamptonshire had been continuously occupied, at any rate in
the lowland areas, for many centuries. Some penetration
of the uplands had also occurred and the Jurassic Way
provided wider contacts with the south-west and north-
east.

Roman Northamptonshire

It is possible that the predilection of archaeologists with the
tangible structural remains of the Romano-British period
and the relief of the historian that here they are at last dealing with a literate culture have exaggerated the effects of the
period of four centuries of peace which the Romans imposed
on the Celtic tribes. It is clear that Roman influence on rural
areas was greatly delayed and even by the third century A.D.
only skin deep.

The immediate impact of the conquerors was, however,
prompt and sharp. Invisible under the stubble on the surface, but its ditches clearly delineated when seen from the
air, a fortress of thirty acres built for both auxiliary and
legionary troops has been found recently at Longthorpe
near Peterborough (Plate 1).[12] It was doubtless connected
with the thrust forward of the Ninth Legion during the
first four years of the conquest, A.D. 43–47, and must have
been an unwelcome addition to the farmers of the Nene
valley. Indeed, their ditched enclosures show a period of
disuse during the occupation of the fort. Another fort, as
yet unexplored, was built at Water Newton (Huntingdonshire). Both were part of a network of garrisons which were

[12] *Britannia,* Vol. II (1971), pp. 264–5.

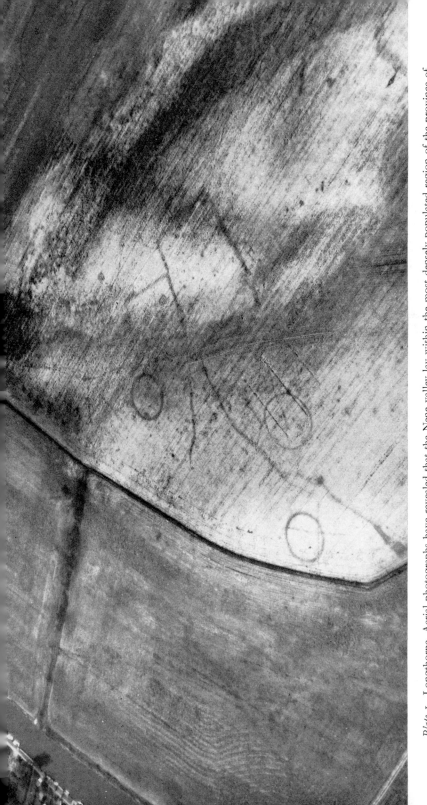

Plate 1 Longthorpe. Aerial photographs have revealed that the Nene valley lay within the most densely populated region of the province of Roman Britain. The river can be seen in the top left-hand corner, the circles are ploughed-out Bronze Age barrows and these are overlain by the deep irregular dykes, funnelled droveways and rectangular enclosure of a pre-Roman Iron Age farm situated on the gravel terrace. A few hundred yards away is the first-century Roman fortress.

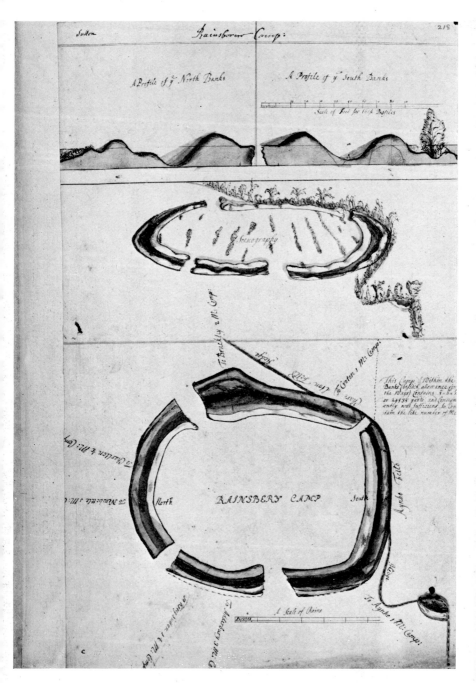

Plate 2 Rainsborough. Eayre's plan and elevation of the univallate Pre-Roman Iron Age hill fort, 1721. The interest in antiquities was already beginning to thrive at this date. This unpublished drawing was commissioned by J. Bridges for his projected *History and Antiquities of Northamptonshire* whose publication was delayed until 1791.

Plate 3 Aldwinkle. The piles and horizontal timbers of the first-century Roman bridge which carried the Gartree road over the river Nene. The metalling of the Roman road surface lies on top of the timbers which are embedded (and therefore preserved because waterlogged) in the clays and gravels of the shifting river bed, which now has a course to the south-east of its ancient predecessor.

Plate 4 Irchester. The location of the small Roman town of 17½ acres is halfway along the minor road linking the two main crossings of the river Nene, Watling Street and Ermine Street. The site overlooking the river is marked by the roughly rectangular area surrounded by substantial earthworks. These defences were added to a pre-existing settlement whose sinuous street pattern is seen on the air-photograph and may even date back to the Belgic period.

stationed in forts a day's march apart round the fens towards the Trent and Humber.

As the legionaries advanced towards the north and west they built roads. A broad swathe of forest was chopped down to remove cover for ambushes; scoop ditches, averaging eighty-four feet from centre to centre on the more important class of roads and sixty-two feet on the secondary class, established what Margery has referred to as the 'road zones'. The straight alignments are a well-known characteristic of Roman roads. A long straight stretch of five miles of Ermine Street passes through the town site of Durobrivae (Huntingdonshire) and crossed over the river Nene by a bridge, traces of which were found on the river bed.

An important junction occurs a quarter of a mile north of the deserted railway station of Water Newton. The secondary road from Thrapston which forded the river at Water Newton meets it, and King Street which goes to Lincoln also probably branched off at this point. The Gartree road, another Roman line of communication joining Godmanchester to Leicester, enters the county at Titchmarsh and crossed the Nene at Aldwinkle by means of a timber bridge (Plate 3). The road metalling was carried on a horizontal wooden framework, eighteen feet wide supported on piling and abutments four to five feet apart.[13] The most impressive stretches of Roman road in Northamptonshire were those of Watling Street, which enters the county at Old Stratford and runs in a rigid straight line for eight and a half miles to Towcester (Lactodorum). It has been greatly widened and otherwise altered in the turnpike era and later, but the stretch between Potterspury and Paulerspury in particular has an embankment up to five to six feet in height with level ground beyond on each side which is the likely remains of a high Roman *agger*. The *agger* was an artificial bank of earth

[13] D. A. Jackson, 'Aldwinkle Roman Bridge', *B.N.F.A.S.*, 4 (April 1970), pp. 37–38.

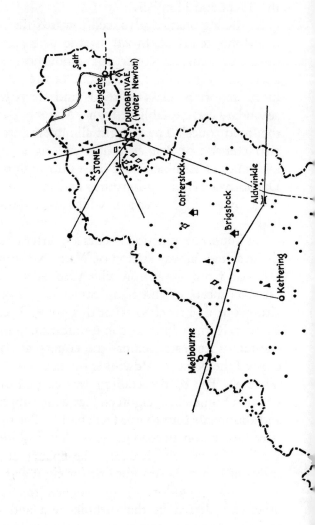

Salt

Fengate

DUROBRIVAE
(Water Newton)

x STONE

Cotterstock

Brigstock

Aldwinkle

Kettering

Medbourne

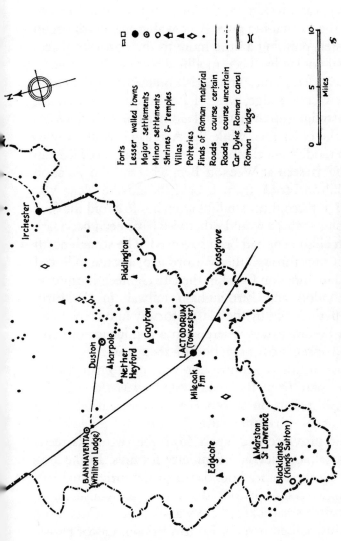

Fig. 3. Roman Northamptonshire

The information on this map has been compiled from the one inch to one mile base map for the Ordnance Survey Map of Roman Britain, 4th edition (forthcoming). It does not contain certain discoveries made since 1970.

on which the road stones were laid, larger at the bottom, tapering off to gravel and small stones on the top. One cannot avoid the feeling that the motive for such substantial earthworks was prestige, something to keep the Catuvellauni and the Coritani in awe. A new alignment was begun at Towcester, pointing a little more to the north. In places the original course has been modified to ease the gradients for later wheeled traffic. The parish boundary at the crossroads near Geese bridge, west of Bugbrooke, for instance, continues straight up the next hill along a line of hedgerows evidently the older line, while the A5 swings some way to the east to modify the climb. An interesting piece of Roman engineering is seen at Weedon Bec, whereby the junction of the Whilton brook from Brockhall and the Nene was negotiated in three short straight stretches to avoid the four river crossings which would otherwise have been necessary if the main alignment had been followed. The stretch north of Weedon runs through the Watford gap, a route followed by the Grand Junction Canal in the late eighteenth century, by the London and Birmingham railway in the early Victorian period, and by the M1 motorway in our own era. There can be few places where such a confluence of communications occurs over a period of 2000 years.[14]

The most distinctive contribution of the Romans to the landscape, apart from the road system, was the artificial imposition of towns on an otherwise almost entirely rural environment. Northamptonshire was a part of the lowland zone of the province and, apart from the two forts mentioned, was almost devoid of military features. In the area delineated by the county boundaries (which originated late in the Anglo-Saxon period) there was one considerable town and three small ones; here was also one of the most heavily industrialised parts of Roman Britain. Castor parish occupies a large part of the extra-mural area of the town of

[14] J. H. Appleton, 'The Communications of Watford Gap, Northants', *Institute of British Geographers, Transactions and Papers* (1960), pp. 215–24.

Durobrivae, which lies south across the Nene, and its
industrial potteries (Fig. 4).[15] The whole site extends four
miles from east to west and two from north to south. The
winding Nene bisects it. We have already noticed how the
Roman roads link it with the rest of the province. On the
east side of a large S-shaped projecting meander of the river
Nene south of the Boat House, a Roman road approaches
and ends in a large depression near the river, suggesting
that there may have been a wharf here serving river transport. "In the adjoyning fields (which instead of Dormanton,
they call Normanton fields) such quantities of Roman coins
are thrown up, that a man would really think they had been
sown there."[16]

There were four well-marked settlement areas here. Air-
photographs show several series of sub-rectangular enclosures, some apparently laid off a roughly east–west ditch,
others lying to the north of a double-ditched trackway
running east–west; still others straggle in long close-like
areas on both sides of Ermine Street. Large quantities of
limestone rubble, roof and box tiles and Roman pottery
have been found in the plough soil. Artis excavated structures, kilns, pits and walls in this area, and he found a
number of large Roman buildings of the villa type which
may well have been the residences of master potters since
they are interspersed between potters' workshops and
kilns.[17]

The quality of the buildings, with fine mosaic floors and
bath suites, shows that pottery-making was an exceedingly
prosperous business, and indeed the products of the Nene
valley kilns in the late part of the second century and the
third century are found all over the province, especially in the

[15] Here Edmund T. Artis, house steward to Lord Fitzwilliam at Milton,
made extensive excavations from 1820–7, which he illustrated in a sumptuous volume of plates, unfortunately published without a text.
[16] William Camden, *Britannia,* ed. E. Gibson (1695), p. 435.
[17] B. R. Hartley, 'Notes on the Roman Pottery Industry in the Nene
Valley', Peterborough Museum Society Occasional Papers No. 2 (1960).

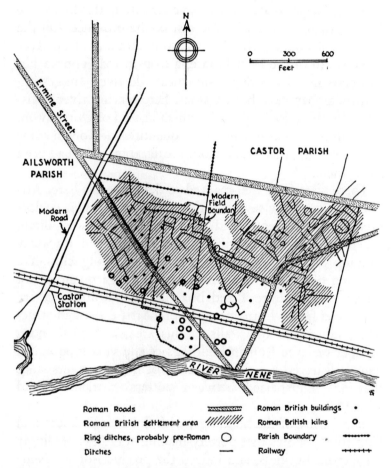

Fig. 4. Part of the Roman-British industrial complex in the lower Nene valley, Castor and Ailsworth parishes

With acknowledgments to the Ordnance Survey, Archaeological Division.

northern military area. We can picture the effects on the landscape of this thriving industry. The river was the controlling factor; none of the kilns was more than half a mile from the Nene, because it gave easy access to the east coast for the transport of these fragile wares via the Wash and via Car Dyke, the Roman canal. The clay seems to have been brought to the kiln sites, possibly from claypits west of Wansford. Immense quantities of brushwood and small branches were needed as fuel and large areas must have been cleared of woodland in the vicinity of the kilns. This may well have led to the establishment of further new kilns away from the presumed original nucleus around Water Newton and Castor. Such an industrial area was located from the air in 1964 at Ecton, four miles east of Northampton, and field-walking produced huge quantities of sandy grey Roman pottery, with patches of burnt clay with grass impressions. Excavation confirmed the presence of pottery manufacture and it is thought that as many as fifty kilns were sited here.[18]

The position of the Roman town of Irchester is marked by the ploughed-down, but in parts still substantial, earthworks defending a roughly rectangular area set on a plateau overlooking on their northern scarp the watermeadows of the river Nene (Plate 4). Aerial photography has revealed that the plan of the town, far from being a rectangular grid in fact, was based on a series of winding lanes and it is evident from Belgic ditches and pits that occupation was virtually continuous from the Pre-Roman Iron Age. An extra-mural suburb seems to have been to the south of the town in the first to second centuries. That the Roman government had horse-rearing ranches in the vicinity is suggested by the epitaph of a *strator consularis* at Irchester, and by the discovery at Thrapston where the road from Durobrivae to Irchester crosses the Gartree road, of an

[18] R. Hollowell, 'Aerial Photography and Fieldwork in the Upper Nene Valley', *B.N.F.A.S.*, 6 (September 1971), pp. 9–11.

inscribed boundary stone apparently marking the separation between public and private land.[19]

The small Roman town of Lactodorum (Towcester) occupied a roughly oval-shaped area on the west bank of the river Tove. An open settlement existed here beside the course of Watling Street and it may well have started life as a staging post between Little Brickhill (Bedfordshire) and Whilton Lodge; in the late second or possibly early third century the settlement was ditched and walled, reducing the area of occupation, and from the late fourth century it lay derelict until it became important as a Saxon frontier post against the Danes of Northampton. Portions of the defensive banks are traceable, notably at the north-west angle, and Watling Street can be seen passing through the town along its longer axis.[20]

The third small town is ten miles north-west of Towcester at Whilton Lodge and is situated at a crossroads on both sides of Watling Street; this is the settlement of Bannaventa mentioned in the *Itinerary* of Antoninus. It has been recognised since the early eighteenth century when Morton observed: "in that part of Whilton Field which adjoins Watling Street old foundations, the stones of ruined walls and the like have been ploughed and digged up and among the ruins some pieces of Roman money". It seems to have covered at least thirty acres and present excavations are attempting to trace the line of the town defences to the east of Watling Street.

The Roman impact on the countryside was complex. To imagine that it simply created a new institution, the villa, and that otherwise traditional life carried on among the inhabitants of the countryside with some Roman 'influence', unduly simplifies the situation, which showed a number of

[19] D. N. Hall and N. Nickerson, 'Excavations at Irchester 1962–3', *Archaeological Journal*, Vol. CXXIV (1967), pp. 65–100, and S. Applebaum, 'Roman Britain', p. 218 in H. P. R. Finberg (ed.), *Agrarian History of England and Wales*, Vol. I, Part 2 (Cambridge, 1972).

[20] *B.N.F.A.S.*, 2 (1967), pp. 19–20.

variants on this basic pattern and considerable development over 400 years. The Roman conquest in fact "opened up a new situation tending to peace and order which greatly stimulated rural development though to different degrees in different places".[21] The demand of the legions for corn undoubtedly extended the area of farm land and it has been claimed that half a million acres of rich fenland were taken into use into what was probably an imperial estate. Aerial photography has revealed that the fenlands in Lincolnshire, in north Northamptonshire and the Soke of Peterborough, around the Wash and in parts of Norfolk and Cambridgeshire were covered with a patchwork of small fields surrounded by drainage ditches and approached by drove roads. An increasing number of small farms of about ten to fifty acres appeared in the second half of the first century A.D. after the Boudiccan rebellion. They tend to be more closely grouped than in the Pre-Roman Iron Age, at any rate on the Welland gravels. At Maxey, a mile south of the Welland between Stamford and Peterborough, there is an area of nearly twenty acres around the Norman church covered by a tangle of boundary ditches, pits and enclosures. Three droveways radiate out—one eastwards to three farmsteads, probably occupied in the late first and early second centuries A.D.; and another goes north to a site inhabited from the Pre-Roman Iron Age until the sixteenth century A.D. The layout, in fact, suggests more the appearance of a village than the centre of an estate. Similar complexes with ditched, funnel-shaped droveways and rectilinear enclosures, with quantities of Nene valley ware found in the plough soil nearby, are in the Fengate area of Peterborough and at Longthorpe (Plate 1).[22]

These ditched droveways leading to the farms represent a

---

[21] H. C. Bowen in A. L. F. Rivet (ed.), *The Roman Villa in Britain* (London, 1969), p. 28.

[22] Royal Commission on Historical Monuments, *Peterborough New Town* (1969), Fig. 1, pp. 5–6, 9–10.

a striking innovation in the Romano-British landscape. It has been suggested that heavier vehicles would now go to the farms, possibly the carts sent to collect the annual levy of grain.[23] More likely, however, is that they are connected with grazing and animal husbandry which was possibly more important than corn-growing in both the Nene and Welland valleys during most of this period. A pattern of farms with drove roads and linear enclosures or paddocks is found all the way up the central Nene valley. How far the enclosures served for cattle and how far for sheep or horses is difficult to determine, but the very large quantity of cattle bones from Chesterton (Durobrivae) just across the river in Huntingdonshire, and the fact that sheep would have fallen victim to the liver fluke in these low-lying river pastures and fens, suggests that the former is more likely. With the clearance of these areas and improved drainage associated with the Car Dyke and other ditch systems it is possible that there was a lowering of the water table by the middle of the Roman period. This may account for the fact that these floodable pastures by the side of both rivers were exploited during this period but not later in the the fifth and sixth centuries when climatic deterioration and the breakdown of the Roman drainage system occurred simultaneously.

There was a good deal of penetration up the side valleys and in parts of the county the settlement pattern was denser in the Romano-British period than subsequently. Isolated farms located by field-walking are found on hillside sites often on cold Boulder Clay in clearings in the thick forest. Two which have been excavated face one another across a shallow valley at Great Oakley and in Geddington Chase. They occur every half-mile or so on either side of the Lyveden valley between Oundle and Brigstock. One can visualise the farmers toiling up the trackway, later known as

---

[23] W. G. Simpson, 'Romano-British Settlement on the Welland Gravels', in *Rural Settlement in Roman Britain*, C.B.A. Research Report 7 (London, 1966), p. 24.

the Harley Way, bringing their votive offerings to the three circular shrines on the top of the hill by Farming Woods. Roman influence does not seem to have been more than superficial in the countryside here, at any rate as measured in archaeological terms: a tendency away from circular to rectilinear building plans; a scattering of coins, and a profuse presence of coarse pottery and the products of the Nene valley kilns. During the construction of the Talavera Way, a high-speed road designed to encompass the newly expanded town of Northampton from the north, roadworks revealed a very extensive Romano-British farm site in 1972. Rapid excavation produced evidence of three phases of occupation; timber buildings stood on the site in the first to second centuries A.D. Stone buildings arranged on three sides round a cobbled yard surface replaced these in the third century. A series of circular buildings, the last with pitched limestone walls and two parallel walls butting on to it, recalled a further circular building found at Moulton a mile away. This continuity of settlement on the same site over 200 to 300 years with frequent rebuildings is of course a commonplace in the medieval period.[24] Doubtless many such native sites remain to be discovered in these less-favoured agricultural areas.

When we turn to the question of the part the villa played in the landscape it is immediately obvious that there was some economic connection and interdependence between villas and towns. Their distribution in Northamptonshire points towards this, as it does, even more clearly, elsewhere. Six villas are sited within a few miles of Durobrivae. Two are close to Lactodorum; and a further four lie between Bannaventa and the large Belgic settlement of Duston. The rest of the county is clear of them except for the isolated examples at Ashley, Weldon, Cosgrove and Brixworth. It has long been accepted that the villa was basically a farm

[24] J. Williams in a lecture given to the Northampton Development Corporation Archaeological Conference, November 1972.

and to be profitable these establishments had to be near to towns and roads to have access to their markets. Examples of the corridor type occur at Apethorpe and at Weldon, the former with wings, and an aisled house has recently been found at Barnack. Mosaic floors, the products of what Dr Smith has called the 'Durobrivan school', have been found at Apethorpe, Castor (Mill Hill), Harpole, Nether Heyford and Great Weldon.[25] The Anglo-Saxon settlers immortalised the discovery of one Roman tessellated pavement by naming a settlement after it, *'Flore'*,[26] and this suggests that in one place at least there was some continuity of habitation into the Dark Ages. The bounds of the estates attached to such villas have not been detected, for the simple reason that these lands have been intensively cultivated ever since and all traces of the Roman fields have been obliterated, and, apart from the fact that these were the first stone-walled and tiled buildings to be seen in the countryside, the known effect of the villa on the landscape remains uncertain and vague.

We have seen how the extension of fenland farming during the early Roman period was almost certainly connected with the increased demand for tributary grain. A navigable canal system provided through-communication by water from the Cambridge and Great Ouse valleys to the river system which flows into the Humber. Using this route, corn supplies could be taken to the military bases of Lincoln and ultimately York. Large stretches of the dyke remain more or less intact north of Stanground between the Nene and the Welland and in its best-preserved lengths such as South Norwoodhouse, Newborough, the ditch is up to fifty feet wide and three to five feet deep to the water level; the east bank here is a massive feature in permanent pasture

[25] D. J. Smith, 'The Mosaic Pavements', in A. L. F. Rivet (ed.), *The Roman Villa in Britain* (London, 1969), pp. 107–8.
[26] J. E. B. Gover, A. Mawer and F. M. Stenton, *The Place Names of Northamptonshire* (Cambridge, 1933), p. 82.

up to sixty feet wide and six feet high, with a flat top twelve feet high, and separated from the ditch by a berm ten feet wide.[27] West of Peakirk the course of the dyke, no longer water-filled, can be made out in two ways. The ditch is visible as a black organic fill contrasting with the lighter brown gravelly upcast of the denuded and ploughed-down bank. Also hedgerows crossing its course dip to show unmistakably the line of the once-busy waterway. Excavation has shown that the Cambridgeshire section of the Car Dyke was constructed in A.D. 50–60 and passed out of use as a routeway late in the second century, when droveways were constructed across it. The other portions, however, including those in Northamptonshire, may well have continued as a valued part of the drainage system of the western fenland for several more centuries.

[27] Royal Commission on Historical Monuments, *Peterborough New Town*, a survey of the antiquities in the areas of development (London, 1969), pp. 40–43.

2. The Anglo-Saxon landscape

Primary and secondary settlements. Village plans. The early Church and the landscape. Anglo-Saxon estate and parish boundaries. Hedgerows. Shire and hundred boundaries

Primary and secondary settlements

SOME IMPACT HAD been made on the natural landscape during the period of Roman occupation but at the beginning of the sixth century A.D. Northamptonshire was still for the most part a wilderness of forest, marsh and fen. During the next 500 years it became a land of villages and the main pattern of settlement which has lasted down to today was established. The work of the Anglo-Saxon migrants and invaders, which may be paralleled by that of the British in North America in the seventeenth and eighteenth centuries, was to accomplish the primary colonisation of the area. The routes of entry of the settlers into the country and the first areas to be occupied have long been the subject of conjecture. There are three approaches to this question, those provided by archaeology, philology and geography.

J. N. L. Myres has recently established that the preliminary stages of the Anglo-Saxon settlement in our area overlapped with the period of Roman occupation.[1] He has suggested that late Roman wheel-made pottery decorated in ways which reflect Germanic taste ('Romano-Saxon wares') may well be material evidence for the presence of friendly barbarian settlers planted in eastern Britain by the Romans

[1] J. N. L. Myres, *Anglo Saxon Pottery and the Settlement of England* (Oxford, 1969), pp. 66–74.

during the last days of their rule as reinforcements or substitutes for garrisons. This pottery has been found south and east around the inner margin of the fens at a number of sites that could be related to the Roman pottery towns at Casterton and Water Newton, notably at Stamford, Peterborough, Woodston and Nassington. This suggests that the countryside was not so densely settled even in these comparatively industrial areas that these 'allies' could not be accommodated.

With the breakdown of Roman rule the East Midlands seems to have been penetrated by Anglo-Saxon migrants from the fifth century onwards and the distribution of the numerous Anglian burial grounds points to an intensive and very early settlement along the middle course of the river Nene and its tributaries.[2] Cemeteries and burials have been found at Islip, Woodford, Irchester, Sudborough, Twywell and in the Ise valley at Great Addington, Barton Seagrave, Cranford, Kettering, Loddington, Newton, Weekley, Thorpe Malsor, Rothwell and Desborough.

It seems from such finds as the Great Addington urn that there were close affinities between this early material and North German and Scandinavian homelands. Myres has demonstrated that there are links between Northamptonshire and Cambridge potters; two who worked for Girton left specimens of their handiwork at Little Weldon and Newton. This strengthens the impression that the migrants came from the east and north-east. That transport and even trade within the area was possible seems clear from the distribution of the work of an Anglo-Saxon potter working in Kettering whose products have been found at Barton Seagrave, and there are connections between both these cemeteries and those of Islip and Newton.[3]

The theory of river penetration is supported by a study

[2] A. Meaney, *Gazetteer of Early Anglo Saxon burial sites* (London, 1964), pp. 186–97.

[3] *Anglo Saxon Pottery*, p. 128.

of the siting of the early place-names. The more ancient place-names of Northamptonshire, which include Fothering-hay, Oundle, Thrapston, Irthlingborough, Hamfordshoe and Billing, are found along the valley of the central Nene. [4] Overlooking the Ise valley are Great and Little Harrowden; the name means a hill marked by some place for heathen worship—a temple or a grove. A few miles up the valley are Kettering and Desborough, where early cemeteries have been excavated. The Stamford road cemetery is midway between the Roman settlement in North Kettering and the original nucleus of the Anglo-Saxon village. The other 'hills with temples or sacred places' are located at Weedon Bec on the upper Nene and Weedon Lois in the south of the county, which shows that even this remote and thickly wooded area was settled before the Christian missionaries arrived in the middle of the seventh century.

The older generation of archaeologists and place-name specialists both suggest that the Anglo-Saxon settlement of Northamptonshire was effected by tribal groups navigating the North Sea and the Wash, then penetrating up the Nene, Welland and Ouse rivers and their tributaries, founding settlements at flood-free points and in areas suitable for cultivation. This theory has been strongly criticised on geographical and chronological grounds. Miss Fuller thinks that it is rash to assume that the Nene and the Welland were navigable much beyond the fenland borders of Northamptonshire.[5] She points out that before their improvement in the eighteenth century, the Nene was navigable only from Alwalton, five miles above Peterborough, and the Welland only below Stamford. With an absence of embanking and straightening it is likely that the course of the river was much more meandering and the

[4] J. E. B. Gover, A. Mawer, F. M. Stenton, *The Place Names of Northamptonshire* (Cambridge, 1933), p. xv.

[5] G. Joan Fuller, 'Settlement in Northamptonshire between 500 A.D. and Domesday', *East Midland Geographer*, No. 3 (June 1955), pp. 25–36.

current would be more sluggish than later, since the thick forest cover would impede run-off. On the other hand we know that the Anglo-Saxons used shallow-draught boats and could well haul them round the shoals. In the early fourteenth century fair-sized vessels were able to go up the old river Nene and its branches as far as the Great North Road. The old Nene was certainly used up to Yaxley in the early sixteenth century.

As well as the rivers it is highly likely that the Anglo-Saxon migrants used overland routes to penetrate North-amptonshire, including Watling Street and the two pre-historic trackways. Banbury Lane, which leads to North-ampton and beyond, and the Portway, which leads to Daventry, were both in use during the Dark Ages. The existence of the Jurassic Way, already mentioned, empha-sises the fact that the uplands were crossed by important trackways from the south and south-west.

The archaeological evidence bears out this thesis that the area later known as Northamptonshire was colonised by Anglo-Saxons coming from the upper Thames valley and the south as well as from the north-east via the traditionally well-known river routes which flow into the Wash. The practice of inhumation was predominant in early pagan cemeteries to the west of Watling Street and cremation to the east. It used to be thought that cremation was evidence of earlier settlement than inhumation. Myres denies this and reckons that the two rites were practised at times concurrently, sometimes one preceding the other and vice versa.[6] These western inhumation cemeteries, therefore, are contemporary with or even earlier than those in the eastern part of the county; if the grave goods are of the Saxon type they may well be the funerary monuments of West Saxons. If we accept this, the Anglo-Saxon penetration possibly occurred earlier in the south than the north and east.

[6] *Anglo Saxon Pottery*, p. 123.

We can picture the Anglo-Saxon farmers plodding along the upland roads into the East Midlands searching for sites suitable for occupation. They were not geologists but they were, from a long practical experience, sensitive to the lie of the land and to the varying quality of the soils as revealed in the natural vegetation. They looked for dry gravelly sites with a steady supply of water and they were interested in warm loamy soils easy to cultivate without too thick a forest cover. The Nene valley gravels, as we have seen, were thickly populated from prehistoric times and it is hardly surprising that some of the earliest Anglo-Saxon place-names are found here. Fotheringhay, 'island of the people of Fordhere', lies on a ridge of gravels between the Willow Brook and the Nene. Oundle is on the spring line between the Great Oolite Limestone and the upper Estuarine Clay. Thrapston (a pre-Christian name), was built at a narrow crossing place of the Nene on the gravel terrace. Irthling-borough, Wellingborough and Great Billing are all on the spring line, the two latter at the junction of the Northampton Sands and the Upper Lias Clay. The importance of springs and wells should be emphasised because streams within the vicinity of a settlement would soon become polluted. A number of villages took their names from springs or wells: Maidwell (the maiden's well), Rothwell (the Red well, red because of the ironstone), Barnwell (warrior's spring), Pipewell (Pippa's spring), Weldon (hill with spring), Twywell (double spring). Some forest clearance would be necessary but the fertile loam soils which surrounded these sites was less dense than on the Boulder Clays of the plateaux. Finally, like many Roman villa sites, these early Anglo-Saxon settlements were on south-facing slopes, probably one reason why the left bank of the Nene was settled first. All except Great Billing were close to the river.

Similar circumstances are found in the valley of the river Ise. Here are four early names and four pagan cemeteries, including Kettering, Harrowden, Arthingworth and Desborough. The settlements are sited along the spring line and provided with more extensive tracts of warm, red, loamy soils than were found in the Nene valley. There is a complete blank area of early names in the area afterwards called Rockingham forest, and the Boulder Clays with their thick woodland cover must have been particularly hostile to Anglo-Saxon farmers. When the Welland valley is reached there are only two early names, Rockingham and Cottingham, both found high up on the steep scarp slope, commanding fine panoramic views, above the gravel terraces, bordering the flood plain of the river Welland. They both lie just below the spring line of the Upper Lias Clay outcrop, the heavy soils of which are lightened with downwash.

When we consider the siting of the earliest settlements in the south-west uplands there seems to be some connexion with the route pattern. Daventry and Weedon Lois both lie close to prehistoric trackways and Weedon Bec perhaps owes its origin to the fact that here Watling Street crosses the upper Nene. Naseby similarly, despite its somewhat inhospitable setting 600 feet above sea level in an area of heavy woodland and clay soils, is close to the presumed course of the Jurassic Way.

Further farms and homesteads sprang up within the area of earlier settlement, the middle Nene valley, and also in areas previously avoided such as the fens and the eastern forest lands. This secondary phase, marked by groups of names with suffixes -*ham* and -*ton* shows that this expansion of settlement had progressed considerably before the arrival of the Danes in the ninth century. Most place-name specialists regard the element *ingas* as deriving from the earliest phase of Anglo-Saxon settlement. There is only one *ing* in the Soke of Peterborough. This was followed by nine *tons*. It may well have been the influence of the monastery at Medeshamstede, endowed with immense stretches of fen and swamp in the seventh century, that led to the foundation of these secondary settlements. They occupied land twenty-five feet or more above sea level; five were on broad stretches of marine gravels bordering the fen, areas where good water supplies and well-drained easily cultivable loam soils were available.

In the middle Nene valley around Oundle a 'filling in' process occurred, with six villages having *ton* elements coming in among the already established settlements. Nassington ('farm of the dwellers on the ness or headland') is on the second terrace gravels of the Nene. Warmington similarly is on a dry gravelly site. Ashton and Pilton are situated on the spring line and Woodnewton is on the southward-facing side of the lower Willow Brook valley. Further up the valley are nine more *tons,* including Northampton itself, on the left bank of the Nene sited between 250 feet and 300 feet on south-facing slopes well above the flood plain. On the right bank is a similar string of spring line sites where villages have grown up.

At least as important as water supply and a dry point site was the availability of land which could be cleared of forest for the plough or for stock-grazing. There are nucleated villages every mile or mile and a half betweeen Northampton and Desborough. The almost geometrically regular spaced pattern of settlement in central Northamptonshire has caused one archaeologist to wonder whether the land was not divided up according to some kind of deliberate plan.[7] Much has been made of the siting of early Anglo-Saxon settlements in areas of easily worked loam soils but it is more likely that what was required was a mixture of soils to correspond with a multiplicity of land use. The strings of settlements on the left and right banks of the Nene between Fotheringhay and Northampton nearly all share a slice of Boulder-Clay-covered upland which would have provided the dense forest cover suitable for swine-herding and for

[7] W. F. Grimes, 'The Jurassic Way', in *Aspects of Archaeology in Britain and Beyond* (ed. W. F. Grimes), 1951, pp. 144-71.

timber and fuel supplies. They also had a predilection for the Northampton sand outcrop—which would provide the cultivable land. Each had a river frontage and a share of the floodable but potentially rich river meadow. In the Ise valley an analysis of the drift cover parish by parish has shown how each had a share of the wide variety of available soils.[8]

It must be confessed, however, that the parish boundaries are not the oldest territorial divisions and date from a comparatively late stage of the Anglo-Saxon period. The large 'primeval' estates probably had the oldest boundaries, and these were mostly natural. Most parishes represent a secondary stage in estate development when a certain amount of sub-division of the primeval estates took place.[9] Consequently any argument trying to make sense of settlement pattern based on the existence of parishes tends to be a rationalisation after the event.

The relative attractiveness of soils seems to have been the key factor in the expansion phase of settlement in Northamptonshire as elsewhere. If we look at the low plateaux of Oxford Clay covered with Boulder Clay on the eastern boundary of the county we find no early Anglo-Saxon names and only a few *tons* suggesting pioneer settlement. This was the *Bruneswald,* a densely forested area on the borders of Huntingdonshire and Northamptonshire which included Leighton, Lutton and Newton. Lutton or 'Luda's farm' was spoken of as being 'juxta Brouneswold' and this place is some eight miles north of Leighton Bromswold. When the third reference, Newton Bromswold, is plotted on the map, some idea of the size of this woodland area can be obtained and we hear that Hereward took refuge here in the eleventh century. These settlements are all situated on chalky Boulder Clay just above the outcrop of Oxford Clay.

[8] K. Farrington and I. Toseland, *Two Studies in Northamptonshire Village Settlement,* Kettering Grammar School Research Paper 3.

[9] Cf. W. G. Hoskins and H. P. R. Finberg, *Devonshire Studies* (London, 1952), pp. 300–10.

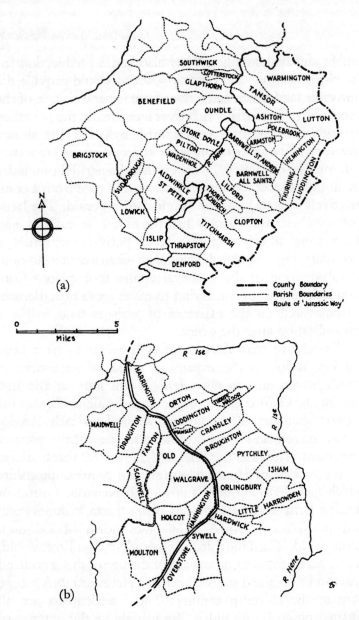

Fig. 5a. A group of parishes in the middle Nene valley. The long narrow linear pattern of the densely settled valley parishes, each with a share of flood-plain meadow, easily worked and well-drained loam soils, and woodland, contrasts with the outsize woodland parishes on the Boulder Clays of Brigstock, Benefield and Southwick.

5b. The prehistoric route known as the 'Jurassic Way' forms the boundary of seventeen parishes over a length of nine miles in this part of north-central Northamptonshire. It is the oldest feature of the landscape.

In the Northampton uplands to the west of Watling Street there was a considerable increase of settlement in the secondary phase marked by twenty-three *tons* and four *hams*. It is noticeable that the bulk of these are at heights between 400 and 500 feet, five are on plateaux or ridges, and nearly all the rest are on the slopes of steep-sided valleys. In the areas between these upland settlements and those of the middle Nene, the upper Nene valley was still unpeopled, and the reason again would seem to be the widely differing soils. West of Watling Street there are wide exposures of the warm red loams of the Northampton Sands, and there are abundant water supplies available at shallow depth; more open woodland on these intermediate soils was also favourable. The uplands to the east have widespread areas of a heavy and cold Boulder Clay with a dense forest cover and they were avoided.

When the Domesday settlement pattern is studied it is apparent that further infilling had occurred later in the Anglo-Saxon period and some Danish influence appeared in the place-names. North, in the Welland valley, were a series of forest farms and clearings. Ashley (Ash tree clearing), Dingley (Dyune's clearing) and Harringworth (the forest enclosure of Hering). Between the Ise valley and the valley of the Brampton Nene many new settlements were established in woodlands. Weekley (clearing or wood by Wic), Cransley (clearing of the crane or heron), Pytchley (Peoht's clearing or woodland), Old (from *weald*, O.E. woodland) and Brixworth (Bricel's clearing), all suggest that inroads were being made on forests. The date when this was happening is impossible to establish with certainty though the fact that there was a church from the late seventh century A.D. at Brixworth does show that there has been human settlement here for at least 1200 years. Even in the Nene valley there was infilling and a multiplication of settlements, resulting in a series of narrow, strip-shaped parishes, contrasting with the huge, rambling, thinly populated areas of the parishes of Rockingham forest such as Brigstock, Benefield and Southwick (Fig. 5a). Such secondary settlements included Wigsthorpe (Viking's farm), Aldwinkle (from O.E., *wincel*, 'corner'—with reference to the big bend in the course of the Nene here) and Tansor (Tan's bank), all sited on the gravel terraces.

These clearings, however, were not the earliest man-made features in the landscape of this area. The prehistoric ridgeway, known now as the Jurassic Way, was (Fig. 5b). It formed the common boundary of no less than seventeen settlements and we can picture the Anglo-Saxon farmers hewing their way uphill through the forests from Orlingbury or Harrington until at length they met on the beaten track of the ridgeway. There are now no villages for ten miles along the A43 Kettering–Northampton road between Broughton and Moulton, but this was not always so. Three settlements came into being in the late Anglo-Saxon period, Mawsley (clearing belonging to the ridge), Badsaddle and Wythemail. All three lasted barely 500 years and failed to survive even to the end of the Middle Ages.

To sum up the position so far. Nearly all the villages to be found on the map today owe their origins to the Anglo-Saxons. This network of settlements was their greatest contribution to the Northamptonshire landscape. The primary colonisation had occurred first in the areas near their routes of penetration, whether prehistoric and Roman road systems, or main rivers. The secondary phase occupied the less favourable soils and the thickly forested regions.

Village plans

Can we still detect the influence of the Anglo-Saxon farmers on the landscape today? One approach to this aspect will be through village plans. Geographers and the historians of settlement refer to the earliest available maps which for Northamptonshire are sixteenth-century surveys such as the

Plate 5 Barnack church. The use of Barnack stone is seen in the long pilaster strips, arched and triangular windows and long and short work in the corners of the late pre-Conquest west tower, crowned by the earliest broach spire in England, dated to the beginning of the thirteenth century. Behind is the large church whose scale points to the prosperity of farming (and quarrying) on the rim of the fen in the eleventh to thirteenth centuries.

Plate 6 Castor and Ailsworth. An RAF vertical taken in 1945, showing the tortuous winding street pattern of the older Anglo-Saxon settlement, centred on St Kyneburga's church, which overlies the villas and industrial workings of Romano-British entrepreneurs who waxed rich on the lower Nene potteries in the third century. Ailsworth to the left is a late pre-Conquest village cleared from the forest, with a linear plan consisting of a High Street and two parallel back streets. Towards the top are faint traces of the last open fields in Northamptonshire to be enclosed, 1898. Both settlements are now being swallowed up by Peterborough New Town.

Finch Hatton manuscripts in the Northants Record Office. They then make the assumption that village plans recorded there survived virtually unchanged from the Anglo-Saxon period. Modern research based on a study of air-photographs, backed up by some excavation, is tending to show that these conclusions are unfounded. Complete replanning and laying out of whole sections of villages, even resiting, could take place in the later Anglo-Saxon and early medieval periods.

Our settlements began as small groups of farms without any obvious pattern, or perhaps single farms, clearings in the forest. The concept 'the village' itself is a development, occurring perhaps over several hundred years and the difficulty is to distinguish between the nucleus of the settlement and later accretions. Only one Anglo-Saxon village plan has been recovered by excavation in the county, at Maxey on the Welland gravels between Peterborough and Stamford, and even here the area uncovered was reckoned to be only one-third of the Dark Age settlement at one period of its life, some time between A.D. 650–850. The buildings were ranged round a relatively unoccupied, elongated space, which may be interpreted either as a single farm complex in which each building had an individual function, or as a village in which each building was a peasant toft and the space a wide street or green. The site of this group of buildings lies east-north-east of the church and nearly half-way towards the present village. It has been suggested that the present village was *Maxey East,* mentioned by Speed in his map of Northamptonshire of 1611 and that it may have been the settlement of Maccus's followers, Maccus being a Dane who perhaps partitioned the island (Macuseige) between his followers in the late 870s.[10]

[10] For Maxey see P. V. Addyman with K. R. Fennell and L. Biek, 'A Dark Age Settlement at Maxey, Northamptonshire', *Medieval Archaeology*, Vol. VIII (1964), pp. 20–74; W. G. Hoskins, *Fieldwork in Local History* (London, 1967), pp. 171–7.

Despite the reservations already expressed about the value of the map approach, it is worthwhile studying early surveys such as the splendid series of villages and their adjoining fields made for the Montagus of Boughton in the 1720s and '30s. A useful supplementary check, admittedly rough and ready since the scale is small, approximately one inch to one mile, is the 1779 map of the county by Thomas Eayre of Kettering. This can be compared with the first edition of the Ordnance Survey, mapped round about 1814–20.

When this is done it is seen that most Northamptonshire villages fall into four main types. The double-loop plan, the green village, the linear village extended along a single street, and the haphazard conglomeration of houses planted with seemingly little relationship to each other or any nucleus.

The double-loop plan was first noticed as appearing along the Ouse valley in north Bedfordshire where the street plan is in the form of two complete loops or a figure of eight.[11] It is found in a number of places in Northamptonshire, especially in the wooded country on the Leicestershire and Warwickshire borders.[12] Ashley (the clearing in an ashwood) is a few hundred yards from a Roman villa whose remains overlie an Iron Age settlement.[13] A stream runs through the village which has the church and manor house at the north-west corner of the western loop and the green contained in a loop formed by Green Lane and Main Street. The northern half of the green has been built over, and this, coupled with the fact that the houses facing the green on the east have now disappeared (they figured in the 1824 Ordnance Survey map) disguises the former existence of the green. Domesday records: "2 acres of spinney [*spinetum*] Woodland, 3 furlongs in length and 8 perches in breadth and in

[11] P. S. McCullagh, 'Twin Loop Villages in Bedfordshire', *East Midland Geographer*, Vol. 3, Part 2, No. 18 (1962), pp. 102–10.

[12] Syresham, Ashley, Braybrooke, Gretton, Weldon, Cold Ashby, Sibbertoft, Spratton, Ringstead, Naseby, Hellidon, Welton.

[13] *B.N.F.A.S.*, 5 (1971), pp. 5–6.

another place there are 4 acres of wood pertaining to this land". The casual and free plan may well reflect a system of agriculture in which field and forest lived side by side.

At Badby, on the Warwickshire border, there is a similar double loop of roads and here "the medieval village had carried through into its period of expansion something of its earliest form of a group of houses in a clearing".[14] The mesh of streets intersect and widen with grass verges into greens now planted with mature chestnuts; to the south the woods come to within two fields' distance of the churchyard.

A third example, this time from Rockingham forest, is found at Weldon, but here the situation is more complicated. In the first place there are two villages now virtually joined together, Great and Little Weldon, with noticeably different plans. The older mother settlement is ranged round two large loops and there are five groups of old houses, many dating back to the seventeenth century and beyond. The northerly loop has the village green in one corner; the church is by the stream in the other loop with the site of the medieval manor house of the Bassets to the south.[15] To the south-west the ground has been much disturbed by stone-quarrying from later medieval times, now grassed over. Domesday mentions woodland, one league in length and three furlongs in breadth, and this haphazard pattern of growth reflects a period when the land was won in clearings, season by season from the forest. It contrasts strongly with the disciplined street village of the offshoot Little Weldon. Here is a plan of great regularity, with the pattern continued in the crofts on the south side of the main street. The grey and yellow limestone thatched cottages of Weldon are now overshadowed by the black skeletal towers and chimneys of Corby's steel works belching out their pall of pink smoke.

---

[14] M. W. Beresford and J. K. St Joseph, *Medieval England, An Aerial Survey* (Cambridge, 1958), pp. 129–30.

[15] W. T. Reedy, 'The First Two Bassets of Weldon', *Northants. Past and Present*, Vol. IV, 5 (1970–1), p. 298.

The village-green plan has survived in a number of places in the county but often later encroachment has disguised the original form. A central green can only have been required by animals, and to drive them into such a stockade protected by a ring of houses with their fenced enclosures would have appealed to Anglo-Saxon stock-rearing farmers farming in troubled and dangerous times. The oval green at Orlingbury, pleasantly wooded, is the focal point of four roads, leading in from the surrounding fields. At Scaldwell the green is triangular and cut up by roads. There is a suggestion that the scrap of green still existing at Ravensthorpe was once part of a much larger rectangular area now encroached on and surrounded by a loop of roads. The church, as is usual in a green village, borders one side. The large green at Creaton, square in plan and bordered by houses facing on it, is reminiscent of those studied by Dr Thorpe in County Durham. At Hinton-in-the-Hedges the small triangular green is still the centre of this tight settlement which has never grown beyond hamlet proportions. Evenley has a large rectangular green, but here the houses sprawl along a road and the open space is at one end of the village. Warkton, situated on a hillslope but below the crest and above possible flood danger from the river Ise, has a plan suggesting that a green once existed. A roughly triangular area, bounded by three streets, has a small fragment of green surviving on the east. The church has been built on the western side of the area, and the fact that the street connecting the village with Grafton Underwood bulges out to avoid the 'green' suggests that it is an ancient feature.

The single-street village plan is much more common.[16] Here, standing at the head of long narrow strips or crofts, were the houses, lying along the street, sometimes flanking

[16] Examples are Charlton, Culworth, Croughton, Barnwell, Grafton Underwood, Yarwell, Wood Newton, Wakerley, Titchmarsh, Upper and Lower Benefield, Bulwick, Deene, Deenethorpe.

it and sometimes set end on. Later infilling has often linked them together as a single frontage and stone and brick has long replaced the Anglo-Saxon and medieval houses. In its simplest form and stripped of houses and fences this plan can be seen in the deserted village site of Nobold between Clipston and Sibbertoft, discovered in the remarkable air-photograph by Dr J. K. St Joseph (Plate 17). Braunston, lying on a ridge of land overlooking the Leam, has its medieval buildings lying along only one street.[17] Church, manor, mill and rectory are grouped together at the western end. The original length of the crofts on the northern side is marked by the Back Lane; the fact that the crofts on the south side are much more irregular and show signs of encroaching on the open fields suggests that the houses originally bordered the northern side of the street only. The single street plan may be the result of a long period of development and the meandering linear shape of Helmdon suggests an expansion during the later Middle Ages both north and south from the settlement with the mill and eleven households mentioned in Domesday Book.

Contrasting with this evolutionary sprawl, some villages give the impression of deliberate planning. Such is the straight street of Eydon with the houses facing each other along the two sides of a main street. The regularity of the pattern is found continuing in the crofts which originally stretched to the straight and parallel back lane, thus forming a well-defined boundary between the village and the open fields. Welford has a similar plan of two parallel streets; here the church and manor house occupy the southern third of the rectangular area thus enclosed. Ailsworth in the valley of the lower Nene has a well-preserved linear plan with two back lanes, each parallel to the original main street which has now become bypassed and the more easterly back lane leads to Helpston, the next village (Plate 6). Until 1898 there were five large open fields, Upton, Wood

[17] *Medieval England, An Aerial Survey*, p. 63.

Dales, Little and Nether fields and air-photographs show
ridge-and-furrow with end-on interlocked furlongs to the
north-east and south-west of the village.[18]

The fact that nearly all the villages to be found on the map
today owe their origins to the Anglo-Saxon settlement
means that the physical remains of Anglo-Saxon domestic
buildings are buried beneath existing villages. Later
disturbances rarely allow traces to survive and the best
chance of recovering evidence about the appearance and
the function of buildings ought to be found on the sites of
deserted medieval villages which were abandoned early.
Unfortunately, "it is very rarely possible to determine the
exact nature of the building from only odd stake holes, post
holes or foundation slots".[19] There are few substantial buildings and no substantial earthworks, but the formidable list
of these early desertions "suggests a major shift in many
village sites during the late Saxon period". Northamptonshire can offer interesting examples of the two main types of
Anglo-Saxon timber buildings: the so-called *grubenhaüser*
or sunken huts, and buildings on the normal ground surface
which have left traces of timbering.

At Upton, two miles west of Northampton, overlooking
the Nene valley, extensive road improvements exposed
forty-two Iron Age pits, several lengths of ditch and an
Anglo-Saxon building.[20] This was of exceptionally large
size, thirty feet by fifteen and was cut four feet into the
natural sand; posts set centrally in the end walls supported
the roof and planks were slotted into the surrounding walls.
Excavations of parallel but smaller structures at the Anglo-
Saxon village of West Stow in Suffolk have raised serious

[18] Royal Commission on Historical Monuments, *Peterborough New Town,* a
survey of the antiquities in the areas of development (London, 1969), p. 18.
[19] M. W. Beresford, J. G. Hurst (eds.), *Deserted Medieval Villages* (London,
1971), p. 90.
[20] D. A. Jackson, D. W. Harding and J. N. L. Myres, 'The Iron Age and
Anglo Saxon site at Upton, Northants.', *Antiquaries Journal,* Vol. XLIX
(1969), Part II, pp. 202–21.

doubts as to whether this sort of building was a 'sunken hut' at all; it is thought that such sunken spaces were in fact cellars below raised planked floors. The presence of about three dozen loom weights at Upton suggested that the main purpose served by the building was that of a weaving shed, and pottery indicates a date perhaps round about the turn of the sixth and seventh centuries A.D.

At Maxey, as we have seen, the Dark Age site lies between the present village and the isolated church and the ridge to the west.[21] We have already noticed that these Fen Margin Gravels were intensively occupied during prehistoric times. *Macuseige*—the early form of the place-name which means Maccus's island—is divided by pit alignments into three, and the 'island' is formed by the Welland and the present parish boundaries of Maxey and Northborough. The whole area was occupied in the Middle Saxon period (A.D. 650–850). Three miles distant is the seventh-century dedication of St Pega's at Peakirk; a Middle Saxon hut has been found at Castor (seven miles away) and there were pagan cemeteries at Woodstone, Stamford and Baston. Excavation before gravel-quarrying revealed seven Middle Saxon buildings and five structures described as 'sunken huts'. The seven rectangular buildings ranged from thirty to fifty feet in length and sixteen to twenty feet in width. They were all of post-hole construction but there were instances of post holes in trenches, post holes joined by wall trenches, and once, a central beam slot. Pits surrounded by post holes suggested either ancillary working huts or the huts of poorer peasants segregated from those of the more prosperous ones. The economy of the site was mixed. Some grain production is indicated by the presence of lava querns and, of the animal bones, cattle and sheep or goat make up almost three-quarters in equal proportions. Pig and horse are relatively

[21] P. V. Addyman with K. R. Fennell and L. Biek, 'A Dark Age Settlement at Maxey, Northamptonshire', *Medieval Archaeology*, Vol. VIII (1964), pp. 20–73.

71

few and bird bones suggest supplementation of the diet by wild fowling as would be expected at the fen edge.

Undoubtedly the most formative influence these Anglo-Saxon farmers had on the landscape was the leading part they played in the forest clearance. Natural oak woods were a major feature of the vegetation in Atlantic times and this vast forest was still largely intact. Frequent references are found to the vegetation in the Anglo-Saxon place-names: Brampton (briar or bramble farm), Oakley (oak clearing or wood, with a secondary colonisation from the mother village producing Little Oakley), Boughton (O.E. Beech farm), Thurning (place overgrown by thorn bushes), Brigstock (birch tree stump or *stoc*), Ashton and Ashley. There are thirty-seven *leys*, twelve *worths* and nine *felds* in the county, mostly congregated in the two ancient forest areas, Rockingham in the north and Salcey and Whittlewood in the south.

Occasionally we get a glimpse of the dangers and uncertainties of this period. Wakerley means the clearing of the Watchers (over the Welland). The animals living in the woods and the hills are recalled. Wolfage, in Brixworth, is probably a reference to an enclosure intended to keep out wolves. Cranford means the crane's or heron's ford; Everdon, wild boar hill; Brockhall, in Nobottle grove hundred, means badger hole. Cathanger farm in Woodend, Blatherwycke, means the wild cat slope. There are many references to the beasts of the chase, Hartwell (Hart's spring), Bugbrooke (brook of the bucks), Hargrave (Hare grove) and Cadge Wood (cadge is a term used in falconry for a frame on which several hawks were carried to be sold). Even insects are mentioned—Warkworth (spider's clearing) and Stuchbury (O.E. *stūt*, a midge or gnat).

Within the woodland, small groups of Anglo-Saxon and later Danish farmers began the slow and strenuous task of clearing. The axes of the new settlers rang out, the great roots were grubbed up, clearings were hacked out or burned. Cattle, sheep and pigs inhibited by their browsing and foraging the natural regeneration of the oak and ash forest. Sometimes the stumps were left in the clearing, hence *Elrenstuble* (elder tree stump) and *Le Stibbynges*. As season by season small patches were added to the total cultivable land of each settlement they were divided up among the families. Little is known about Anglo-Saxon fields but in Northamptonshire the open-field system, with a two-field rotation and strip cultivation, seems to have been universally practised. Glimpses are seen from the field names. These strips were referred to as 'lands' and often their size and shape were noted as in *Scortleande, Langland, Wobland* (crooked strip) and *Wrangland* (twisted). Other words of similar meaning were *dal* (dole—as in *Le Weldole, Le Thakedole*—whence thatching material came, and Thistledole) or *furlangs*. Boundary stones were necessary to demarcate holdings (hence *Steane*—at the stone). Heavy oxen were used to plough—hence Oxendon (the field of the oxen), and Bulwick (bull farm). Some indication of the variety of the crops can also be derived from place-names. Wetleys' wood in Syresham in the forests of the south of the county means 'a wheat clearing'. The Middle English element *breche*, 'land broken up for tillage', is often found compounded with wheat and pease, hence Wetebreche, Pesebreche and Medowbreche. Woad was extensively grown judging by its frequency in field names—Wadcroft, Wadground, Wad Cabin, Wadborough and Wadhill. As Morton says, "of all the Midland counties, this, I am pretty sure, either is, or has been, *woaded* most".[22]

The early Church and the landscape

Although individual missionaries are known to have penetrated into the land settled by the Middle Angles round about the middle of the seventh century A.D., it is clear that

[22] J. Morton, *Natural History*, p. 17.

the foundation of the great Mercian monastery of Medeshamstede about 657 gave a powerful impetus to the work
of the Church in the area. In common with the experience
of other areas the conversion proceeded from the top down-
wards and this first monastery was the creation of Peada,
king of the Midland Angles and Oswiu, brother of King
Oswald, to commemorate the revival of Christianity in his
kingdom after the death of his father, the pagan king Penda
(632–654).

When one views the rather ugly town of Peterborough
from the south across a web of railway lines, pylons, power
cables and the chimneys of engineering and brick works it
is difficult to believe that once this was unreclaimed, remote
and swampy land. Medeshamstede is a name derived from
the meadows which lie on each side of the river Nene. It is
not clear whether the earliest building of the monastery was
of stone or wood. Hugh Candidus, the twelfth-century
monkish chronicler of Peterborough, refers to "*immanissimos
lapides*" and says that the foundation stones were so large
that eight yoke of oxen could scarcely draw one of them.
This, however, could refer to the stone church erected in
the seventh century and destroyed by the Danes in 870 when
Abbot Hedda and all his monks were slain. The gutted site
lay desolate for nearly a century, until, as the *Anglo-Saxon
Chronicle* says, "Bishop Aethelwold came to the minster
called Medehamstede which was formerly ruined by heathen
folk; but he found there nothing but old walls and wild
woods . . . he then ordered the minster to be rebuilt and
set there an abbot who was called Aldulf; and made monks,
where before was nothing."[23]

Aldulf, abbot from 972 to 999, cleared the woody and
solitary swamp by degrees and built manor houses and
granges. It may well be that the hamlets of Dogsthorpe,
Newark and Eastfield in the Little Borough Fen began as
colonies or granges upon the Medeshamstede fields. The

[23] *Anglo-Saxon Chronicle,* Everyman edition (London, 1938), pp. 92–93.

arable area eventually came to be laid out in two great divisions of fields, for the East and West Fields can still be identified lying east and west of the cathedral. The southern boundary of the East Field was Car Dyke and beyond it stretched the fen and the waters against which it was a protection. Mill Field was a division of the West Field and the Boon Fields (from *Bondfields*—the strips of the bondsmen of the abbey) a division of the East Field. Abbot Kenulf (992–1005) made a wall round the minster and changed the name Medeshamstede to Burgh but we cannot necessarily jump to the conclusion that the village had become a borough in the tenth century.[24] The place of the possible Anglo-Saxon borough in the present townscape will be discussed in a later chapter.

The early Church could therefore take a lead in the economic development of areas under its control. The pastoral and missionary activities also left their impact on the landscape. These tasks were carried out from mission stations known as minsters and these owed their foundation to a king or bishop or important monastery. Its parish might be an estate belonging to the founder, or what Bede calls a *regio* or *provincia,* an area occupied by a particular tribe. The minster itself would be situated in the village which was the administrative centre of the estate or *regio,* and minster parishes covered an enormous area containing a number of centres of population, with no set parish boundaries but merging into the forest and fen. An example from the neighbouring county of Leicestershire shows Friduric, a Mercian nobleman, giving land at Breedon to the monastery of Medeshamstede on the express condition that the monks should found a monastery at Breedon and there appoint a priest of good repute who would minister baptism and teaching to the people assigned to him.[25] According to Hugh

[24] *Victoria County History, Northamptonshire,* Vol. II, p. 424.
[25] G. W. O. Addleshaw, *The Beginnings of the Parochial System,* St Anthony's Hall, York (1970), pp. 12–13.

Candidus, the monastery at Medeshamstede began to send out missionaries and religious colonies and one of the earliest was that established at Brixworth. [26]

This great church, whose ironstone and red-tiled walls still tower above the village, dominating the upland country between Northampton and Market Harborough, has been justly described by A. W. Clapham as "perhaps the most imposing architectural memorial of the seventh century yet surviving north of the Alps". [27] The nave and presbytery have survived intact though shorn of the porticus or side chapels which were originally built out from the side walls. Its monumental proportions suggest a deliberate attempt to create a building to awe the newly converted. It is likely that the gallery at the west end was designed to take the catechumens, or pagans under instruction, and from here they would have an impressive glimpse of the liturgical drama below. Constructed apparently largely of Roman materials, some of which may have been brought from the Roman town of Leicester, planned like a Roman basilica and located near the great Roman Watling Street connecting London with the north-west, Brixworth may well have been inspired by Theodore of Tarsus, Archbishop of Canterbury 668–90. Its strategic position certainly suggests its link between the group of stone churches founded by Augustine in Kent and the later stone churches of Benedict Biscop and Wilfrid in the North of England.

A second very early centre of Christianity in Northamptonshire was at Oundle. Here Wilfrid founded a minster among the Middle Angles and he ended his stormy career here in 709. Bede refers to the province of Oundle (*in provincia Undalum*). The town and surrounding district were given to the abbey of Peterborough and the charter of restoration or confirmation dating from 972 shows that it

[26] F. M. Stenton, 'Medeshamstede and its colonies', in *Historical Essays in honour of James Tait* (Manchester, 1933), pp. 313–26.

[27] A. W. Clapham, *English Romanesque Architecture before the Conquest* (Oxford, 1930), Vol. I, p. 33.

was then the local government centre for 'eight hundreds' and that it had a market. St Ethelwold visited the place in his endeavours to restore the abbeys ravaged by the Danes.[28]

A surprising number of the early religious centres in the area are associated with the pious activities of women of high rank. Guthlac, the hermit of the fens who founded Crowland abbey among the dense haunted marshes and agues of South Lincolnshire, had a sister, St Pega. After burying her brother she is reputed to have lived a solitary life in a cell four leagues to the west of Crowland, traditionally associated with the village of Peakirk (Pega's kirk or church), and here she died in 716. North-east of the church, which contains late-Anglo-Saxon masonry, is a small late-thirteenth-century building, the traditional site of St Pega's cell, but called, in the only place in the records in which a title is attached, the hermitage of St Bartholomew.

St Werburgh, daughter of Wulfhere, who had a general supervision of monasteries in Mercia, founded a cell at Weedon Bec. The choice of this place is interesting because as we have already noticed the place-name means 'hill with the temple or sacred place'. The Christian missionaries deliberately took opportunities of re-using sites already endowed with sanctity during the pagan period. Peterborough Abbey lay between two tumuli, one gave its name to Howgate (later Midgate), the other lies to the south of the abbey. St Kyneburgh, sister of Wulfhere, was the abbess and founder of a Christian colony at Castor whose Norman church is dedicated to her. Her name is also preserved in a ridge known locally as Lady Conyburrow's Way.

It is likely that, apart from the building of minster churches and the founding of small religious settlements, the first visual sign of the Church in most parts of the county was the raising of standing crosses to mark Christian graves or the site of a battle, to commemorate the dead, and

[28] W. de G. Birch, *Cartularium Saxonicum* (London, 1885–93), Vol. III, p. 582.

to Christianise some spot in the open air for preaching and
the celebration of the liturgy in the field. Radstone in King's
Sutton hundred probably denotes a stone used as the socket
of a rood (O.E. *rōd*) or cross. The name Steane, a deserted
village site near Brackley with only a great house and chapel
left, means 'at the stone', though whether a boundary stone
or a standing cross is not clear. Fragments of crosses have
been found in many places, often built into the walls or
under the foundations of churches.[29] A finely ornamented
cross base with decoration of interlaced work and winged
dragons was formely in the churchyard at Castor; it has now
been taken inside the church. Other notable cross shafts
have been found at Desborough, Longthorpe, Moreton
Pinkney, Moulton, Nassington, Northampton St Peter's
and Peakirk. The carved stone about two feet long, tapered
with interlacing pattern on one side and a vine scroll on the
other, built into the late Anglo-Saxon tower at Stowe Nine
Churches, is also likely to be one of these cross shafts.

Domesday Book shows that over large parts of England
the old minster system had been displaced by the parochial
system, whereby the Church's pastoral care was exercised
through small rural and urban units coterminous with single
villages and estates, each unit having a church with its
endowment and its priest. Domesday records only three
churches in the county, at Guilsborough, Halse and
Pattishall, but there some sixty-one priests recorded in
connection with sixty villages. The fact that Domesday
fails to mention churches in places which have surviving
Anglo-Saxon structures only emphasises that it was not
meant to be an eleventh-century version of Crockford's
clerical directory. These parish churches were founded by
local lords to serve the needs of the communities on their
estates. Thorpe Achurch recalls the foundation of a church
belonging to a man called Asi or Asa.

"In the popular mind of the eleventh century the typical

[29] A list appears in *V.C.H. Northants*, Vol. II, pp. 187–99.

thegn was a man with a specific duty in the king's household, who possessed a church and a kitchen, a bell house, a fortified dwelling place, and an estate assessed at five hides of land."[30] At Earls Barton we have the remains of such a complex. The church has a commanding position beside an early fortified mound and ditch, on high ground 320 feet above sea level and 170 feet above the river Nene. The tower, although magnificently large, sixty-eight feet eight inches high and twenty-four feet wide and covered profusely with the matchstick-like decoration of pilaster strips and arches and triangles, cannot compare, aesthetically speaking, with Barnack in the far north of the county. It would seem to have been originally turriform in plan, with the lowest floor of the tower serving as nave, and a short chancel, narrower than the tower to the east. Here then was the church and bell house in one, side by side with the fortified dwelling. A second example of a Saxon thegn's establishment with a hall more than eighty feet long, a chamber block at the other end, a detached kitchen and a stone tower, thirty-five feet by thirty was found in recent excavations at Sulgrave under a Norman ringwork.[31] It is significant that the church is directly north of the fortification (which is known as *cherche knabbe* in the Canons Ashby cartulary) and has an Anglo-Saxon feature, a triangular headed doorway, in the west tower.

Other Anglo-Saxon work is found in the stout tower at Brigstock, and fragments can be detected at Geddington, Helpston, Moulton, Nassington, Pattishall, Tansor and Wansford, in addition to the six already mentioned. But the tower of Barnack church is perhaps the finest piece of Anglo-Saxon architecture in the county (Plate 5). Incorporated in it are quantities of long and short quoins and pilaster strips and the source of this was the quarries now

[30] F. M. Stenton, *Anglo-Saxon England* (Oxford, 1962), p. 480.
[31] *Medieval Archaeology*, Vol. XIII (1969), p. 236; *Current Archaeology*, Vol. XII (1969), pp. 19–22.

known as the 'hills and holes' situated south of the village
(Plate 11). They are now grassed over and the habitat of
rare orchids. It is difficult to believe that out of these holes
came the prized Barnack rag which went to build the major
churches of Peterborough, Ely, Thorney and even Norwich
Cathedral. Jope[32] has shown that bulk transport of stone
over long distances (up to seventy miles) overland as well as
by inland and coastal waters became a regular part of Saxon
building operations from at least the ninth century onwards.
In the time of Edward the Confessor, Ramsey Abbey was
licensed by Peterborough, the owners of the quarries, to
take "werkstan at Bernak and Walstan at Burgh" while in
return they furnished 4000 eels for the Lenten fare of the
monks at Peterborough. Barnack stone was used in the long
and short quoins on the exterior at Wittering and provided
the cyclopean slabs which are such a striking feature of the
chancel arch of this church. It had a far wider distribution
than this and one of the aspects of the landscape at the end
of the Anglo-Saxon period was the creaking waggons and
boats taking Barnack stone as far south as Strethall in north-
west Essex, Milton Bryan in Bedfordshire and Walkern in
Hertfordshire.

Anglo-Saxon estate and parish boundaries. Hedgerows

Recent studies of Anglo-Saxon charters in other areas
suggest that the boundaries of estates described in them
were frequently coterminous with those of modern parish
boundaries.[33] There are sufficient charters involving estates
in Northamptonshire to test out this thesis. A simple
example is the village of Twywell.[34] King Aethelred II

[32] E. M. Jope, 'The Saxon building-stone industry in Southern and
Midland England', *Medieval Archaeology*, Vol. VIII (1964), pp. 91–118.
[33] W. G. Hoskins, *Fieldwork in Local History* (London, 1967), pp. 34–40;
C. C. Taylor, *Dorset* (Making of the English Landscape series) (London,
1970), pp. 47–72.
[34] *Place Names of Northants.*, p. 188.

Plate 7 Barton Seagrave. Taken from an early-nineteenth-century engraving. The twelfth-century Norman church (its fine tympanum is no longer hidden by the small porch) and the Queen Anne period rectory now lie uneasily beside a yellow brick council housing development overlooking the river Ise.

Plate 8 T. Eayre's view of the Nene valley three miles east of Northampton, 1721. The ridge-and-furrow of Little Houghton open field leads the eye to the wooded Norman motte of Clifford's Hill dominating the river crossing. The steeples of Great Billing, Little Billing and Weston illustrate the close spacing of the medieval Nene valley villages. The view encompasses the area currently being developed in the eastern expansion of Northampton.

Plate 9   The deserted medieval village of Newbold. The former streets show up as hollow-ways between the roughly rectangular tofts and house platforms separated by boundary mounds and shallow gullies. The village site is an island in a sea of ridge-and-furrow, the medieval open fields which underlie the straight hedgelines of parliamentary enclosure.

Plate 10   Wollaston. Ridge-and-furrow taken from SP903634, looking south-south-east, in February 1969.

granted three and a half hides to his thegn Northman at
Twywell in 1013 and the bounds very briefly described run
along the stream forming the southern boundary parish to
ðrawoldeswelle, presumably the tiny stream which forms the
western boundary of the parish. The boundaries go up the
shallow valley to a triangular projection (i.e. the gore) where
they take two sharp right-angled turns, a vivid indication that
there was a clearing of this field shape at this early period.
The antiquity of the road connecting Slipton and Warkton,
suggested by the broad grass verges with the hedgelines
well back, is demonstrated by the fact that it forms the
parish boundaries of successively Cranford, Twywell and
Slipton.

A second example from the valley of the lower Nene is
Ailsworth (Aegel's farm), where the charter of A.D. 948 gives
us the bounds and, as at Twywell, they closely follow the
modern parish boundary.[35] Starting at the Nene they go
to the old *dic* on the boundaries of Sutton—this must be the
old Ailsworth–Sutton road, thence they go to the old *stræt*
—a clear indication of the route of the Roman road being
visible in the landscape of the tenth century. The *agger* of
Ermine Street, north-east of Castor station, still shows the
stub ends of ridge-and-furrow coming up to it, and its
massive appearance is due to its use as a headland in the open
fields. Thence, the bounds go north to the 'common thorn',
on the Upton boundary, south-east of Upton manor house.
They now go through woodlands (Domesday mentions
"Wood(land) 3 furlongs in length and 2 furlongs in breadth")
and on to Ailsworth heath. At this point in the far north
of the parish the bounds now turn west and go to the
Castor boundary. Through Castor Hanglands (a term met
with in a *c.* 1400 document meaning 'the woods lying on the
side of the hill') and so to the road which runs alongside
the old *dic*, thence to the Nene. The gravel in the south of
the parish is covered with prehistoric ring ditches, pit

[35] *Place Names of Northants.*, p. 228.

alignments and Romano-British linear ditches and it is not clear whether the old *dic* is one of these.

It is in the charter of A.D. 944 making a grant of thirty hides at Badby, Dodford and Everdon to Bishop Aelfric that one can come closest to an appreciation of the Anglo-Saxon landscape in Northamptonshire.[36] The boundaries begin to the north-west of Badby at the little cloven hill which is probably the prominent isolated hill known as Studborough hill: thence to the *wearge dun* between the two little hills. This is Big hill—and the boundary still runs between two areas marked by 700-feet contours. The boundary next runs north along the little *dic* at the end of the grove to the small thorns. The zigzagging mentioned in the charters is still to be seen in the parish boundary and it is likely that the deflection can be accounted for by the statement that the king granted to Aelfwine and Beorhtulf the *leah* and the *hamm* to the north of the little *dic*. The next points mirror the forested nature of the landscape brilliantly. To the hollow road, thence to hind leap, from the hind leap to the spring at the top of the clearing, from the spring to the harts' wallowing place, from there to the *leah* (a clearing in the forest) near Burntwalls farm and so to 'the Old Burh', Borough hill camp. The boundary now runs due east to the north of Mazedale (boundary valley) and thence to Watling Street. It turns west to what is now the Queen's Head Inn where it takes a southward turn to the old mill pool where the willows stand. This can be identified with the present site of Dodford mill, an example of a watermill dating back to the mid-tenth century. The boundary, followed by the present parish of Great Everdon, goes south and at Everdon Stubbs a heathen burial place, now vanished, is one of the landmarks pointed out. It then went west to the end of the hedge on the boundary of the men of Weedon, thence straight to the stump on the east side of the *leah* and then due south to the *stræt*. The *stræt* is the road which used to lead

[36] For a full discussion see *Place Names of Northants.*, pp. 10–13.

from Stowe to Preston. Two further *leahs* are mentioned, more evidence of haphazard clearance taking place at this time in broken country, then the boundary hits the old salt *stræt*. Other Salt roads are recalled, in Salterestrete in Rothwell (1330), Saltwei in Boughton (*c.* 1250), Saltweie in Braunston (1294), and in other places. It is a reminder that if few other commodities were imported from the outside world into these remote settlements, at least salt was vitally necessary. Domesday records extensive salt production around the Wash, especially in south Lincolnshire. As the boundary is followed over the ridge separating Fawsley from Badby the landmarks change from being dykes and roads to references to vegetation; from the apple tree which stands west of the way through the *leah* to the great hazel thicket, and then down to the black rushes and from there to the little hedges by the road from Badby to Charwelton. Such a charter shows that not only the parish boundary had been settled by the mid-tenth century. The countryside had also been enmeshed by a system of roads, some already 'Old', dykes had been dug in numerous places, and the landscape was being opened up by hundreds of clearings. The fact that individual trees—the 'apple tree', the 'stump'—are mentioned, implies that the forest cover was already becoming thin in some places for these to be noticed.

It is also quite clear that hedges were being planted and had become a part of the landscape in the late Saxon period. Recent studies by Dr Max Hooper of the Nature Conservancy, Monks Wood Experimental Station, have suggested that it is possible to date hedges by counting the number of flowering shrub species on both sides of a sample thirty to fifty yards in length.[37] The age is calculated by multiplying the number of shrubs by ninety-nine and subtracting sixteen. This method has been checked against those which can be

[37] N. W. Moore, M. D. Hooper and B. N. Davies, 'Hedges, Introduction and Reconnaissance Studies', *J. App. Ecology*, 4 (May 1967), pp. 201–20. Also M. D. Hooper, lecture given in Northampton, June 1971.

firmly dated from documents. The reasons are obscure: it may be that some hedges are remnants of former woodland where the fields they enclose are cut directly from the forest. A second possibility is that there has been a change in the fashion of planting—that the Saxons liked ten species, the Tudors five to six and the Victorians one. This is unlikely since the Saxons favoured hawthorns (O.E. hedge thorn). A more credible explanation is that hedges simply demonstrate the botanical law of succession. If you start off with a hawthorn hedge a succession of different species are likely to come in at different times. Under the shade of the hawthorn, a soil favourable to ash develops; then field maple colonises. As the hedge gets older some species like alder might get shaded out by the more dominant species. Spindle might be more successful than the elder. And so the ancient hedgerow goes on becoming richer in species as each century passes. A further useful comparative dating agent is the fact that *Crataegus Oxyacanthoides*, the two-styled hawthorn, is by far the more ancient and may well be found in hedgerows 1000 years old; *Crataegus Monogyna,* the common hawthorn, is only 200 years old. A fifty-yard stretch of the parish boundary hedgerow just described in the Badby charter north of Staverton lodge yielded nine species, sycamore, elder, wild rose, hawthorn, bramble, crab apple, oak, woody nightshade, blackthorn. This would give a date 100 years later than the date of the estate charter. Dr Hooper has studied the hedges of the parish of Polebrook and has shown that there was very early enclosure in the open fields with five to six species, reversed-S-shaped hedges, denoting consolidation of the strips as early as the fourteenth century. These contrast with the two species straight hedges of the 1759 enclosure onward. What is needed is a series of studies undertaken in the county, if we are to have a proper appreciation of the evolution of the hedge pattern.

Shire and hundred boundaries

The earliest reference to the shire by name is *Hamtanscir* in the *Anglo-Saxon Chronicle* for 1011, and it is generally accepted that the origin of Northamptonshire lies in the district occupied by a particular Danish army (*here*) based on Hamtun. The full form of Northampton does not appear until 1065, presumably to differentiate the town from South-hampton. The original county certainly included Rutland and it is possible that Watling Street may have been its first boundary towards the west.

Like the other English counties, the shire was divided into smaller units called hundreds and there were twenty-nine hundreds in Northamptonshire recorded in Domesday Book. Hundred court meetings were held in the open air and as such their locations are a part of the history of the landscape. Usually some prominent hill or perhaps a tree or grove was chosen; sometimes fords and road junctions. In a number of cases, such as sites sacred to pagan worship, it is clear that the place of assembly had a far older origin. In most cases tracks and routeways converge on the hundred meeting place and along these came the suitors prepared to transact the administrative and judicial business of the hundred. Morton recalls, for instance, "the famous Beech tree in Fawsley Park under which the Hundred Court call'd Mangrave was formerly kept". The Mangrave or 'common-grove' was at the Knob, on the highest point of the ridge, over 500 feet above sea level, 150 yards north of the junction of the parishes of Badby, Fawsley and Everdon. Similar hilltop sites are found in Spelhoe hundred (it means the hill of speech) and at Hamfordshoe, where "Low Hill alrode in the feld in the particion between Barton Feld and Ashebye" has been identified with the field called Round hill—where there is a small mound in a commanding position with a view over the whole countryside.

A name like Modley (O.E. *mōt Lēah*, moot clearing) is the

clue for the Greens Norton hundred meeting place and old
tracks lead to these fields on the Towcester–Litchborough
road to the west of Field Burcote. The hundred of Nassaborough was in the far north of the county, the *næss*
being the nose or promontory which juts into the fens
between Welland and Nene, 'borough' being the abbey of
Peterborough. The meeting place was at Langdyke Bush
where the parishes of Ufford, Helpston and Upton join.
Here also is the junction of King Street, the Roman road
which pursues its rigidly straight alignment from Nene to
Welland and thence north to Sleaford, and the east and west
ridgeway which connects Stamford to Peterborough. In the
tenth century this spot was referred to as *Dicon,* the plural
of *dic* (dykes), and three hundred years later evidently the
drainage ditches of the roads were still sufficiently marked
to justify the fourteenth-century name for the meeting place
as the 'Abbots hundred of Langdyke' (Plate 26).

Occasionally an individual imprinted his name on the
administrative map. Nafarr was some powerful Viking
settler who gave his name to the ford, the brook, the grove
(*Naveres Lund*—part of Huxloe hundred) and to the hundred
of Navisford itself. The meeting place here was at the river
crossing of the Nene where the parishes of Aldwinkle,
Thorpe Achurch and Titchmarsh meet. Just as we have seen
evidence for continuity in the use of pagan sacred sites as
the locations for churches, there are at least two examples of
hundred meeting places having far older associations. Such
is Harrow hill, the likely hundred meeting place of Nobottle
grove hundred. A number of tracks lead to it and the name
itself (O.E. *hearg*, sacred grove) goes back into the heathen
past. A similar sacred site, 'Hoc's *hlaw*' or his barrow,
served as the meeting place of Huxloe hundred. This is
found sited about half a mile south-east of Lowick church.[38]

[38] *Medieval England, An Aerial Survey*, p. 260 for Nassaborough. *Place Names of Northants.*, p. 9 (Fawsley), p. 137 (Hamfordshoe), p. 38 (Modley), pp. 223–4 (Nassaborough), p. 216 (Navisford), p. 280 (Nobottle), p. 177 (Huxloe).

If we break off our consideration of the Anglo-Saxon landscape at this point it is not because the Norman Conquest marked a watershed in any sense in the development of the Northamptonshire landscape. The area of cultivation continued to expand, the forests were nibbled away year by year, new settlements were founded. The countryside went on evolving in its own way despite the wholesale changes in land ownership brought about by the Conquest.

3. The early medieval landscape: the countryside

Domesday Book. The open fields. Land hunger and the expansion of settlement. The forests—assarting. Reclamation from the fen. Secular buildings in the landscape. Castles and manor houses. Moats and fishponds. Monasteries and churches in the landscape

Domesday Book

DOMESDAY BOOK is a convenient starting point for a consideration of the early medieval landscape, since for the first time we have a detailed documentary record of towns, villages and hamlets, methods and varieties of farming, the proportions of arable, waste, forest and meadow, population, the distribution of mills and churches and the development of the infant industries of Norman England.[1] The main motive behind this enormous undertaking, in Stenton's words, was William's "desire to learn the essential facts about his kingdom . . . 'how it was peopled, and with what sort of men'." The amount of information, though vast, is very condensed, often incomplete and at times exceedingly difficult to interpret. To extract a picture of the eleventh-century landscape requires considerable disentangling.

The clearest fact that emerges from the Domesday statistics is the comparative density of settlement in the

[1] For Domesday Book see J. H. Round's text in *V.C.H. Northants.* (London, 1902), Vol. I, pp. 301–56.

Nene valley, occupying the centre of the county.[2] This is not indicated by the distribution of villages but by the relatively greater population figures and numbers of plough teams. In this region the densities of plough teams (3–8 per square mile) and of population (9·2 per square mile) contrasts greatly with the much smaller figures found in the North-amptonshire Heights region in the west of the county. In the Guilsborough hundred for instance there were only 1–3 teams and 4–5 persons per square mile. The clay region to the east of the Nene had only sporadic settlement, noticeably in the Higham Ferrers hundred where there were only 2 teams and 4·8 recorded persons per square mile. Whittle-wood and Rockingham forests were both sparsely settled with little cultivated land in the eleventh century. The density of plough teams and population are only about half those recorded per square mile in the Nene valley. The Soke of Peterborough shows few vills and some are very large such as Werrington which had 28 plough teams and a recorded population of 57. If we take the area corresponding to a plough as most frequently equivalent to 120 acres and assume that 'ploughlands' as a rule designated land in arable use, then we come to Postan's remarkable conclusion that the totals of Domesday plough teams and ploughlands in Northamptonshire, as in most Midland counties, "would correspond to an acreage under plough larger, sometimes much larger than it was to be at the highest point of English arable husbandry in the second half of the nine-teenth century".[3]

This emphasises the point that Domesday Book records the state of the primary colonisation of Northamptonshire near the *end* of the long process. The total number of separate places mentioned in the area included in the modern

[2] H. C. Darby and I. B. Terrett, *The Domesday Geography of Midland England* (Cambridge, 1971), pp. 416–19.
[3] M. M. Postan (ed.), *Cambridge Economic History of Europe, I, The Agrarian Life of the Middle Ages* (Cambridge, 1966), pp. 549–663.

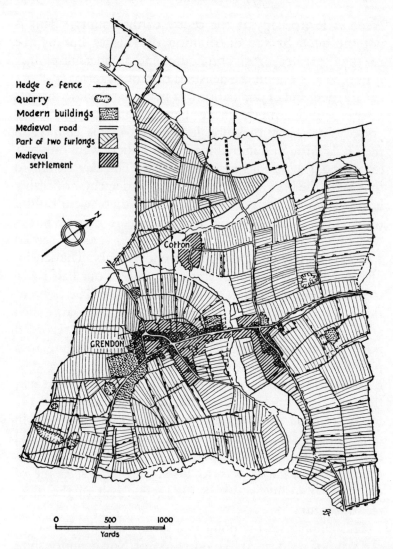

Legend:
- Hedge & fence
- Quarry
- Modern buildings
- Medieval road
- Part of two furlongs
- Medieval settlement

Cotton

GRENDON

0   500   1000
Yards

Fig. 6. The medieval landscape of Grendon, based on a map by David
N. Hall of Rushden

Mr Hall has been studying the distribution of ridge-and-furrow in the
eastern part of the county. By skilfully combining the evidence of
documents, ancient estate maps, air-photographs and field survey, he
is succeeding in recreating vanished landscapes such as this one round
the village of Grendon in the central Nene valley.

county seems to be 324. There are in fact only forty modern villages which are not mentioned in Domesday Book. Although the documents of the twelfth and thirteenth centuries abound with references to recent reclamation, especially in the forest and fen area, as will be seen, it can no longer by assumed that the main work was done during this period. Not only had the basic settlement pattern been laid down by the middle of the eleventh century, but in large parts of the county the cultivated area had also reached its maximum extent.

The open fields

We might well ask at this stage, what was the appearance of these field systems surrounding these Northamptonshire villages of the early Middle Ages? How far have features from them been preserved in the modern landscape? It has long been realised that there is some connection between the surviving visible remains of 'ridge-and-furrow' and medieval field systems. These wave-like undulations found in fields throughout the Midlands show up particularly well early in the morning or late in the evening of a sunny day. They are accentuated in pasture during dry seasons where the humped back of the former ridges is parched, while the furrows remain green. In winter the furrows retain the snow longer and a curious corrugated effect is seen (Plate 10). In ploughed land for a time their presence is shown by bands of different colouring in the soil or crop. In many areas, especially in the north of the county, they have been ploughed out and it is only in the air-photographs of the 1940s and early 1950s that the original extent can be traced for many parishes.

When viewed from the air a number of interesting features immediately leap into view. The ridge-and-furrow is seen to be older than existing overriding hedges; the frequent changes of direction of the ridge-and-furrow is accounted for by the fact that they are in blocks or furlongs, which in turn are subdivided into long narrow strips called *selions* or *lands*. These strips frequently are shaped with the so-called 'aratral curve', a reversed S which derives from the problem of turning a team of beasts in a tight circle. By swinging left some yards before the land end, the turning circle is increased to bring the oxen drawing the plough into position for the return furrow. Each unit from furrow to furrow marked a single strip in the open fields. As they were ploughed separately, year after year, gradually ridges were built up towards the centre of each strip. In addition to lengthwise ridging, the plough dragged soil forward and, on turning, soil was deposited at the ends of the land; the heaps were called *heads* and where two furlongs with lands met at right-angles, the first land of one was made up of the smoothed-out heads of the others and was called the *headlands*. I live in a road in Kettering known as Headlands; a glance at the pre-enclosure map of Kettering confirms that my house lies at the head of a group of furlongs which met another block at right-angles.

The earliest open-field maps are the Elizabethan surveys of the late sixteenth century. The pre-enclosure map of Strixton, dating from 1583, shows a close similarity between the surviving earthworks of ridge-and-furrow in the parish today and those facing the Elizabethan surveyor. Again, at Weston Pinkney, aerial photographs of the ridge-and-furrow show a close correspondence with the strips drawn in the 1593 map in All Souls College. But these maps delineate the system after a good deal of the medieval complexity had been pruned; they give no indication as to how the scattered pattern of ownership developed.[4]

When one is walking over the gently undulating ridges

---

[4] For Strixton see D. N. Hall and N. Nickerson, 'The Earthworks at Strixton', *Journal of the Northampton Museums and Art Gallery*, 6 (1969), pp. 22–34. For Weston Pinkney see M. W. Beresford and J. K. St Joseph, *Medieval England, An Aerial Survey* (Cambridge, 1958), pp. 33–35.

and furrows which marked the multiplicity of strips making up the individual holdings of medieval families and which are found intact round so many Northamptonshire villages, particularly in the south of the county, the question of the origin of the system comes to mind. It is obvious that the oldest strips are likely to be near the edges of the built-up area of the village because while some are overlain by the crofts of subsequent expansion these represented the land first cleared. Since each addition to the cultivated land from the waste was a co-operative venture it is highly likely that the newly cleared land was allocated to the families who had assisted in the clearing and ploughing. But it is equally likely that in some places partible inheritance could lead in several generations to the fragmentation of farms originally in the form of consolidated fields into smaller holdings. A further possibility is that the subdivision of fields among co-heirs would produce a pattern of unenclosed parcels in intermixed ownership. We know that peasants on the Peterborough Abbey estates bought and sold land frequently in the thirteenth and early fourteenth centuries.[5] The needs and resources of individual families were too unequal and too unstable to allow family holdings to remain uniform or unaltered in size. In fact the open-field landscape of thirteenth-century Northamptonshire was in a constant state of flux as peasants sold or sub-let their holdings *propter paupertatem, propter impotenciam* or *propter senectutem* and other peasants bought and consolidated theirs. Their charters give a picture of the medley of cultivators and their intermixed holdings all known and named. An example of this can be seen in a grant of about 1303 by Simon Gere of Dogsthorpe and Mabel his wife to Simon in *Le Wro*, Agnes his wife and their heirs, of one acre in Dogsthorpe in the furlong called *Apeltre*, between the land (strip) of Richard of Crowland and of Robert Alred—and a headland called

[5] C. N. L. Brooke and M. M. Postan (eds.), *Carte Nativorum*, Northants. Record Society, Vol. XX (1960).

Heyehevedlond abutting to the east on the land of Gilbert Gere
and to the west on the land then held by William, then
abbot's carter; and one acre of meadow in Edgerley between
the monks' meadow on the east and Robert Sewale's on the
west, abutting on the Causeway to Oxney at one end and the
abbot's meadow at the other. In this case Agnes is Simon's
daughter so we are seeing the fragmentation of a peasant
holding taking place.[6] The area described is now on the
outskirts of Peterborough. The long pale pink fingers of
ribbon development and post-World War II housing stretch
over the open fields once worked by these peasant tenants of
Peterborough Abbey.

In another of these charters there is mention of a green
road among blocks of furlongs between Garton and
Newark[7] and this draws attention to the problem of access
to the fields. Detailed study of the location of ridge-and-
furrow in relation to the hollow-ways and common baulks
across the fields has suggested that curving lanes were
driven out from the original nucleus of settlement, and
clearing began on either side—with the furlongs laid out
either parallel or at right-angles to the tracks. The remaining
irregular areas between these orderly encroachments were
those last brought in from the scrub, forest and waste, and
the arrangements of the furlongs here are a haphazard
affair.[8] The hollow-ways which are such a distinctive
feature of deserted medieval village sites imply heavy
transport, and Lynn White has pointed out how the invention of improved and larger wagons coincided with the
increase of distance between the margins of cultivation and
the village in the boom period of thirteenth-century
agriculture.[9] Archaeological sections across village roads,
as at the deserted medieval village of Faxton, have revealed
that early hollow rutted lanes were metalled in this period

[6] *Carte Nativorum*, p. 39, No. 120.   [7] *Carte Nativorum*, p. 4, No. 4.
[8] D. N. Hall, Lecture at C.B.A. conference at Wolverton, November 1971.
[9] Lynn White, *Medieval Technology and Social Change* (Oxford, 1962), p. 68.

and deep drainage ditches carved out on either side. These took the increased wear of two- and four-wheeled carts which have left traces in strake nails and linchpins picked up on sites such as the medieval industrial site at Lyveden.

Land hunger and the expansion of settlement

Despite the fact that there were great stretches of the county which appear to have been already fully occupied by the time Domesday Book was written, there are unmistakable symptoms of a pressure of population on land, and a resultant land hunger in the early medieval period which have left their mark on the landscape.

Medieval population statistics are notoriously difficult to interpret but some indication of changing trends is given if we compare the numbers recorded in Domesday Book (1086), the tax returns of 1301, and the poll tax of 1377.

South-west uplands

	1086	1301	1377
Astwell	17	35	57
Canons Ashby	16	18	82
Fawsley	17	44	90
Purston	7	16	
Stuchbury	10	21	59

Western uplands

Elkington	17		30

Upper Nene valley

Brockhall (with Muscott)	6	48	
Glassthorpe	6	14	

Centre

Faxton	21		94
		(with Mawsley)	

North

Wothorpe	16	19	40

These figures are all from villages which subsequently disappeared.[10]

A second sign of expanding settlement is the appearance of numerous daughter hamlets and villages budding off the older settlements. A few of these are distinguished in Domesday Book. Upper and Nether Heyford in the upper Nene valley, for example, appear as *Heiforde* and *Altera Haiford*; Great and Little Weldon are represented as *Weledene* and *Parva Weledone*. Great and Little Addington are a further instance of a pair of settlements. *Edintone*, the parent vill, was divided into two manors and here Hugh held one and a half hides from the bishop of Durham, and the abbey of Thorney held two hides. Domesday also mentions another *Edintone*, which is doubtless Little Addington. Here Osmund held one hide and one virgate. The parish is rectangular in shape and is sandwiched between the extremely ancient settlement of Irthlingborough and the larger bounds of the parent village of Great Addington. The parish boundaries zigzag with many right-angled turns and returns and it is likely that their jagged edges represent the margins of the fields already ploughed—each straight stretch a block of furlongs. The waste and forest between Little Addington and the two older villages had already been largely cleared along the northern and southern edges of the parish by the time the boundaries were demarcated. Only to the west are there long straight stretches suggesting an arbitrary line drawn through unmapped oaks and undergrowth.

Great and Little Brington are another pair of settlements. *Brinintone* is mentioned in Domesday Book. There were two manors—William de Cahagnes had half a hide and William Peverel one and a half hides here. The secondary settlement of Nobottle 'the new building (or grove)' is also referred to among Peverel's lands. This is in the southern part of the

[10] K. J. Allison, M. W. Beresford, J. G. Hurst, *The Deserted Villages of Northamptonshire* (Leicester, 1966), passim.

parish, and indeed the fields of Nobottle extended in a long wedge-shaped tongue towards Harpole. There is no mention of Little Brington, however, which is likely to have been a post-Conquest offshoot receiving its first reference in an *Inquisitio Post Mortem* of 1284. Hereafter Great Brington is sometimes distinguished by being called Church Brington.

At times we come across the ecclesiastical division of a pair of settlements, the senior one taking its name from the parish church and the other from the chapel. Domesday mentions only one Brampton. When the parish was carved into two, Church Brampton retained a long narrow strip of land which stretches only one field width to the Nene in the south and up to the 350-foot contour line of the hill by Holdenby East Lodge to the north. The first mention of the two separate settlements comes in the thirteenth century (when they are referred to as Great and Little) and the first use of the prefix Church comes in 1287. Bridges says there are only "very imperfect traditions" of the chapel which gave its name to the junior village. Stowe Nine Churches, mentioned in a land charter of A.D. 956, had a secondary settlement, Upper Stowe. In the same area, Weedon Bec or Church Weedon had an offshoot to the west known as Upper Weedon. There is a tendency for these secondary settlements to be strung along a road, presumably already in existence, while the founders of the parent village, inhibited in no way by pre-existing clearance, scattered their homes round a tangle of lanes, loops and greens. They are also often found further up the side of the valley.

A third sign of an expansion of cultivation on the fringes of the area already cleared is seen in the appearance in the records of the twelfth and thirteenth centuries of isolated farmsteads, built well away from the earlier nucleated settlements. Although they are not mentioned until this date, the Anglo-Saxon elements in their names sometimes suggest a pre-Conquest origin. This development can be seen going on in the upland area of the west of the county.

Byfield, a nucleated village adjoining the Warwickshire border, with the double-loop plan we have noticed as characteristic of this area, has a straggling extension to the west known as Westhorp. Both are mentioned in Domesday Book, Earl Hugh holding eight hides in Byfield, with land for twenty ploughs, and Gunfrid holding half a hide in Westhorp. In the north of the parish are two isolated farms, Ludwell (Lord spring) and Pitwell, first mentioned respectively in 1247 and 1285. Both stand high, over 500 feet above sea level. We know that the fields attached to these villages stretched out as far as Charwelton hill by the middle of the thirteenth century since it is described as *"le Graundone* [big hill] *que jacet inter campos de Charwelton et Bifeld"*. Greens Norton, a mile to the north-west of Towcester, also mentioned in Domesday Book, has four isolated settlements in the north of the parish which are first mentioned in the thirteenth century. Caswell (Cress spring) *c.* 1200, Duncote (Dunnas' cottages) 1227, Field Burcote (peasants' cottages) *c.* 1200 and Potcote Farm (cottages in the depression) 1202. They all lie high on the 400-foot contour line.

We can trace a similar process but on a larger scale in the forested south-east part of the county. Syresham is another good example of the double-loop plan found in heavily wooded areas, and here the church occupies the northern-most of the loops. The village was divided into three portions at the time of Domesday of which the largest, two hides in Earl Aubrey's fee, is dealt with alongside Brackley and Halse. There were also two smaller holdings, of half a hide and one and a half hides. The farms towards the edges of the parish first mentioned in the thirteenth and fourteenth centuries reflect in their names the fact that they were won by clearing from the thick woodland: Fernily (Ferny clearing or wood) 1365, Hazelborough Lodge (Hazel Hill) *c.* 1220, Wetleys wood (wheat clearing) 1287, Whistley (clearing in soft ground) *c.* 1200, Wold House (from O.E. *weald*—wood) *c.* 1220, Crowfield, 1287, Langley, *temp.*

Edward I, and Kingshill, *temp.* Henry II. The small and irregular shapes of the fields also suggest forest clearance. The fact that a number of these settlements have disappeared from the map indicates that the lands so won may well have been marginal in quality. Birchenhoe (found *c.* 1200 and into the fourteenth century) is now lost; so is Fernily.[11]

The forests—assarting

This discussion has led us into the forests and a study of Domesday makes clear that one of the outstanding facts about the mid-eleventh-century landscape of Northamptonshire was its wooded aspect.[12] When the recorded wood is mapped it falls into two main areas. The northern area corresponds in a general way to the present-day forest of Rockingham and it can be further subdivided into two belts of woodland. The one to the east of the Nene between Nassington and Woodford is mainly on the Oxford Clay and Cornbrash. We have already noticed that this was the area called the forest of Bromswold. The other lies along the north-western boundary between Easton-on-the-Hill and Brampton Ash and here the underlying rocks are mostly Northampton Sands. Domesday settlements are particularly sparse and the population density was at its lowest in this region. The southern area was confined largely to the Boulder Clay and the Lias Clay of the Tove valley and to the Northampton Sands in the west. This is the area later known as Whittlewood and Salcey forests.

It is futile to attempt to calculate the area occupied by woodland recorded in Domesday Book because most of the entries are given in the form of linear measurements. At Benefield, in the heart of Rockingham forest, for instance, there was woodland "one league in length and half a league

[11] *Place Names*, pp. 33, 18, 59, 60.
[12] J. M. Steane, 'The forests of Northamptonshire in the early Middle Ages', *Northants. Past and Present*, Vol. V, I (1973), pp. 7–17.

99

in breadth". Nor is the position much clearer when acres are mentioned as at Barton Seagrave, where there were recorded eight acres of wood, because we are uncertain as to what area was implied by an acre. Where, however, Domesday is unequivocally helpful is when it gives information about the economic uses of woodland.

The wood at Aldwinkle measured two leagues in length and one in breadth; "it is worth 15 shillings when it bears *mast*". In other counties, especially to the east and south, woodland was measured in terms of the numbers of swine which fed upon acorns and beechmast. Manuscript illustrations show them to have been bristly woodland beasts, not the plump, pink porkers of today's factory farms.

The entries for Corby and Gretton demonstrate the close connection between wood and ironworking. "Many things are wanting to this manor which in King Edward's time belonged to it in wood and ironworks and other matters." At Deene, Greens Norton and Towcester smiths are mentioned rendering considerable sums and all these places were located in well-wooded areas where the supply of charcoal was abundant. Archaeological evidence for iron-smelting in the former woodland area of the forest of Rockingham at Lyveden in the early twelfth century has been found, and the siting of the pottery industry in this settlement from 1200 to 1325 was no doubt connected with the availability of brushwood and timber fuel in large quantities. Oak, field maple and hawthorn have been identified in charcoals found in twelfth- to thirteenth-century levels here.[13]

The Fotheringhay entry gives information on a further use of the forest "when it bore mast, *and the king does not hunt in it it is worth 10 shillings*". The crown, in fact, had already begun to use the area as a hunting reserve and it is likely that

[13] *Medieval Archaeology*, Vol. XIII (1969), pp. 285–6, Vol. XIV (1970), pp. 203–5. *Journal of Northampton Museums and Art Gallery*, 5 (1969), pp. 1–50, 9 (1971), pp. 1–94.

the afforestation of at least three large tracts in the county
was the outcome of Norman and Angevin rule. A charter
of William Rufus confirming to the abbey of Peterborough
a tithe of the hunting in Northamptonshire is witnessed by
Richard Engaine at Brigstock,[14] and we know that the
Engaines of Pytchley held their lands by the service of
chasing wolves from those coverts. Their seal has a running
wolf with two pieces of broken spear above and the head
of an axe below.[15] A writ of William Rufus to Richard
Engaine and others commanding them to safeguard the
rights of the abbot of Thorney in Charwelton and Twywell
is dated at King's Cliffe 1094–1100.[16] Both documents were
doubtless issued during the king's periods of hunting in the
forest of Rockingham.

Apart from the royal castles of Northampton and
Rockingham the Norman and Angevin kings had six houses
all of which are likely to have been connected with the
pursuit of hunting in the royal forests. Geddington was a
hunting lodge in Rockingham forest; the site of the house
was to the north of the church and tiles and pottery were
found in digging trenches for the housing estate which now
overlies it. Henry II and Richard I were frequent visitors and
repairs and reconstructions were carried out here, particularly
during Henry III's reign, and from time to time during the
reign of Edward I. At Brigstock the site of the house is
unknown, but a field, Fish Pond meadow, to the north of
the village preserves the memory of the royal ponds where
pike and bream were kept. King's Cliffe was a royal manor
which gave its name to one of the three bailiwicks into which
Rockingham forest was divided, but all that remains of the

---

[14] *Regesta Regum Anglo-Normannorum*, Vol. I, No. 446. I owe this reference
to Dr Edmund King, University of Sheffield.
[15] A. L. Poole, *Domesday Book to Magna Carta* (Oxford, 1964), p. 31,
L. C. Lloyd and D. M. Stenton (eds.), *Sir Christopher Hatton's Book of Seals*,
Northants. Record Society, XV (1960), plate iii, No. 120.
[16] D. M. Stenton (ed.), *Facsimiles of Early Charters*, Northants. Record
Society (1940), p. 8.

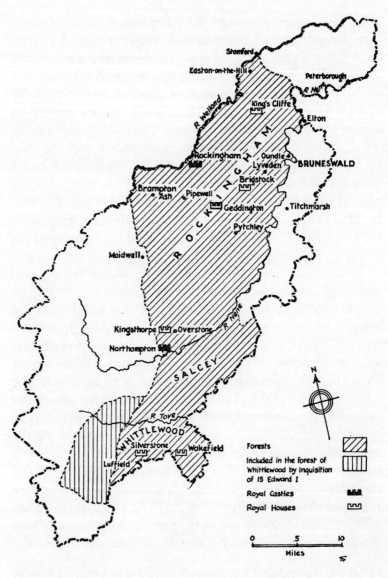

Fig. 7. The extent of the royal forests of Northamptonshire in the
thirteenth century

With acknowledgments to M. L. Bazeley, 'The extent of the English
forest in the thirteenth century', *Royal Hist. Soc. Trans.*, 4th series
(1921).

lodge are the earthworks of the fishponds now breached and overgrown with trees to the south of the church. Kingsthorpe lay in the forest of Rockingham and adjoining the royal park of Moulton which was attached to Northampton Castle. The lodges at Silverstone and Wakefield frequently figure in the royal records of the twelfth and thirteenth centuries for rebuilding and repairs but again the fishponds attached to them are the only discernible traces on the landscape.

Occasionally among the records of innumerable prosecutions for poaching in the forest eyre rolls are incidental glimpses of the woodland landscape. We find that William of Northampton and Roger Tingewick were on their way to the pleas of Salcey when they heard that poachers were in the *Lawn* of Benefield. Lawns were enclosed pasture within the forest, originally to provide grazing and hay for deer. They ambushed five poachers, "one with a cross bow and four with bows and arrows standing at their trees . . . [they pursued] the aforesaid malefactors so vigorously that they turned and fled into the thickness of the wood. And the foresters on account of the darkness could follow them no more."[17]

The extent of the forests is known from the perambulations made at intervals. The enormous size of Rockingham forest is seen from the survey made in 1286. It stretched from the south bridge of Northampton to the bridge of Stamford, a distance of thirty-three miles, and from the river Nene on the east to the Welland and Maidwell stream on the north-west—an average breadth of between seven and eight miles. These perambulations remind us that the royal forest was not a vast extent of woodland but simply an area within which forest law operated. Whole villages with their appropriate complement of arable and pasture lay within the boundaries of the royal forest. The bounds of the forest of Whittlewood for instance in the perambulation

[17] G. J. Turner (ed.), *Select Pleas of the Forest*, Selden Society, Vol. XIII (1901), p. 28.

of 1299 went "between the fields of Great Denshanger
and Little Denshanger to the Portway" (an ancient road
through the forest in the direction of Northampton).[18]
Richard de Clare, it was alleged in 1252, chased with his
hounds a hart from the wood of Micklewood "as far as the
field of Desborough above Rothwell" (*in campum de
Deseburg supra Rowell*).[19] There were also enclosed fields.
The perambulation just mentioned, traces the bounds "between the fees of Passenham and Wykedyve to the garden of
Elias de Tyngewyk and so by a certain ditch including the
said garden . . .". There were areas of private woodland,
and grants of liberties and franchises such as free warren
were made to the owners of lands and woods within the
area technically forest. Such were the woods of Cosgrove
and of Furtho belonging to the prior of Snelshall, Elias de
Tyngewyk, John FitzJohn and John de Bernevyll.

In the thirteenth century the main interest that the forests
held for their lords was hunting the beasts of the chase.
Their function as a reservoir of timber both for fuel and for
building was destined, however, in the long run to be more
important. Thus Henry III gave valuable timber in one year
to such personages as the Countess of Cornwall (five oaks),
Reginald de Plesset (seven oaks), William de Swineford
(six oaks) and the Friars Minor of Stamford, who were
given fifteen oaks to help construct their schoolhouse. Also
for his own building he sent orders to Hugh of Goldingham,
the warden of the royal forests between the bridge of Oxford
and Stamford, to provide the sheriff of Northampton with
twelve oaks from the royal forest of Salcey and eighteen
oaks from the royal enclosures at Handley for the works of
the castle of Northampton and twelve oaks from the forest
of Dersley for the royal works at Geddington.[20]

[18] G. Baker, *History and Antiquities of Northamptonshire* (1836–41), Vol. II,
pp. 75–76.
[19] *Select Pleas of the Forest*, p. 34.
[20] *Cal. Close Rolls*, 1254–6, pp. 85, 138, 290, 112, 117.

The axes of the royal foresters were not the only ones at work. The sinister sound of felling by night was heard by the foresters of the lord king in 1251 as they walked in the park of Brigstock. They found a trap set in *Aldnatheshawe* and heard a man cutting wood by night in the park; later they met Robert (Le Noble of Sudborough chaplain), "who came from the wood and carried in his hand a branch of green oak and an axe". They arrested him, searched his house at Sudborough and found further incriminating evidence including barbed arrows and the woodwork of a deer trap. The chaplain was held at Brigstock until his case came before the justices.

Offences against the *vert* (vegetation conserved for animals in the forest) figure frequently in the pleas of the forest. In 1253 we read that Walter Kakilherd, the man of Sir Hugh Goldingham, the steward of the forest came into the forest of Geddington at Westleigh and "felled to the ground two oaks in the demesne woods of the lord king and a third oak in *Themanneshedge* in the demesne woods of the lord king— And the said oaks were carried to Oakley to the house of the said Walter." And again we hear that "William Wick took a sapling in Springshedge in the demesne wood of the lord king: by what warrant they know not." The vicar of Geddington living right under the nose of the royal servants of the king's hunting lodge was more fortunate than his colleague at Sudborough: he had two trees delivered for fuel "of the gift of the lord king".[21]

These minor depredations affected the forest cover only to a small extent by comparison with the wholesale clearance resulting from the increased pressure of population on land which reached its height in the county during the thirteenth and early fourteenth centuries. *Assarting* means the uprooting of trees and the reduction of the land on which they stood to cultivation. It was necessary to enclose an assart to keep the beasts of the forest from trampling down or

[21] *Select Pleas of the Forest*, pp. 94, 110, 116.

feeding on the crops planted thereon. The punishment for making illegal assarts was an amercement at the next forest eyre and also a fine on the crops sown on it, something like one shilling for every acre of winter-sown corn and sixpence for every acre of spring-sown corn.

The monasteries of Midland England were in the forefront of this process as improving landlords and we can follow their activities in the forests by taking three detailed examples from different parts of the county. Luffield Priory, founded *c.* 1124 deep in Whittlebury forest on the border with Buckinghamshire, was poorly endowed at the outset. The monks, however, are soon found increasing their properties by assarting. William de Stapleford released to the priory his right in the wood and the monks' assart which they had in the demesne wood of Norton, saving his right, in common with the whole countryside, to pasture there when the crops had been carried (1235–45). John Marshal granted to the priory an assart situated between the one the monks had received from William de Clairvaux and the wood on the one side and the assart of Henry de Perio and the wood on the other (1225–35).[22] The right of droving was safeguarded when roads were driven through the forests. Between 1216 and 1225 Geoffrey de Insula bargained with the priory to have "a drove road running northwards from the land of Robert de Pavely to the wood of Norton which should be four perches wide, by the perch of 16½ feet as far as the land of Gregory de Towcester next the ditch of the Countess and from the land of Gregory to the wood of Norton it shall be 3 perches wide".[23]

Peterborough Abbey possessed lands in the most densely wooded part of the county.[24] Domesday records a large stretch of woodland at Oundle, three leagues by two, which

[22] G. R. Elvey (ed.), *Luffield Priory Charters*, Part 1, Northants. Record Society, Vol. XXII (1968), pp. 162–3.

[23] *Luffield Priory Charters*, p. 175.

[24] I am grateful to Dr Edmund King for allowing me to read Chapter 4 of his book on Peterborough Abbey in typescript.

may mean four and a half miles by three. The forest eyres
show that the monks were clearing here in 1163 and 1167.
A comprehensive charter from Richard I in 1189 confirmed
400 acres of assarts. These clearances naturally needed farms
from which they were administered and stocked. Such
unlicensed encroachments involving building or enclosure
were known as *purprestures*. An example was *Novum Locum*
(New Place), the foundation of Abbot Benedict (1177–93),
of whom it is recorded:

"He also built *Novum Locum*, which was a purpresture
made by Fulk of Lisours, the chief forester, on the abbey
manor of Oundle. He obtained it in a case against William
of Lisours. All that pertained to *Novum Locum*, namely nine
carucates of land and the woods of Sywardeshaw and
Frendeshaw and all the rights of the church in that area, he
either vigorously retained or else justly recovered by law or
force of arms."

In 1209 the regarders presented a further 'old assart' of
eighty acres at *Novum Locum*, two-thirds of it sown with
oats and the rest with wheat, and assarting was still going on
here in the fourteenth century.

Biggin Grange, a mile to the west of Oundle, was a new
manor, entirely carved out of forest land; it grew much
larger than the manor of Oundle from which it was founded.
In 1301, 180 acres were sown at Oundle and 482 at Biggin
Grange. In 1321 there were 200 acres of arable land in
demesne and other 200 acres newly brought under the
plough and therefore worth only a penny an acre; also a
park. The country is still well wooded in this area. Thick
wedges of trees crown either side of the valley leading west
from Oundle towards Brigstock. Between Lyveden and
Benefield is Banhaw wood. Humphrey of Bassingbourne
obtained licence to enclose "a hundred acres of waste . . . in
his wood of Banho, which is within the bounds of the forest
of Rockingham, and reduce it to cultivation as the said
waste is distant one league from the covert of the forest and

is not a frequent resort of the king's deer". [25] The high proportion (twenty per cent) of deer among bones excavated in the thirteenth-century levels of the deserted medieval settlement at Lyveden in this same valley belies the royal record. The potters of Lyveden evidently made use of the king's deer in supplementing their meat diet and in making tools for their trade from the dense deer bone. [26]

An interesting parallel process is seen at work in the abbey estates in the far north of the county, where the work of clearance started to gather pace in the mid-twelfth century and was at its peak in the period 1175 to 1225. Two charters of Stephen confirmed to the abbey "200 acres of assart" in the Soke of Peterborough, 115 acres in Longthorpe, 55 acres in Walton and 70 acres in Castor and Ailsworth. (This comes to 240 acres in fact.) In the eyres of Alan de Neville the abbey is found alongside its knights and free tenants in the Soke, paying fines for assarting in this area. Lists of assarts were made in 1209. There are seventy-eight entries and the total amount is only 145 acres. The parcels of land are small: five acres is counted as a large holding and amounts of half an acre frequent: Matilda of Scotendon for instance held three acres in Dogsthorpe, and parcels of two acres, one rood, half an acre and one acre in Peterborough. Abbot Robert of Lindsey (1214–22) farmed a grange in the manor of Castor which he granted to the cellary comprising: "All our new assarts in Nassaburgh, that is to say *Belsize* with all its dependencies, and Glintonhage and the assarts of Estmede, and Fraenhame bought up from William de Guthiges and all the meadow bought in Northborough."

He built houses at Belsize, now a farm in the north of Castor parish, and planted hedges and drained the land around it. There seems to have been some encroachment on other men's rights because Richard de Waterville, a knight, and other free men of Castor and Marholm brought an

[25] *Cal. Patent Rolls*, 1313–17, p. 453.
[26] *Journal of Northampton Museum and Art Gallery*, 9 (1971), pp. 90–92.

assize of Novel Disseisin against the abbot.[27] The fields around Belsize are small, with many turns and returns; large amounts of woodland still remain in irregularly shaped patches to remind us that in the thirteenth century this was an area of colonisation from the forest. The name indicates that already men had begun to appreciate the beauties of the landscape. 'Belsize' means 'beautiful site or spot'. Perhaps it seemed to the monks a pleasant spot by comparison with the flat and largely featureless fen to the north and east.

Reclamation from the fen

The last areas in Northamptonshire not yet colonised in the twelfth century and still open to large-scale reclamation were along the western rim and islands of the great fenland marshes. It is difficult when travelling through the fens north and east of Peterborough today to form an impression of the conditions facing the medieval farmer. The straight causewayed roads of the eighteenth- and nineteenth-century enclosures stretch ahead. The black peaty soils below the level of the roads are criss-crossed by innumerable drainage dykes. Above the fields and bounded by embankments, the slow-moving waters of the fenland rivers make their way towards the Wash. Yet this land in the twelfth and thirteenth centuries was a maze of waterways, twisting among the sedges which grew to man-height. Myriads of water fowl lived among the reeds.

Rising from the marshy levels were ridges and islands of higher land. Such was Eye (O.E. island) four miles north-east of Peterborough. The village now consists of one long wide street on a ridge of gravel, originally an island in the fen. Although it receives no mention in Domesday, Eye was probably included among the eight hides of Werrington which belonged to the abbey of Peterborough. In 1125 there

[27] *V.C.H. Northants.*, Vol. II, p. 474.

were thirteen half virgaters here, paying "an annual rent of XVI s. and 12 skips of oats, for dead wood, 40 hens and 320 eggs". They had six carucates of which they ploughed 26 acres yearly. A century later there were fifteen full virgaters here, together with twelve smallholders. By 1300 these smallholders had become 'old cottars' and these had been joined by nineteen 'new cottars' whose holdings can only have been reclaimed from the fen.

The abbey was prominent in developing the area. Abbot William of Woodford (1295-9) built a windmill and began a hall there which was finished by his successor, Abbot Godfrey (1299-1321), who also built a new house with a bakery and dairy and enclosed land for keeping wild beasts. This sounds like the origin of the abbots' park at Eyebury, mentioned in the fourteenth century. The outlying farms of Northolm (1247), Eyebury and Oxney (*c.* 1200) all owe their siting to the same cause, being built on ridges running north and south of the main settlement. The high road to Thorney went along the causeway through Eye. In 1305 the abbot of Thorney complained that Godfrey, abbot of Peterborough, and others "lately by night raised a dike across the highroad at Eye leading from Peterborough to Thorney" and which was used by the abbot for carrying corn and other necessities. The quarrel was settled by the intervention of Walter de Langton and Thorney was allowed "to use that highway, to the breadth of fifteen feet with their carriages, horses and drift of cattle to farms and markets without any molestation". This "drift of cattle" reminds us that the droveways, already noted in the Romano-British fenland, continued to be a feature of the early medieval landscape.[28]

The reclamation of the fen was almost entirely for the sake of rich pastures. The abbot of Thorney, for instance, in 1330 gave up all the right which he had claimed to common of pasture in Northolm and Eye, in such places as

[28] For Eye see *V.C.H. Northants.*, Vol. II, pp. 490-1; J. Bridges, *History*, Vol. II, p. 513.

had been enclosed by a ditch or hedge reserving to himself the right of common in the marsh which he had always enjoyed. Northolm, a mile to the north of Eye, was founded by Abbot Godfrey in 1304, "where no manor had been before for it had lain as pasture". He enclosed the pasture of Cranemore and in its west part planted a wood which he called Chidholm. Oxney, again originally an island in the fen a mile south of Eye, had one inhabitant in 1125, a cow-herd; his stock was twenty-three cattle. The site of the grange is now occupied by a damp farmhouse and remains of its former importance can be seen in a fourteenth-century stone-vaulted room, now used as a kitchen. Outside in the plough soil a scatter of pottery including developed Stamford wares shows that occupation was continuous here from the twelfth century.

The same process of reclamation from the fen is found at Glinton, four miles north of Peterborough, where Domesday records ten villeins, six bordars and eight sokemen in the abbey's manor. In a survey of 1230, twenty-five cottars made their appearance. There were 100 acres of meadow mentioned in 1086. By 1300 there was a surplus capacity of meadow available for leasing to other people of 165 acres including nine and a half acres in *Le Newedik* and forty in *Le Inham,* both revealing field names. Werrington, the next village to the south, also had twenty-seven acres in *Le Inham* and forty-two acres in *Le Newefrithede.* The Inhams on the map today are the fields and farm immediately to the east of Car Dyke and it is significant that the parish of Werrington crosses the dyke at this point to include them. The area was claimed to be tithe-free as having formerly furnished grass or rushes to strew the church of Werrington on the feast Sunday the first after midsummer day.

Even when unreclaimed the fen provided, in the words of Hugh Candidus, the twelfth-century chronicler of Peterborough, "no small benefit to the bordering people; for there they have wood or other fuel for the fire, and hay for fodder; as also reed for thatching of their houses; with many other necessaries. There are likewise divers rivers, waters and great meers for fishing, the county abounding in such things."[29] Among the tenants of the manor of Glinton in 1125 was a fowler who held seven and a half acres for a rent of ten wild geese. This was still remembered in the eighteenth century. Bridges, writing about Eye which was surrounded by water before the draining of the fen, states that "formerly the inhabitants supported themselves by fishing and fowling".

Secular buildings in the landscape

The pressure of population on land, land-reclamation from forest and fen, and the increased demand of agricultural output led to technical innovations in farming and an increased investment on buildings, equipment and mills. Mills are mentioned in connection with 161 out of the 314 Domesday settlements in the county and from their distribution it is clear that they were closely associated with the principal rivers of the county. There was in fact a mill for (roughly) every thirty-two units of recorded population. The annual value of these mills would range from as little as eight pence (Easton Maudit) to as much as forty shillings (Warmington). The fact that in seven places the rent was paid for partly in eels shows that there must have been fisheries in these places. They were all located in the Nene valley between Warmington and Raunds. It seems from early-twelfth-century surveys such as the *Liber Niger* of Peterborough that the miller was often a peasant who combined an agricultural holding with his occupation of a mill.[30] Oundle and Warmington were examples where they were let along with a virgate of land.

[29] W. Dugdale, *The History of Imbanking and Draining of Divers Fens and Marshes* (2nd edn. 1772), p. 367.
[30] R. Lennard, *Rural England, 1086–1135* (Oxford, 1959), p. 284.

Plate 11 Barnack. The field of 'hills and holes' south-west of the village. These abandoned medieval quarries, worked from pre-Conquest times to the sixteenth century, provided stone for abbeys and churches throughout the East Midlands and East Anglia. From the air they look like pock marks in the landscape; on the ground they are grassed over and colonised by orchids, one of the most delightful places for hide and seek in the county.

Plate 12 Canons Ashby. A truncated fragment of the early-thirteenth-century church of the Augustinian canons, apart from Peterborough Cathedral the most considerable monastic ruin in the county. From Baker's *History and Antiquities of Northamptonshire*, 1825–41.

Plate 13 Woodcroft Castle. A surprising fragment of a late-thirteenth-century castle rises from a moated site on the edge of the fen between Stamford and Peterborough. The plan, with circular corner towers, suggests affinities with the Edwardian castles of North Wales (as does Barnwell). Behind is a Tudor range of buildings.

There were undoubtedly considerable earthworks associated with these mills which often have survived although
the mill has long disappeared. At the Domesday mill of
Newton, for instance, a weir a mile up the river Ise channels
off the mill race which pursues a more direct but roughly
parallel route between enbankments to the site of the mill
a few hundred yards to the east of the deserted village of
Little Newton. The course is now choked with reeds and
overgrown with trees but the stone-lined sluice and bed
for the wheel can still be found. At Weekley, the next mill
down the Ise, there is a similar long and tortuous embanked
mill race, which was necessary to gain a head of water
sufficient to turn the mill wheel. Mills were often adapted to
other mechanical tasks than grinding. Fulling mills built by
the abbey of St James, Northampton, are found in the
thirteenth century at Billing and Cotton 'Marsh'. It seems
likely that most of these early water-driven mills were built
of timber. William, son of Robert Ratele of Paulerspury,
and William, brother of the same William, were arrested for
burning the mill of Geoffrey of Braddon at Easton Neston.[31]
Later in the Middle Ages multiple mills were built under
one roof as at Ditchford (three) and St Andrews, Kingsthorpe (four).[32]

Many people lived in flat areas where rivers ran too
slowly to turn a wheel forcefully or where the building of
a dam brought the dangers of flooding. The first documentary reference to a wind-driven mill in England is found in
1185 at Weedley in Yorkshire, but before Henry II's death,
four years later, one of his constables handed over a windmill near Buckingham to Oseney Abbey. During the next
hundred years windmills became one of the most familiar
features of the landscape all over northern Europe. Wind

[31] M. Gollancz (ed.), *Rolls of Northamptonshire Sessions of the Peace*, 1314–16,
1320, Northants. Record Society, Vol. XI (1940), p. 75.
[32] G. H. Starmer, 'A check list of Northamptonshire Wind and Watermills', *Bulletin of Industrial Archaeology in C.B.A. Group*, 9, No. 12 (April 1970).

was a more constant element than water, particularly in the eastern part of England where the distribution of windmills for grinding corn follows the grain-growing and low-rainfall areas. Moreover in winter, unlike the water-mill, they could not be stopped by freezing. In *c.* 1220–5 the Luffield Priory charters contain a reference to the land necessary for the erection of a windmill. The prior and convent of Chicksands handed over land in Sutfelde in Whittlebury, fifty feet long and half an acre broad *"ad construendum ibid ibi molendinum suum ad ventum."*[33]

These early windmills were post-mills and to keep the sails turning into the eye of the wind the body of the mill, containing the gearing and the stones, would be pivoted upon an upright post firmly fixed to cross timbers or a stone foundation sunk in the ground. The traces left by medieval mills on the landscape are of two kinds. The earthworks, sometimes mistaken for prehistoric tumuli, are simple circular mounds piled up with the original intention of supporting the legs of the mill and surrounded by a ditch. Where a post-mill site has been ploughed, limestone cobbling which formed the hardstand round the base of the mill can be seen. The site of Strixton post-mill within a few yards of the Wollaston–Newport Pagnell road shows up as a mass of yellow limestone rubble on an otherwise dark-brown ploughed field. In addition we found pieces of fragmented millstones and medieval pottery. The windmill mound, a quarter of a mile to the north of Great Oxendon, wrongly interpreted by Pevsner as a barrow, shows another feature which frequently gives a clue to the landscape historian. Paths cutting across the former open fields converge on the site. Again we picked up four millstone fragments on the mound and in the ditch.

An interesting example of the historical sequence of the technology of medieval milling is seen in South Goodmans Mill field a mile to the west of Pipewell Upper Lodge. Here

[33] *Luffield Priory Charters,* p. 75.

is the revetted stone embankment of a massive mill dam—
now breached. Above it, a few hundred yards to the north,
is a windmill mound nine and a half feet high, eighty-four
feet across, situated about 400 feet above sea level. This may
well be one of the windmills referred to in the complaint by
the monks in 1323, "built at the expense of the woods of St
Mary of Pipewell". An excavation of a windmill mound at
Lamport revealed cruciform walls supporting the cross-
trees of the original mill, two feet eight inches thick, spanning twenty-one feet two inches. The mill had been perched
on the walls for a sufficient time to weather them but
difficulty of access due to the height above ground level
(five feet), the usual danger of exposure to the wind, and
the need to add strength to the foundations, necessitated
the throwing up of the mound. Pottery dated the structure
to the thirteenth to fourteenth century.[34]

Castles and manor houses

We are reminded of two essential differences between our
society and that of the early Middle Ages when surveying
the grassy or tree-grown mounds, banks and ditches of
earthwork castles and manor moats. Life was insecure, and
society was feudally ordered. It has recently been suggested
that defensive residential enclosures are found in late Anglo-
Saxon Northamptonshire at Sulgrave and Earls Barton but
this hardly yet amounts to a demonstration that the origin
of the castle is pre-Conquest.[35] In fact the castle was a
Norman invention. Domesday mentions only one in the
county, at Rockingham, "it was waste when King
William ordered a castle to be made there", but this is
hardly surprising because a castle was a cause for expenditure not a source of income. The new Norman landholders

[34] M. Posnansky, 'The Lamport Post Mill', *Journal of the Northamptonshire Natural History Society and Field Club,* Vol. XXXIII (1956), pp. 66–79.

[35] B. K. Davison 'Excavations at Sulgrave, Northamptonshire, 1968', *Archaeological Journal,* Vol. CXXV (1968), pp. 305–7.

quickly threw up earth-work castles which are still prominent features in the landscape.[36] Some were never finished,
like the huge undocumented mound of Clifford's Hill
towering over the Nene, three miles east of Northampton (Plate 8), others dominated boroughs and route centres.
Simon de Senlis, first Norman Earl of Northampton, built
a mounded castle to command the valuable strategic site of
his town, and the crown, recognising its significance "in
the middle of the kingdom", took it over in about 1111.
Saxon houses had been destroyed to make way for the
earthworks and we know from Speed's 1610 plan of the
town that there were outer and inner wards and at least
four great towers. Recent, and unfortunately as yet unpublished, excavations demonstrated the wealth of architectural ornament lavished on the building which became a
royal residence and fortress in the Angevin period. A second
of Simon's castles was at Fotheringhay and, over-looking a
farmyard by the Nene, the powerful motte and bailey are
all that survive of a castle described by Leland as "fair and
meately strong with double ditches and a kepe very anncient
and strong". At times the awesome proportions of these
Norman mottes are blanketed by a thick cover of trees and
undergrowth as at Castle Dykes, one mile north of Farthingstone church, and Castle Yard, half a mile north-east of
Sibbertoft. We can imagine the timber towers either with
their foundation posts deeply buried in the mound or
revetting the earthen filling. Excavations of so called
'ringworks' as at Sulgrave and at Long Buckby make it
clear that the final form of these earth castles was the result
of a long series of adaptations. Mottes were a later accretion
in some cases and at Lilbourne on the Warwickshire
border there seem to have been no less than three on massive

---

[36] A list occurs in *V.C.H. Northants.*, Vol. II, pp. 403–12, but for an up-to-
date appraisal of castles and an annotated but incomplete gazetteer see D. F.
Renn, *Norman Castles in Britain* (London, 1968). For Northampton Castle,
Medieval Archaeology, Vols. VI–VII (1962–3), p. 322, Vol. VIII (1964), p. 257.

ramparts with segmental banks added. From the tops of these mottes can be seen hollow-ways stretching into the ridge-and-furrow corrugated fields. This emphasises the place of the castle in the landscape of Norman Northampton-shire. It was meant to dominate and to act as the administrative centre of an estate, the *caput* of an honour.

As life became more secure, and the economy more prosperous in the relative peace of the long reign of Henry III, more comfortable but still fortified stone manor houses began to be built. A few are found in the north of the county. Longthorpe Tower on the outskirts of Peterborough was occupied and added to by Robert Thorpe, appointed steward of the abbey in 1309. Southwick Hall has a similar mighty tower of the early fourteenth century, the core of a later medieval complex of buildings. Easily the most attractive is the moated and turretted fragment of the manor house of the Preston family at Woodcroft in Etton (Plate 13). The windows with their shouldered lintels and transoms are, as Pevsner notes, characteristic of the Welsh Edwardian castles. Barnwell Castle (Plate 18), on an unimpressively flat site by the watermeadows of the Nene, is best seen in spring when its towers rise behind hazel thickets from carpets of daffodils. It is interesting to note that its monumental square plan with circular and trefoiled towers, probably the work of Berengar le Moyne *c.* 1266, predates Harlech Castle by twenty years.[37] It may well be regarded as a prototype for the Edwardian castles of North Wales.

Moats and fishponds

Stone manor houses surviving from as early as the thirteenth century are rare; far more frequently we come across moated sites. Although these have as yet been imperfectly

[37] E. C. Rouse, *Longthorpe Tower*, H.M.S.O. Guides (London, 1964). For Southwick see *V.C.H. Northants.*, Vol. II, p. 592. For Barnwell see N. Pevsner, *Buildings of England, Northamptonshire* (Penguin, 1961), pp. 96–97.

surveyed and gazetteered in the county, their distribution tends to bear out the thesis that most are found in areas of late colonisation. There is a concentration of eight on the Oxford Clay region between the Nene and Ouse valleys east of Oundle, and four are found around the forests of Salcey and Whittlewood, but only four are in Rockingham forest and the rest are thinly distributed in the more upland areas to the west and south-west. The moated monastic grange of Evesham Abbey at Badby has been recently excavated and it seems here that the moat, enclosing about an acre, was dug first, the upcast being used for levelling the site before the erection of stone hall, chapel, chamber and other domestic buildings dating from the thirteenth century. Apart from this, hardly any scientific excavation has been done to reveal the inner structures of moated sites. At Quinton substantial stone buildings, including a first-floor hall, kitchen and workshop, were surrounded at a later and uncertain period by a moat added as an after-thought. The defensive potential of moats was small; their drainage capacity perhaps helpful in a period of deteriorating weather conditions. Above all, they were somewhat unsavoury and unhygienic status symbols.[38]

Certainly fish would have been bred in these moats until pollution drove them out. Many villages were furnished with fishponds which were by no means a monopoly of monasteries and manors.[39] Fish were a vital augmentation to a sparse meat diet and a virtue was made out of necessity. The ponds were constructed in several ways. A valley might be dammed and the overflow stream diverted round the pond by means of a trench cut deeply in the side of the valley forming a dog-leg as at Pipewell, Yardley Hastings and

[38] An incomplete list of 32 moats appears in *V.C.H. Northants.*, Vol. II, pp. 412–13. See also *Medieval Archaeology*, Vol. VIII (1964), pp. 219–22. For Badby see *Medieval Archaeology*, Vol. XIV (1970), pp. 191–3. For Quinton, lecture by R. Taylor at Wellingborough, 1971.

[39] J. M. Steane, 'The Medieval Fishponds of Northamptonshire', *Northants. Past and Present*, Vol. IV (1970–1), pp. 299–310.

King's Cliffe. They might be stepped as advised by Norden: "I could wish some cost to be bestowed here in making a fishpond nay it would make at least two or three, one below the other." This has been done at Brampton Ash and at Pilton where thirteenth-century pottery was found in the upcast. A third method was by excavating a shallow rectangular basin and lining it with banks, two parallel with the stream and two across it as at Silverstone, Slipton, Welford and Maidwell.

Monastic and baronial establishments had earthworks on a larger scale. The knights hospitallers who held Harrington from 1232 to the Dissolution possessed one of the most magnificent sets in the Midlands. The main fishpond, trapezoidal in shape, measures 140 paces on its northern, 90 on its southern, 173 on its western and 113 on its eastern edge. It is fed by two deep supply channels. Above it, also containing banks, is a smaller chamber probably for a different type of fish. A relief channel for surplus water runs outside both ponds to the west. There are traces of stone revetting on the inside faces of the main banks. Braybrooke 'Castle' where Thomas, son and successor to John de Latimer, obtained licence from the crown (*temp.* Edward I) to embattle his manor house, is surrounded by elaborate earthworks which make little military sense, but would have made admirable fishponds, enclosing a large lake with small islands whose centres are lower than their ramparts, likely breeding tanks.

These medieval fishponds are now mostly dry. Their containing dams are often breached, as at the royal hunting lodge of Silverstone where medieval pottery can be picked up in the stream-made cut in the great dam straddling the valley. Their embankments were the most substantial earthworks to date in the landscape, if we except the prehistoric hill forts, and are additional witness to the tremendous surge forward of agriculture in the early medieval period. In other places only a field name betrays the former existence of ponds. The royal house and fishponds at Brigstock have completely disappeared from the visual scene; only a name on the tithe map survives.

Monasteries and churches in the landscape

William of Malmesbury writing after the Norman Conquest stated: "Everywhere you might see arising, in a new style of building, churches in the villages, and monasteries in the suburbs and the towns." The Laws of William I recognised three grades of churches, the mother church which might be a cathedral or abbey, the parish church, and finally the chapel. There was no cathedral in Northamptonshire during the Middle Ages; the county was in the See of Dorchester from the mid-ninth until the mid-eleventh century when it was removed to Lincoln. The greatest church was the pre-Conquest Benedictine foundation of Peterborough, the sole Saxon monastery in Northamptonshire (Plate 25). This was rebuilt magnificently in the early twelfth century and is one of the finest extant major Norman churches. We have already noticed the crucial influence the abbey had on the landscape within the forests and fens of its vast endowed estates.

Little survives above the ground of the six other Benedictine houses. The site of Luffield Priory, the church which is in Northamptonshire and the buildings in Buckinghamshire, is ironically under the middle of the Silverstone motor racing circuit. Only the thick surrounding woods recall the pioneer work of clearance carried on by the monks in the thirteenth century. The small alien priory of Everdon, a grange dependant on Bernay, was founded before 1100 and dissolved in *c.* 1399; it eventually came into the possession of Eton College. Bridges stated that "the remains of it, which bear many marks of antiquity, are still to be seen in the Lordship house . . . in a close adjoining are the appearance and hollows of ponds". These have now disappeared but the quotation reminds us that frequently there are considerable earthwork remains of monasteries, when the masonry buildings have almost completely disappeared as so often happens on Midland sites. Three examples show this.

The Augustinian priory of Canons Ashby was founded in 1147–51 by Stephen de Leye for thirteen canons. In his original endowments he included the church of Ashby, with four virgates of land, a fishpond, a mill, *Rudemede*, the enclosure of *Segeho*, twenty-six acres in Ashby field and the houses and crofts as far as the principal gate. [40] All that remains of the conventual church is a truncated fragment (Plate 12); the fine Early English arcaded west front gives some indication of vanished glories. Excavation in 1828 established foundations running more than 100 feet east of the present building. Recently the south-west corner of the cloister was uncovered. There are, however, a stone medieval wellhouse and a walled garden locally believed to have been the vineyard. Also the moat, enclosure banks and ponds to the south-east survive in part, despite recent filling and ploughing. The village has almost completely disappeared but its area is clearly outlined by ridge-and-furrow. A flat-topped motte (wrongly identified by Pevsner as a barrow) stands in the deer park; it was doubtless the precursor of the manor house of the Copes who were granted the site in 1538 (see Fig. 15).

A better-preserved monastic complex comprising moat, fishponds, a hollow-way (probably the old road from Cottesbrooke), and contemporary field banks, is found in Cottesbrooke parish. They are the remains of the Premonstratensian cell of Kaylend founded by William Buttevillan *c*. 1155. It had a short life and may well have disappeared by 1291. Bridges reports "large foundation stones have within these few years been dug up in Kalendar meadow, and the cell when standing appears to have been moated round".

[40] *V.C.H. Northants.*, Vol. II, pp. 130–1.

The name is present in Calendar farm. Kaylend was a cell of
the abbot and convent of Sulby.

The Premonstratensian abbey of Sulby was founded about
1155 and Bridges describes the site as "well wooded and
watered with springs on all sides . . . the whole manor-
comprehending the abbey and Old Sulby . . . contains
upwards of 1500 acres".[41] The abbey occupied the farm
just north of a stream which now runs from the Naseby
reservoir to the Welford branch of the Grand Union Canal.
A massive mill dam was built across the valley at this point
and a chain of fishponds constructed. To the east are more
fishponds, now dry, and a long linear earthwork which is
connected with the medieval cultivation of the fields.
Further considerable linear earthworks survive on the hill
towards Naseby. Curiously enough a possible derivation of
the place-name from O.E. *sulh* 'furrow, trench' may refer to
this. Of the abbey only a few fragments of building, a
floriated cross tombstone and some pieces of lead and tiles
survive; they are kept in a small shed attached to the deserted
farm buildings.

The impact that the monasteries made on the landscape
in the thirteenth and fourteenth centuries can be demonstrated in two strongly contrasting examples. The Lincolnshire abbey of Crowland held manors in Northamptonshire,
Peakirk, Elmington and Glapthorn, Wothorpe, Badby,
Great Addington and Wellingborough. This last place, in
the hundred of Hamfordshoe, was the chief of these manors.[42]
We know from a survey that Wellingborough manor had
its administrative centre in the *curia* of the lord's demesne
where lay the hall, chamber, kitchen, grange and other farm
buildings which included a stable, cowshed and granary
with two dovecotes, garden and bakehouse. All these have
vanished but the complex was centred near the house behind

[41] J. Bridges, *History*, Vol. I, pp. 557, 597.
[42] F. M. Page (ed.), *Wellingborough Manorial Accounts, 1258–1323*, Northants. Record Society, Vol. VIII (1936), p. xiii.

Sheep Street now called 'Croyland Abbey'. The shell of the six-bay tithe barn, buttressed and built of local ironstone with limestone courses, its thatched roof recently gutted by fire, still stands to the north-west of the house. It could well become an arts' centre for the expanding town.

The arable land of the manor of Wellingborough lay in three fields in which both the abbey and their tenants had their share, each holding being composed of half-acre strips lying in different parts of the three fields. Great quantities of wheat, malt, pigs, geese and pigeons were sent annually to the central larder at Crowland. The landscape at the turn of the fourteenth century must have been alive with the carters and creaking wagons taking the produce to Crowland. "Item for the fodder of the carthorses of Croyland and the carthorses of Hoyland carrying the grain of Wellingborough to Croyland 5 quarters 3 bushels: 1 quarter by tally against Hugh the Carter."

Along the droveways to the north were driven a large number of the year's lambs to the great sheep farm where they grazed on the river meadows of the Welland. Wellingborough was included in the well-organised system of sheep farming developed by the abbey and in 1291 the profits of the flocks were especially mentioned. We can picture the temporary wooden buildings where the sheep were folded. "For buying three cartloads of brushwood for making the bedding of the ewes at the sheepfold and for thatching the said sheepfold extra firmly on account of the wind ... Item for the wages of one carpenter cutting up timber at the sheepcot . . . 16d."[43] Each year from 1296 to 1306 the Wellingborough rolls record that the annual wool crop had been sent entire to 'Simon Kynne', the chief shepherd.

The effect of a monastery on the landscape was sometimes destructive. At Pipewell, a village community which had a recorded population of nine in Domesday Book was eliminated by the predatory monks who placed their abbey

[43] *Wellingborough Manorial Accounts*, pp. 132, 125.

east of the village in 1143, and the site of the former peasants' holdings was incorporated in the West Grange. The foundations of the monastic church were excavated in 1909 and are now grassed over, their shape is just recognisable from the air.

Indications of the agricultural activities of the Cistercian monks of Pipewell are still to be seen in the surrounding landscape. The original name of the abbey was *Sancta Maria de Divisis*, so called because the demesne lands lay on both sides of Harpers brook which here divides Corby and Rothwell hundreds. The area was densely forested in the twelfth century and there is still plenty of woodland; to the north are *Rawhaw* wood ('Roe enclosure' or 'enclosed wood'), *Barrowdykes* wood ('dikes or ditches in the woodland'), *Askershaw* wood ('Asketill's enclosure'), Little Haws wood, Monks Arbour wood. All these names indicate that the wholesale conversion of woodland to tillage was going on and recall the complaints made about the grievous waste of the property of the abbey in the thirteenth century. *Colleshawe, Rahage* and *Otha* woods were entirely cleared and Wilbarston and *Pykemede* were grubbed up as early as 1237. What is a little difficult to fathom is the reason for the complaints. If the monks lost their woodland they undoubtedly increased the area of tillage and pasture. The depredations of fuel-gatherers who went out daily into the woods to procure supplies of thorns and briars, green wood and the tops of young oaks or their roots were enumerated and deplored. It was claimed that great numbers of people came by day and night to plunder the woods of Desborough, Stoke Albany, Wilbarston, Charlton, Oakley and Rushton. Great men, whom the monks feared to oppose, obtained large quantities of timber from the woods of the abbey for private purposes. Walter de Langton, bishop of Lichfield and treasurer of Edward I, was accused of stripping the Pipewell woods of timber for building himself a sumptuous mansion at Thorpe Waterville. Licence to crenellate was given him in 1301. At Thorpe Waterville near the deserted railway line a farmhouse stands within a moated enclosure. On one side of the yard now used as a barn is the mighty hall of Walter de Langton—with circular windows and a a fine chimney leading to a fireplace in the upper room. The single framed roof with tie beams and kingposts reminds one of the anguished prayers of the monks of Pipewell as their finest oaks were removed by their powerful neighbours.

The interest of Victorian topographical antiquaries was focussed on the parish church and the manor house; a natural tendency arising out of their frequently clerical and genteel origins. To their emphasis on architectural style and the development of the plan has now been added a new dimension arising out of our present generation's obsession with economic and social history. The historian of the medieval landscape now asks what the church is built of, where did the materials come from, how were they paid for? Does the style give any indication of the movement of the masons? Most important, it is being increasingly realised that the fabric of the medieval church with its great complexity of building sequences may well reflect economic expansion or decline of the population it served at different periods. Its siting again can sometimes demonstrate that the pattern of a late Saxon or early medieval village has been changed with substantial replanning.

Although Norman churches in the county are undated with the sole exception of the fine cruciform church with sumptuous crossing tower at Castor, dated by a dedication tablet to 1124, it is clear that a good deal of building and rebuilding took place within a century of the Conquest. Small village churches with bellcotes substantially survive at Peakirk, Northborough and Werrington—towers were added as at Maxey, St Peters, Northampton and Spratton.

Monasteries, as the patrons of churches or the owners of tithes, sometimes undertook their building or reconstruction. At Barton Seagrave, for instance, where the advowson was held from the early twelfth century by the priory of Kenilworth, a three-cell plan with nave, central tower and chancel was constructed *de novo* (Plate 7). This largely Norman building is a fitting resting place for the county's greatest historian, John Bridges, who was buried here in 1724. A more unusual monastic essay in parish church design is seen in the unique double nave under the same roof at Hannington. Here the Gilbertine order of double monasteries of monks and nuns held the advowson and built the church in the thirteenth century.

Spired steeples with half pyramid or 'broach' coverings are a characteristic regional feature of this area. The spires at Barnack and Elton are among the earliest in the country; indeed the origin of the spire could be claimed to be in Northamptonshire. Doubtless local rivalries contributed to their astonishing proliferation and variety but the distribution of these noble stone steeples suggests that economic considerations played a large part.[44] To pay for churches on the scale of Warmington (Plate 14) and Raunds would have required a large agricultural surplus; a tribute to the success of the thirteenth-century exploitation of arable cultivation in the Nene valley. Spires require dressed ashlar blocks in quantity. The fact that they are found in large numbers in the north-eastern part of the county as far south as Northampton and especially along the valley of the Nene near the east border is linked with the easy accessibility of this area of fine building stone, brought in by water from quarries at Barnack, Weldon and Ketton. The old saying, Northamptonshire "a county of spires and squires", is not strictly true, however. It has well over 200 medieval parish churches but no more than about eighty spires including those which are no longer in existence (Fig. 8). Pevsner analyses their aesthetic attractions with perception and rightly regards the recessed spires of Oundle, Kettering

[44] T. D. Atkinson, *Local Styles in English Architecture* (London, 1947), pp. 89–91.

Fig. 8. Medieval spires of Northamptonshire

Only the principal freestone quarries operating during the Middle Ages have been located. The pronounced distribution of the eighty or so spires in areas within easy reach of water transport and near the quarries is noteworthy. It is possible that the distribution also gives some indication of the wealthier agricultural areas from the thirteenth to fifteenth centuries.

and Higham Ferrers as the finest in the county. So often it
is the situation of the church in the landscape which brings
out its inspiring quality. I remember stepping out of the
train on my first visit to Kettering in 1964: I raised my eyes
from the soot-blackened Derbyshire sandstone and red
brick of the Midland railway station to the astonishing
spire rocketing out of a tall tower crocketed up the edges
like a swordfish, brilliantly yellow as it caught the afternoon
sun against a lowering storm cloud. The superb spire at
Higham similarly dominates a ridge over the Nene valley.
Oundle on the other hand lies low on the gravel spit on
which the town is built. Its slender tower with elegant bell
openings and tapering needle spire is one of the master-
pieces of the English Decorated style (Plate 27).

There is not a great deal of church architecture in the
Perpendicular style in the county, but the contribution to
the landscape of such buildings as Lowick church, Fotheringhay and Whiston is out of all proportion to their numbers.
For one thing they are securely dated; they occupy commanding positions in the countryside; they exhibit the
finest craftsmanship and sense of design particularly in their
splendid towers. Lowick was built by members of the
Greene family. Everyone remembers Bushy, Bagot and
Greene, executed by Bolingbroke in 1399. Henry began the
nave and aisles; Ralph continued the chancel and was buried
there in 1417, and Henry was responsible for the tower
which was completed *c*. 1470, perhaps two years after his
death. The tower has an octagonal lantern from which
shoots a forest of pinnacles. The prototype for this type of
top stage was Ely octagon built 150 years earlier. A similar
tall and graceful lantern shimmers above the watermeadows
at Fotheringhay, rising from the truncated collegiate
church founded by Edmund de Langley, son of Edward III
and continued by the Duke of York. We have a rare contract
dated 1434 between Richard, Duke of York and the freemason William Horwood, for "a new body of a kirk,

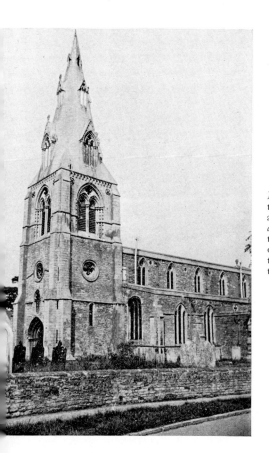

Plate 14 St Mary's church, Warmington, unusual because it is stylistically all of one build, dating from between *c.* 1180 and *c.* 1280. Situated among the rich cornfields and watermeadows of the middle Nene, a monument to the success of medieval farming in the thirteenth century.

Plate 15 Geddington. The thirteenth-century bridge across the river Ise. The two pointed arches and cut-waters are original but the semi-circular one dates from 1784. An impressive approach to the hunting lodge frequented by Henry III and Edward I. The Eleanor Cross is a hundred yards up the village street on the left.

Plate 16 Peterborough. Aerial view of the historic core of the city. The cathedral church with its monastic precinct dominates the central layout. To the left the rectilinear grid of Abbot Martin's early medieval urban settlement. Bridge Street (formerly Hithegate) alters course at the market place outside the Minster Gate, becoming Long Causeway. The railways and river hem in the centre of the city from the west and south. The beginning of nineteenth-century development can be seen at the top in the straight streets lined by Victorian terrace housing parallel with the railway.

joyning to the quire of the college of Fordringhey, of the same hight and brede that the said quire is of",[45] but unfortunately the chancel was pulled down after the Dissolution by John Dudley, Duke of Northumberland, to whom Edward VI had granted the college.

There were other parochial losses in the Tudor period when the greatest revolution in landownership since the Norman Conquest loosened traditional loyalties and made churches in some places as vulnerable as monasteries to the greed of local potentates intent on erecting their own palatial residences. Such was the probable fate of Wothorpe church where Richard Cecil had the advowson in 1540. Both church and village vanished when Burghley House and Wothorpe House were built. All Saints, Irthlingborough, went the same way. John Mountsteven wrote to Sir William Cecil in 1562 telling him "that there ys a certen church wyth in this diocese, called Arthelborough . . . devastated and in uttr ruyne . . . And I, havinge intellygence thereof and remembringe your honour's dayle necessitie of lead, wherewyth the saide church ys keverid . . ." He went on to say that he would put in a good word with the dean and the bishop on Cecil's behalf. By the middle of the next century the church had been so completely destroyed that even its site was forgotten until bulldozing hit burials in 1965 and its ground plan was recovered.[46]

[45] L. F. Salzman, *Building in England down to 1540* (Oxford, 1952), pp. 505–9.
[46] G. Brown, 'All Saints, Irthlingborough', *Northants. Antiquarian Society*, Vol. LXV, Part I (1964–5), p. 5.

I

4. The early medieval landscape: communications and towns

Roads, bridges and waterways. Markets and towns

Roads, bridges and waterways

THE ROMAN ROAD system in the East Midlands did not completely break down during the period of the Anglo-Saxon settlement: indeed it is likely that Roman roads were favoured routeways of the immigrants. The fact that parishes frequently took their boundaries from them suggests that parts of them were still recognisable features in the landscape of the late Saxon period. Anglo-Saxon land charters sometimes mention short stretches of road in their descriptions of boundaries but unfortunately never say where they are going to or coming from. The charter, for instance, granting land at Denshanger in Passenham in A.D. 937 refers to the *Stanweg* of Watling Street which still forms the eastern boundary of the parish.[1] The name Old *Stratford*, the part of the town of Stony Stratford which lies on the Northamptonshire side of the Ouse crossing, is another reminder that stone-paved roads were sufficiently unusual to be recorded in the place name. The declining importance of Watling Street, however, is suggested by the break in the alignment for two miles which occurs between Kilsby and Crick. The Scandinavian settlement of Kilsby deflected the course of the road to itself and a similar pull away from Watling Street was exerted by Northampton which began in the late Saxon period to draw traffic eastward through

[1] *Place Names of Northants.*, p. 101.

Catthorpe, Lilbourne, Yelvertoft, Winwick and West Haddon. The most famous Roman road in England at this point degenerates into a derelict green lane, much overgrown with bushes. It was not until the road improvements of the eighteenth and early nineteenth centuries that it regained its former importance.

By the eleventh century a web of roads had grown up in the county connecting incipient towns and markets which displaced the Roman system and emphasised the regional grouping of the area. The Anglo-Saxon term for such routeways is *portstræt*. We have references to the *portstræt* in the Newnham charter of 1021–3 which must refer to the Banbury–Daventry and the Weedon–Daventry roads. There is also *the Portwey* in Easton Neston (*c.* 1226) and *Le Portestrete* in Welford (1439) and *Portwey* in Everdon (1240), probably Bridges' Portway from Woodford to Preston Capes. Commodities carried on the roads sometimes gave their names. There was a *Sealt-stræt* in Everdon, and salters' streets, ways, gates and fords are found in Rothwell, Braunston, Easton-on-the-Hill, Oakley, Quinton and Evenley. There was a *Fisshewey* in Evenley and a *Berestrete* (a 'corn street') in Boughton. The local militia marched along *Le Ferdeweye* in Wilbarston.

A study of medieval road-names reveals that others have disappeared from the modern map. The 1228 forest perambulation includes as its bounds, from the west side of Market Harborough bridge, "according as the road called *Bedeford Weye* goes to Arthingworth bridge and then by the same road to the cross which stands on the bounds of Harrington and Kelmarsh and so by the same road to the watercourse which comes down between Maidwell and Draughton". This can be traced by following tracks and footpaths, but at times the course peters out altogether in country where farmers have been ploughing footpaths for some years. One can pick up the trail a mile north of Arthingworth bridge. Thence south of the bridge for a mile along an existing road. At this point the Bedford Way becomes a footpath which strikes a small stream, still the parish boundary between Draughton and Maidwell. The main Northampton road carries the old route along through Lamport and then it turns across country, along lanes by Old and Walgrave in an easterly direction towards Bedford. [2]

It is possible to reconstruct the itineraries of the early medieval kings from a study of the places where their charters were issued. In this way a vivid picture of relatively high-speed movement of the courts and their retinues emerges.

King John, for instance, restlessly energetic, and a great hunter, left Lincoln on 26th November, 1200, reaching his hunting lodge at Geddington two days later. On the 29th he arrived at Northampton. Thence he moved south through Oxfordshire into Wiltshire and Hampshire. He was back in the county on 3rd January and stayed at Silverstone. On 6th, 7th and 8th he was in residence at Geddington and by the 12th he had returned to Lincoln. [3] Kings sent justices riding in eyre and sheriffs bustling between castles, parks, shire and hundred courts. The government was interested in maintaining communications and consequently intervened from time to time for the repair of causeways and bridges, but in general the local communities were supposed to maintain the highways.

An example of this occasional intervention still detectable in the landscape can be seen in the neighbouring county of Huntingdonshire. In 1252 Henry III ordered the sheriff to clear the Great North Road of underwood against ambushes. A study of the two-and-a-half-inch Ordnance Survey map north of Alconbury shows Ermine Street going up *Stangate Hill*. Parallel to the course of the road and set back about 200 yards, are the hedgerows and patches of woodland (Upton, Coppingford and Archers Wood) which

---

[2] *Place Names of Northants.*, pp. 5–6, 26, 4.
[3] A. L. Poole (ed.) *Medieval England* (Oxford, 1958), Vol. I, p. 200.

were the result of this order. Their distance from the main road is a bowshot, as the seven-hundred-year-old writ demands. The 1285 Statute of Winchester insisted that "the highways leading from one market town to another shall be broadened, wherever there is ditch or underwood or bushes, so that there be neither dyke, tree, nor bush where a man may lurk to do hurt within two hundred foot of the one side and two hundred foot on the other side of the way".[4]

These medieval highways were unfenced and unpaved along many stretches, as is suggested by the numerous cases involving destructive encroachments on roads by predatory priests and peasants. In 1377 the jurors of Polebrook hundred complained that a bridge for horses and men on foot at the west end of Warmington was broken, that a causeway for men was impassable in rainy weather and should be repaired by the men of Barnwell: and that a road called *Medeweye* at *Sampittes* which was the king's highway between Thorpe and Thrapston was straightened by wells made there by the men of Titchmarsh to the nuisance of all passing by.[5] The parson of Rushden church in 1418 had planted a hedge too near (*nimis prope*) the king's highway at *Munkesyerd*. Henry Newell was fined twopence for occupying the king's highway (*regiam viam*) with branches in 1434. In 1452 another Rushden man, William Robyn, was amerced for digging on the king's highway at *Sandpittes* on *Galowhill*. John Abthorp was fined fourpence for ploughing away the common road at *Persones cropsende*, while in 1474 Richard Wynde of Stanwick had to pay twopence for erecting a cottage on the king's highway.[6]

Although there is little evidence that medieval roads were

[4] W. Stubbs (ed.), *Select Charters* (9th edn., Oxford, 1913), p. 468. I owe this reference to Stangate Hill to M. D. Hooper.

[5] C. T. Flower (ed.), *Public Works in Medieval Law*, Selden Society, London, 1923), Vol. II, p. 102.

[6] 'Court Rolls of Higham Ferrers', *Architectural Societies Reports and Papers*, XXXIV (1917–18), pp. 72–73.

paved except in towns, considerable efforts were made to improve river crossings to cope with heavier traffic. In particular fords were replaced by bridges. Medieval bridges are characterised by their narrowness, normally one wagon's width or exceptionally two; by their length, they carried their approach roads on long causeways above flood level; by their cutwaters or refuges, usually on the upstream side but at times on both. They present fascinating puzzles in archaeological interpretation. Periodic storm drainage necessitated repairs in varying materials. Different styles of building are accounted for by divided responsibility of rival townships for building and maintenance. As traffic built up with the centuries, road widening, detectable when one peers under the arches, was carried out. These bridges, now sometimes bypassed, are worth preserving as footpaths and local roads; they also add beauty and interest to the landscape.

Take, for example, the thirteenth-century bridge at Geddington, perhaps the loveliest of the county (Plate 15). It stands next to a ford through which I once drove in a mad moment and stalled in midstream. As the water gushed into the corroded underbody of my car I reflected ruefully on the enduring value of the bridge. Its sturdy stone arches are a fitting approach to the exquisite Eleanor Cross a few yards up the street and, beyond, the now-extinct royal hunting lodge.

Trains of packhorses were a more usual form of transport than wagons at this time. Charwelton is fortunate in having a late medieval packhorse bridge only three feet wide, preserved when the main road was slightly realigned.

The Nene, as the county's principal river, acquired a series of important bridges in the Middle Ages. Peterborough's bridge dates from at least as early as the time of Abbot Godfrey, who built or rebuilt it in 1308, but the abbey declined responsibility for its maintenance and it was repaired against Edward II's coming only on sufferance twenty years later. It was evidently of timber, judging from the town bailiff's account book of 1560–86 which records purchases of baulks of wood and iron bolts. The rickety trestle construction figures in the watercolour of Thomas Fayre in 1721 (Plate 25), and was only replaced by a more substantial Victorian bridge in 1872.[7] Peterborough was not in fact on the main medieval route system at all. Seven miles to the west was one of the most important bridges of the county, Wansford. Here roads converged from Peterborough, Oundle, Huntingdon, Stamford and Leicester. Again the thirteenth-century structure was of timber; Henry III in 1234 granted oak from the forest of Cliffe "for the work of the bridge". In 1221 Bishop Hugh Welles of Lincoln had granted a release of ten days' penance to those contributing to its repair. A bypass has now removed the stress of modern traffic. The twelve grey stone arches divided by frequent cutwaters are of three dates; the northernmost seven are in Northamptonshire and are inscribed 'PM 1577'; the next three spanning the main stream were rebuilt in 1672–4 after flood damage; the last one as recently as 1795.

A distinctive feature of the landscape of the middle Nene valley is the long causewayed roads strung out over the flood plain, with raised footpaths, sometimes planked, bordered by willows and wreathed in winter by fogs. The course of the river before embanking in the eighteenth century must have been shallower and more sinuous in the Middle Ages. Hence the great length of the bridges at Oundle, Irthlingborough and Thrapston. As he thunders over the Nene at Irthlingborough on the monstrous concrete viaduct of the 1930s which disfigures the landscape at this point, the motorist is perhaps unaware that a few yards to the north are the placid grey limestone and red ironstone arches and refuges of a major piece of fourteenth-century

---

[7] *Historic Peterborough*, catalogue of an exhibition of documents held in Peterborough, Northants. Record Office (1971), p. 13.

engineering. The Kettering–Huntingdon road still makes
its way over the multiple arches of the much mutilated and
widened bridge at Thrapston. "At the very end of Thrapes-
ton Bridge," wrote Leland in the 1540s, "stand ruins of a
very large hermitage welle builded but a late discovered and
suppressed." Unthinking destruction was not the monopoly
of the Tudors; the County Council propose to destroy this
ancient bridge to ease the flow of traffic through Thrapston.
The juggernaut car sweeps all in its path.

Despite the fact that the Nene is a considerable river,
large-scale water transport was only possible on its lower
stretches until the navigational improvements in the
eighteenth century. Its course has varied in complicated and
frequent meandering but it was undoubtedly used to transport heavy commodities such as stone from the late Anglo-
Saxon period onwards. Local tradition maintains that
Barnack stone was dragged six miles overland to Gunwade
Ferry, one and a half miles east of Castor, on the Nene. Two
stones called *Robin Hood* and *Little John* stand in a field a few
yards above a northerly loop of the river and can be seen
from the road between Wansford and Peterborough.
Norton states, "they were set up for Witnesses, that the
Carriages of Stone from *Bernack* to *Gunwade Ferry*, to be
convey'd to *St Edmund's Bury*, might pass that way without
paying Toll".[8] The accounts of Trinity College, Cambridge,
1560–1, show that Weldon stone was carried by carts from
the quarry to *Goonward* or *Gornward* ferry where it was
loaded into barges for the journey to Cambridge. Why was
it brought so far, bypassing Wansford and other embarka-
tion points? Purcell suggests the obvious advantage of a
place where the road is close to the river yet well above its
flood level; weirs, mills and other hindrances to navigation
upriver doubtless restricted its use.[9]

Blocks of Barnack type stone have been found in the

[8] J. Morton, *Natural History*, p. 551.
[9] D. Purcell, *Cambridge Stone* (London, 1967), pp. 41, 99.

bottom of Car Dyke in Lincolnshire.[10] This suggests that portions of the Roman dyke remained in use during the Middle Ages; on its north–south route it cut both the Welland and the Nene and would greatly have shortened the distance between Stamford and Cambridge. The Ketton, Stamford, Clipsham (and Weldon) quarries all lie closer to the Welland than the Nene.

In the late fifteenth century a celebrated attempt to control the waters of the lower Nene was made by John Morton, Bishop of Ely (1478–86) who had a channel, known now as *Morton's Leam*, cut, twelve miles long, forty feet wide and four feet deep, from Stanground near Peterborough to Wisbech.[11]

South of Morton's Leam the ancient course of the lower Nene also connected by a winding waterway to Whittlesey Mere. Further blocks of Barnack stone have been dredged from its now-drained bed: these were doubtless sunk *en route* for Ramsey or Sawtry Abbey. On the western rim of this former sheet of water was the petty borough of Holme. Its single street encircles the edge of a small island in former fenland just east of Ermine Street. A lawsuit of 1314 stated that "merchants came up the river from King's Lynn and especially to the king's town of Holme, situated on the river with its market and fair".[12] Goods were unloaded from ships, and carts creaked with sea produce through Glatton, past the Salters' Way, to Great Gidding and into the county at Winwick. The Northamptonshire Assize Roll of 1202 records that Geoffrey Cardun had been levying new and unprecedented customs from carters going through his lands at Winwick. The goods involved were eels, fresh fish, salmon and herrings, whereas he ought, the jurors claimed, to take toll from the salters only and give them in return

---

[10] C. W. Phillips, 'The Present State of Archaeology in Lincolnshire', *Archaeological Journal*, Vol. XCI (1934), p. 121.

[11] H. C. Darby, *The Medieval Fenland* (Cambridge, 1940), p. 168.

[12] Quoted in M. W. Beresford, *New Towns of Medieval England* (London, 1967), p. 455.

free bread and pasture in case of a breakdown of their carts. D. M. Stenton assumes that the Winwick mentioned is in Guilsborough hundred and that the salters came from Cheshire in the north-west. The commodities involved, however, being perishable must have had a more direct sea origin and it is reasonable to suppose that here in fact is evidence for a road and river route connecting the county to the Wash, the Lincolnshire salters and the North Sea fisheries.[13]

Markets and towns

Settlements sited near river crossings which attract converging routes might acquire markets and eventually grow into towns. *Stamford*, part in Lincolnshire and part in Northamptonshire, came into being in this way. The Roman road, Ermine Street, crosses the river Welland half a mile upstream from the stony ford which gave the Danish borough of Stamford its name. What interests the landscape historian of Northamptonshire is that King Edward in A.D. 922 ordered a *second* borough to be built on the south side of the Welland for the Anglo-Saxons. The fortification was on the site afterwards occupied by the nunnery of St Michael, now in Little Wothorpe, and the borough is the settlement known as St Martin's Stamford Baron. It consists of one main thoroughfare, High Street, running south–east from the bridge, but it is difficult to know whether this was a piece of deliberate Anglo-Saxon town planning or a spontaneous and gradual ribbon development.[14] Webstergate, Burleygate and Highgate are mentioned in medieval deeds, but, as with Peterborough, these probably referred to streets rather than gates (Old Norse *gata*, road). One large courtyard house of medieval origin adjoining the George Hotel

[13] D. M. Stenton (ed.), *The Earliest Northamptonshire Assize Rolls 1202 and 1203*, Northants. Record Society, Vol. V (1930), pp. xxiii, 10–11.
[14] A. Rogers (ed.), *The Making of Stamford* (Leicester, 1969), p. 19.

survives, but the long narrow tenement plan, which would only have been built on at the street end, predominated in Stamford Baron. Some tenements had 'broad gates' or an archway, giving access to a stableyard or small farmyard; an example is 25 High Street, St Martin's. Mercantile activity is displayed by the fine stone-vaulted cellars or undercrofts as at 24 High Street, St. Martin's. Coin evidence clearly shows this double trading community of Danes and English flourishing, separated only by the river which brought traders in boats from Lynn and the ports of the Wash.[15]

The distribution of the distinctive early glazed Stamford ware pottery demonstrates trade links with the countries round the North Sea and along the trackways west to Chester and south into the Oxford region.[16] It is likely that the potters from the industrial settlement at Lyveden, twelve miles to the south, came to Stamford market to buy their schist hone stones imported from Central Norway and their lavaquerns, brought in from the Niedermandig quarries in the Eifel. They marketed their distinctive jugs here and their packhorses (whose shoes outnumbered those of the draught oxen by twenty to one) trotted laden with Lyveden wares west to Leicester, east to Cambridge and south as far as Badby.

There was a mint in Stamford Baron belonging to the abbot of Peterborough for a long period before the Conquest and it continued at least as far as Henry II's reign. Such a flourishing commercial centre had a full complement of ecclesiastical and charitable institutions. All Saints used to stand by the bridge in Water Street. St Martin's church, the burying place of Lord Burghley, is now almost entirely of fifteenth-century work. To the south of it was the hospital

---

[15] A. Rogers, *The Medieval Buildings of Stamford*, Stamford Survey Group Report I (Nottingham, 1970), pp. 8–9.

[16] G. C. Dunning, 'The Trade in Medieval Pottery around the North Sea', *Rotterdam Papers* (1968), pp. 35–58.

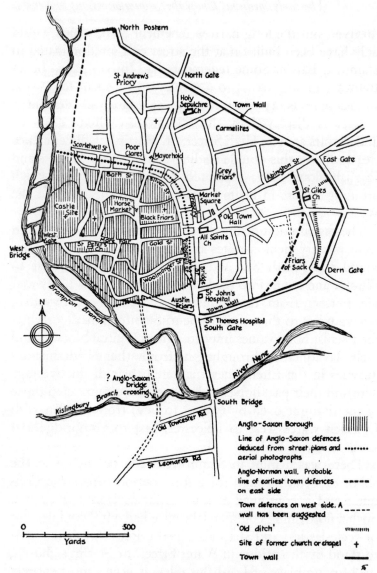

Fig. 9. Medieval Northampton

The likely position of the Anglo-Saxon borough and its line of defences, together with the possible bridge crossings to the south, are taken from the map accompanying Frank Lee's article. Most of the other medieval features are deduced from the 1610 map of John Speed, but he wrongly places the Grey Friars where in fact the house of the Carmelites was, and his version of the course of the Brampton branch of the Nene to the west of the town is highly dubious.

of St Giles; to the north the house of St Sepulchre. The Burghley hospital adjoining the bridge over the Welland on the west side is joined to a twelfth-century building at its north-east angle.

The Anglo Danish borough of Stamford seems at the time of the Norman Conquest to have served as a county town to South Lincolnshire, and when we turn to consider the medieval townscape of *Northampton* we find that it also originated as the military and administrative centre of a Danish army whose territory stretched as far as the Welland. Reconquered in 918 by Edward, it became the chief town of one of the new shires carved out of the former Danelaw. Its favourable geographical position where the Jurassic Way crosses the Nene made *Hamtun* a natural focus for trading, and already by 1010 it is described as a 'port'. The frequency of early road-names in the county like *Hamtuneweie*, *Hamtunegate* (Braybrooke 1199) and *Hantuneford* (Welford *c.* 1190) speak of its early importance as a communications centre.[17] The Danish-Anglo-Saxon borough was sited on a sandstone bluff above the river. As Frank Lee pointed out in an ingenious and convincing argument, which has not, however, been backed up so far by archaeological evidence, the pre-1066 borough was centred round the north–south, east–west crossing of Horsemarket–Horseshoe Street, and Mare Fair–Gold Street. He reckons that the original southern bridge crossing was one and a half furlongs to the west of the present south bridge, and certainly the line of the approach road from Towcester and the street plan of the Anglo-Saxon borough strongly support this thesis. In particular the curved alignment of Bath Street, Silver Street, College Street and Kingswell Street suggests a previous line of fortifications—Lee's so-called 'palisade'.[18]

Domesday Book mentions a 'Novus Burgus' which has

[17] *Place Names of Northants.*, p. 6.
[18] F. Lee, 'A New Theory of the origins and early growth of Northampton', *Archaeological Journal*, Vol. CX (1954), pp. 164–74.

been added between 1066 and 1085 to the north of the Anglo-Saxon *enceinte*. This was centred on the *Marehold*, now absurdly spelt *Mayorhold*. The Norman castle, the work of Earl Simon de Senlis I (1090–1111), was thrown up on top of the Anglo-Saxon houses in the western sector of the old borough. Their remains in the form of hearths, post holes and pits have been found sealed below the earthworks of the castle and these demolished dwellings are mentioned in the Domesday account which states that nearly ten per cent of the 230½ houses belonging to the old and new boroughs were waste or in ruins. Four churches survive from Norman Northampton. The Saxon foundation, St Peter's, was rebuilt magnificently *c.* 1160, doubtless because of its proximity to the castle. Earl Simon is also credited with the foundation of All Saints and the round church of the Holy Sepulchre. St Giles served the eastern end of the expanded town. A new route, Bridge Street, was built to connect the enlarged Norman town to an improved and now single south bridge. This was joined to the old Towcester road by a short link, and the London road was slightly realigned to the east at the Queen Eleanor cross, Hardingstone, to meet the new bridge (Plate 24).

In these ways the Normans had decisively shifted the centre of gravity of the town towards the east.

The present street-names indicate the marketing centres of the medieval town. The fairs held in the church and churchyard of All Saints which is described in 1180–3 as *ecclesia de foro in Northampton* were the precursors of the market. Henry III in 1235 forbade the continuance of this and ordered the markets or fairs to be held henceforth in a waste and empty place to the north of the church. This is the beginning of what Morton described in 1712 as "The Market Hill . . . lookt upon as the finest in Europe; a fair, spacious, open Square." Mercers Row, where the dealers in silks and velvets were to be found, lies to the south of the market. On the west side of the square were the various *rows* of the wimplers, mercers, cobblers and maltsters where today a line of shops separates the Drapery from the market place. The Drapery was a place where cloth was made. Further evidence of the importance of wool and cloth in the town's early economy is seen in Woolmonger Street, running south-west from the Drapery, Sheep Street (*shepes market* in 1540) and Scarletwell Street (from the dyeing trade). Gold Street takes its name from the goldsmiths who had workshops on the east side. The Horsemarket and Hogmarket lay in what became the north-western quarter.

Perhaps the most fascinating feature of the street pattern of medieval Northampton is the series of narrow passageways or 'jitties', piercing the likely line of the Anglo-Saxon fortifications at intervals; like Francis Jitty, connecting Bridge Street and Kingswell Street, Jeyes Jitty, connecting the Drapery and College Street, and the alley connecting Silver Street and Bearwood Street (from 'keeper of performing bears'—a common sight in the Middle Ages).

The medieval town was dominated on the west by the royal castle and on the north by the powerful Cluniac priory of St Andrew which had the presentation of all nine churches in the town by the year 1200. It stood between Brook Street and Lower Priory Street; Monks Pond Street runs across the site of its fishpond. Only the names recall its former greatness. The Friars (the Salvation Army of the thirteenth century) also colonised the town in force. No fragment remains of the houses of the Friars of the Sack, Dominicans, Poor Clares, White and Austin Friars. The Franciscans settled in the town in 1226 and their site is under municipal car parks due north of the market place. It gives its name to the present Greyfriars Street and is being currently excavated. The recovery of the total plan of what Leland described as "the best builded and largest House of all the places of the freres" is an exciting possibility. The only other medieval buildings surviving in the townscape are the substantial red sandstone almshouses and chapel of St John's

Hospital dating from the fourteenth to fifteenth centuries. Recently restored by the Roman Catholics, they stand on the east side of Bridge Street near to the site of the South Gate.

This reminds the landscape historian that Northampton was a walled town. It is possible that the ditches and earthworks were begun by the founder of the castle, Earl Simon de Senlis I. Grants of murage were made to the town in 1224, 1251 and 1301. The wall ran east and north of the town, and to the south-west and west the river and the castle provided adequate defences. Its course is still traceable from its north-west corner on the Brampton branch of the Nene. The prior of St Andrew's was supposed to have treacherously weakened the stretch bounding his convent's property to allow a royalist breach in the siege of the town in 1264. The story can be discounted. Public works like town walls were perennial problems for penny-pinching burgesses. They frequently fell down of their own accord! The line of the wall and ditch ran along the south side of St George's Street (North Gate), Campbell Street, the Upper and Lower Mounts (East Gate), York Road, Cheyne Walk (Dern Gate—the 'secret' or 'hidden' gate), Victoria Promenade (South Gate), Weston Street (now almost obliterated) across the Gas Works Site (Marvell's Mill postern) and so up by the river to the West Gate near the Castle. We know from an inquisition of 1278 that the wall between the East and North Gates was crenellated and much used for walking purposes by sick burgesses when they needed fresh air, by all who wanted to take short cuts to avoid the muddy lane below in winter and by the nightwatchmen on the lookout for malefactors.[19]

From the thirteenth century there are references to houses in the suburbs and burgesses doubtless settled outside the walls to escape the burden of taxation. To the north and

[19] *V.C.H. Northants.*, Vol. III, p. 30. R. F. Treharne, 'The Battle of Northampton', *Northants. Past And Present*, Vol. II, 2 (1955), pp. 13–30.

east where the town fields extended to the parishes of Kingsthorpe, Abington and Weston Favell, there were houses
outside the North Gate along the road to Market Harborough. Between this and the Kettering road the remains
of the town fields are visible in the large open space known
as the Race Course—once Northampton Heath. South of
the town between the walls and the river, grew up the south
quarter, still containing many waste places in 1430. This was
laid out in neat rectangular blocks delineated clearly on the
1747 plan of Noble and Butlin. Cow Meadow, Calvesholme
and Midsummer Meadow, although overshadowed by the
giant concrete cooling towers of the East Midlands Electricity Board, still recall the agrarian pursuits of the early
burgesses. A suburb developed to the east of the abbey of
St James, founded by the Austin Canons *c.* 1100 on the west
side of the Nene. Known as St James' End, the earliest
reference (*Brodende Sci Jacobi*) dates from 1285. South of the
river in Hardingstone parish Cotton End (1199, *Cotes*, 'the
cottages'), or St Leonard's End, grew up along the London
road round St Leonard's Hospital and Chapel. The last
traces of the latter were destroyed in the early nineteenth
century.

From this it is obvious that the present central area of the
county town retained the medieval street plan and street
names intact until 1971. These were more important
reminders of the time when Northampton was one of the
greatest towns in the kingdom, frequented by kings and
their councils, by meetings of the great international
monastic orders, and by scholars and merchants, than the
few remaining, and one hopes, well-protected medieval
buildings. It is all the more a pity that the planning proposals for the central development of the town seem to
imply the obliteration of the ancient street plan which has
remained almost unchanged from the Middle Ages, surviving even the considerable reconstruction which took place
after the Fire of 1675. In particular the interesting double

line of streets inside and outside the defences of the pre-1000 town seems doomed to destruction—a senseless capitulation to the havoc which the motor car makes on all our lives.[20] The historic heart of the medieval town has been ripped out.

A far more sympathetic approach to the past has been made in the case of projected modern developments in *Peterborough*. It also offers a strong contrast to Northampton in its origins and evolution.

We have noticed how the Anglo-Saxon abbey became a centre from which the colonisation of the middle Nene valley and the fen was attempted in the early Middle Ages.

The monastery had been refounded after its partial or total destruction at the hands of the Danes in the ninth century by Ethelwold, Bishop of Winchester in 966. Abbot Kenulf (922–1005) made a wall round the minster and changed the name Medeshamstede to *Burgh*. It is risky to jump to the conclusion that the village had become a borough in the tenth century. Borough status implies a mint, market place, possibly a court and a defence circuit. Perhaps the monastery had simply become 'like a city', a strong place and a burh. One or two clues, however, suggest otherwise. The find of a coin with the inscription suggesting Medehamstede (not Burgh) might just provide evidence for a mint. Scrutiny of the street plan illustrated in the 1721 Eayre map (more useful than the Speed map of 1610 which is simply a sketch plan) shows a likely site for a Saxon market place to the north-east of the minster.[21] The remnants of burgage plots seem to straggle east and west from the street frontage. If one adds to this the possibility that there may have been a ford well to the east of the present bridge and that this linked up to the 'market place'

[20] Northampton Civic Society, *Comments and suggestions on the Planning Proposals for the Expansion of Northampton* (1969), Appendix B.

[21] B.M. Add. MSS. 32467 No. 188. A number of suggestions in this paragraph were made by D. Mackreth in a lecture to the Middle Nene Archaeological Society, January 1973.

on the same north–south alignment as the old Lincoln road which went out north via Dogsthorpe and Paston, the supposition becomes closer to likelihood. The existence of a bank and ditch surrounding the burh which is suggested by the layout of Eayre's plan is still to be proved, but one other factor, the siting of Thorold's motte to the north-east of the monastery, would be conveniently placed to overawe the putative borough as well as the rebellious Anglo-Saxon monks.

Whatever the extent of the Saxon burh, the small vill with its church to the east of the monastery was found to be inconvenient. It was sited on the clay and prone to flooding. Accordingly Abbot Martin (1133–55) "changed the situation of the monastic gate, the market place, the hithe for the boats, and the vill itself to a much better position and made many improvements".[22] The modern layout of central Peterborough has been determined by the presence of the powerful monastery which dominated the little town growing up beneath and outside its walls to the west (Plate 16).

A detailed description of the monastic precinct is found in Henry VIII's patent setting up the new see of Peterborough in 1541.[23] When this is compared with Speed's plan of 1610 and the fine map of Thomas Eayre, 1721, the generous scale of the grounds of the monastery can be realised—quite a quarter of the whole of the medieval town. Within the walls was a stream running north–south towards the Nene; it flowed into a great fishpond or *vivarium* known as the Derby Yard, an area now a temporary car park between Bishops Road and the river. A series of dykes, including 'the Bull Dyke' on the east and the common sewer on the west, drained the site towards the south. The walled

[22] W. T. Mellows (ed.), *The Peterborough Chronicle of Hugh Candidus* (Peterborough, 1941), p. 65.
[23] W. T. Mellows (ed.), *The Foundation of Peterborough Cathedral A.D. 1541*, Northamptonshire Record Society, Vol. XIII (1941), pp. 11–12.

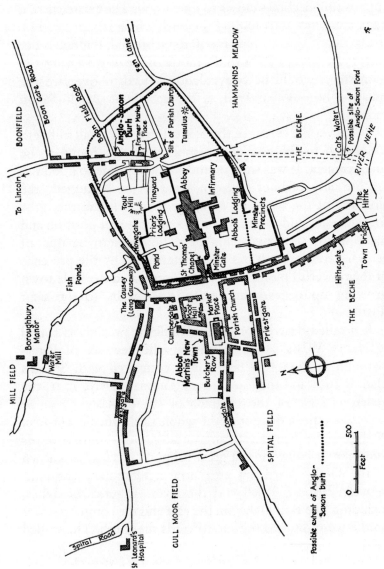

Fig. 10. Medieval Peterborough

MILL FIELD

BOONFIELD

Boon Gate Road

Boon Field Road

Fen Lane

Anglo-Saxon Burh

To Lincoln

Former Market Place

Site of Parish Church

Tumulus

HAMMONDS MEADOW

THE BECHE

Cat's Water

? Possible site of Anglo-Saxon Ford

RIVER NENE

Tout Hill

Vineyard

Abbey

Infirmary

Howegate

Prior's Lodging

Abbot's Lodging

Minster Precincts

Fish Ponds

Pond

St Thomas' Chapel

Minster Gate

The Hithe

Boroughbury Manor

The Causey (Long Causeway)

Cumbergate

Moot Hall

Market Place

Parish Church

Hithegate

The Beche

Town Bridge

Water Mill

Abbot Martin's New Town

Butcher's Row

THE BECHE

Westgate

Priestgate

N

Cowgate

SPITAL FIELD

GULL MOOR FIELD

Possible extent of Anglo-Saxon burh ●●●●●●●●

500

0   Feet

Spital Road

St Leonard's Hospital

precinct enclosed an area now defined on the south by Bishops Road and on the east by Vineyard Road. We know that the old vineyard of the monastery lay to the east and the southern part of this was where William Morton, almoner of the abbey, 1448–67, grew his herbs and leeks.[24] The precinct then cut across to a motte known as *Tout Hill*, thrown up by the first Norman abbot, Thorold, to overawe his rebellious Saxon monks. The wall turned south, parallel with Long Causeway; the entrance to the town was at Minster Gate; and it continued south bounding the abbot's lodging (later the Bishop's Palace). The houses— now shops—of Long Causeway and Bridge Street abut against the precinct but recently St Peter's Road has been driven through to service them from behind.

Abbot Martin's vill was given the rectilinear layout of a planned town similar in some respects but not as ambitious as the monastic foundation of Bury St Edmunds in Suffolk. It was orientated east–west to connect it with the road to Thorpe. There were three main streets called *gates*. Abbot Martin built a bridge over the stream already mentioned which gave access from Westgate to Howegate. This is now known as Midgate but the original name was derived from some now forgotten tumulus; a second can be found just

[24] P. I. King (ed.), *The Book of William Morton*, Northamptonshire Record Society, Vol. XVI (1954), p. xxx.

Fig. 10. Medieval Peterborough.

The tangled lanes of the pre-Conquest settlement to the east of the abbey precinct were succeeded as the centre of activity by the grid-like street plan of the new town laid out in the twelfth century by Abbot Martin around a large rectangular market place to the west of the Minster Gate. This was encroached on in 1402 when the parish church was re-erected in its western quarter. Hithegate reminds us that there was a wharf by the Nene before a bridge (first mentioned in 1308), which later changed the name to Bridge Street. The open fields of the burgesses lay to the north of the town. This map is compiled from one by W. T. Mellows, now in the Dean and Chapter library, and other features are from T. Eayre's plan of *c.* 1720.

north of Gravel Walk to the east of the cathedral, reminders
that the site chosen by the seventh-century monks was
already long hallowed. Cowgate, the second main street,
where cows were bought and sold was parallel to Priestgate.
The nucleus of the vill was the wide market place, immediately adjoining the minster gate. Here, during the year, three
fairs were held each of a week's duration. In 1402 the new
parish church of St John was built in the middle of the
market place from materials taken from the former church
to the east of the monastery and the nave of St Thomas'
chapel.²⁵ The great size of the market place was again
reduced by the building of the handsome guildhall, the
present structure of which dates from 1671.

The trades practised during the Middle Ages have provided further street names in the centre of the town.
Butcher's Row was the name for the west end of the present
Market Street. Cumbergate was the street of the wool-
combers. St John Street was earlier known as Bondegate,
possibly from having been the home of the 'bonds' or
peasants, as distinct from the burgesses. Saltersgate, Cook
Row and Souter Row (the shoemaker's quarter) have now
vanished. As the population increased, the town became
more densely built up and such descriptive street names as
Dedmanslane, Gropelane (a very dark thoroughfare) and
Rotonrowe, a term of contempt for a tumbledown street,
came into use.

The vill was connected to the Nene by Hithegate, which
led to the hithe or landing place. Abbot Godfrey's construction of a bridge at this point in 1308 changed the shape of
the town by pulling it to the south. Burgess holdings, their
rectilinear shape, contrasting with the more haphazard and
sprawling layout of the agricultural vill around St John
Street, lined both sides of the broad thoroughfare leading
down to the bridge. A Bridge Fair on St Matthew's Day,
held on the south bank, was granted in 1439, but there was

²⁵ *The Book of William Morton*, p. 122, fn. i.

no expansion of the town to the south until the nineteenth century.

Boroughbury (modern Lincoln Road) was a street leading off Westgate but only as far as a mill and the monastic fish-ponds. Travellers going north in the direction of Lincoln, went, as we have seen, by way of Bondegate which also connected the town to the East Field and so to the fenland island settlements of Eye and Thorney. Buried under the streets of the late-nineteenth-century expanded town lies the ridge-and-furrow of the two great open fields of the burgesses and bondsmen of Peterborough Abbey. The East and West Fields can still be identified lying to the east and west of the cathedral.

In the far south of the county *Brackley* affords an interesting example of a seignorial borough which grew to a modicum of prosperity in the early Middle Ages and then decayed.[26] It failed to spring into new life in the Tudor period and was untouched by the Industrial Revolution. Its comparative insignificance in the twentieth century in terms of size is balanced by the fact that here we have the best example in the county of a medieval planned borough; if conservation areas had been invented twenty years sooner the county could have preserved intact a charming town now in process of being wrecked by the motor car and unfeeling development.

The origin of Brackley is to be sought in the cluster of farms two and a half miles to the north. Here was the centre of the old Saxon parish of Halse with a church mentioned in Domesday Book. The 'Old Town' marks the site of Bracca's 'leah' or clearing. It was chosen for its rich soil, good water supply and because of its proximity to a ford over the Ouse leading to a road to Buckingham. Of the two springs one was called Goldwell (the golden spring)

[26] M. W. Beresford and J. K. St Joseph, *Medieval England, An Aerial Survey* (Cambridge, 1958), pp. 208, 209. Also M. W. Beresford, *New Towns of the Middle Ages* (London, 1967), pp. 468–9.

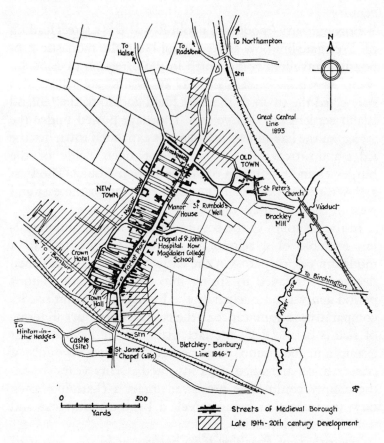

Fig. 11. Brackley

The curving loops of the lanes in the 'old town', with St Peter's church nearby, point to the site of *Bracca's leah*. The lords of the short-lived castle dominating the stream crossing (to the south of the road leading to Hinton-in-the-Hedges) created the new town with its long High Street and parallel back street with burgage tenements strung out in between. Despite the brief prosperity of the coaching age and the arrival of two railways in the nineteenth century, Brackley remained virtually unchanged as a small market town for the agricultural south of the county, with no industry to speak of, until the motoring age, which threatens to destroy it.

and the other, St Rumbold's well (named after a local Anglo-Saxon saint who came from King's Sutton). The fields cleared by the followers of Bracca extended as far as the Northampton road. The new town was probably a late-twelfth-century seignorial creation, deriving from the short-lived castle. The earthworks, now shrouded in allotments, command the river crossing to the south but not the hill on which the town stands. "From this bridge," wrote Leland, "the greate streate of the towne goith up apon a pratie hille: at the pitch whereof there turnithe a nothar streat by este to Saint Peters, the heade churche of the towne." The prosperity brought by the marketing of wool in the broad High Street in the thirteenth century enabled the burgesses to rebuild St Peter's with a fine Early English west tower and south aisle, and to found St James' chapel at the foot of the castle (demolished in 1836). A hospital dedicated to SS. James and John stood half-way up the High Street. The Saxon Old Town is distinguished by its huddle of houses round a tangle of streets; the New Town has a strictly linear layout with one back lane only (Manor Road) parallel to the High Street servicing the long narrow burgess crofts on the west side. It is possible that the fall of the ground explains the shorter crofts—or maybe the clearing from the Old Town had progressed this far. Certainly the burgesses of the New Town had their fields on the north and west sides of the town.

The town fell on hard times in the late Middle Ages and Leland remarked that "Brakely market is now desolatyd." The buildings of St John's Hospital were given a new lease of life by William of Waynflete, Bishop of Winchester, when he used them to endow his foundation of Magdalen College, Oxford (1458). The Fellows hurriedly established a free school there in 1548 and saved their chantry from dissolution. The thirteenth-century hospital now serves as a chapel to the school; the western part may have been used as an infirmary for the sick.

Brackley became a classic example of a 'rotten' borough (there was even *the Ratoun Rewe* or rat row in 1365!) with a closed franchise returning two nominated scions of the aristocratic Stanleys, who provided the town's most notable building in 1706, a fine town hall whose arched ground windows originally provided an open market space (Plate 35). The town attracted some coaching traffic in the eighteenth century. The Crown Hotel on the west side of the market place has a central carriageway and a Palladian window above it, and there are several good Georgian town houses, indicating that Brackley was not devoid of some prosperity and its accompanying taste in the eighteenth century. The Bletchley–Banbury branch railway in 1846–7 brought convenience but made little impression on the town; the Great Central line (1893) with its mighty viaduct across the Ouse similarly brought nothing in its train except an outsize station peculiarly called Brackley Central (it is in fact on the northern fringe of the town).

Higham Ferrers is a second example in the county of a Saxon village which expanded under seignorial patronage to borough status.[27] The A6 from Kettering to Bedford sweeps up the hill from the medieval bridge crossing at Irthlingborough to the 'High ham'. Here above the 230-foot contour line was a Saxon settlement which had acquired the unusual distinction of a market mentioned in Domesday. The 1959 edition of the six-inch Ordnance Survey map shows the name *Bury* close beside the terminus and goods shed of the Midland railway station. If this clue is followed back to the 1789 plan made for the Duchy of Lancaster we notice three large closes, all bearing the name *Bury*, which have a markedly rectilinear boundary, suggesting that here is the outline of a Saxon burh protecting the houses of the first Higham.

William Peverel held Higham in 1086 and his family built an earthwork castle, the remains of which, obscured by

[27] M. W. Beresford, *History on the Ground* (London, 1971), pp. 153–79.

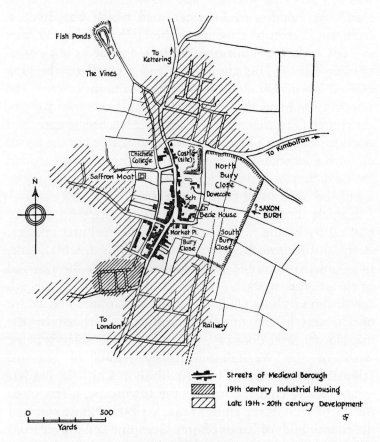

Fish Ponds

To Kettering

The Vines

To Kimbolton →

Chichele College

Castle (site)

North Bury Close

Saffron Moat

Dovecote

Sch

? SAXON BURH

Ch

Bede House

Market Pl.

South Bury Close

Bury Close

To London

Railway

N

0   500
Yards

━━━ Streets of Medieval Borough

▨ 19th century Industrial Housing

▨ Late 19th - 20th century Development

SF

Fig. 12. Higham Ferrers

The suspiciously rectangular boundaries of the three fields called *Bury Closes* (in the 1789 map) suggest that they outline the Saxon burh. If so, the first Norman castle was built in the north-west corner of this rectangle. William de Ferrers created a new borough in 1251 for ninety-two burgesses, whose tenements are grouped around the triangular market place and along both sides of the main road. As at Brackley, there is a parallel back lane to the west, and a shorter back lane to the east.

scrub, overlook a municipalised park laid out in the outer ward. The castle garrison and household attracted trade along the London to Leicester road which was diverted from the Ditchford crossing to the Higham bridge at least as early as 1227. William de Ferrers obtained the right of holding fairs at Higham in 1250 and a year later the king created a borough along both sides of the main street, the London road and the central market place to the west of the church. The triangular market place has been encroached upon by a block of buildings on the west side but the broad cobbled area where the buying and selling went on around the market cross which dates from 1280 still gives a spacious air to the main street of this little town.

Burgess holdings stretched in long strips to a long parallel back lane similar to so many agricultural villages. Barns and farmyards are to be found along the back lane, their limestone rubble walls contrasting with the raw red brick of the workshops added during the nineteenth century and its boom in the boot and shoe trade. The wealth of Higham in the thirteenth century is attested by the magnificent west doorway, the sculpture of which was the work of the Westminster Abbey school of masons. Higham's most famous son, Archbishop Chichele, has left three notable contributions to the townscape, a school to the north-west of the church (1422), a Bede House south of the church built of bands of grey limestone and ginger ironstone (1428), and the college abutting on to the main street (1431).

To the casual visitor, perhaps coming to take his schoolboy son out for the afternoon, *Oundle* gives the impression of being a sleepy little stone-built town, a creation mainly of the seventeenth or eighteenth century. The historian of the townscape, however, will detect in the layout of the streets a far earlier agrarian origin. We have already seen that it was one of the earliest Anglo-Saxon settlements in Northamptonshire; it was referred to as an ancient regional centre in the eighth century and there was a monastery founded by St Wilfrid who died here in A.D. 709. The focus of pre-Conquest Oundle may well have been north-west of the present church (a late medieval building) between the rectory and the vicarage where there was formerly a house known as *Berrystead* (O.E. *burh-stede*).

The abbey of Peterborough controlled the fortunes of the town from A.D. 972 when it was restored to the monks until the Dissolution. Peterborough Abbey used it as a centre for the administration of 'the eight hundreds' in the late Anglo-Saxon period. Its early ecclesiastical and administrative importance attracted traders and there was a market before the Norman Conquest here which was already worth twenty-five shillings in 1086.

Six roads converge on its two river crossings (Plate 27). "The river Avon (Nene) so windeth about Oundle town," wrote Leland in 1540, "that it almost insulateth it, saving a little by west-northwest." The main street runs along a low limestone ridge which lifts the site on a spur above the floodwaters of the Nene. Behind the almost continuous façades of dignified town houses of the late-seventeenth- and eighteenth-century Oundle merchants and innkeepers is a jumble of outbuildings and walls only partly concealing the long rectangular crofts of the early medieval burgesses. As at Higham these lead to two parallel back lanes (now called Milton Road and South Road) which provided access to the river meadows on the south and the town fields on the north and west. Fifteen burgesses are mentioned in the twelfth-century *Liber Niger* rendering thirty shillings. The same document refers to twenty-five men holding twenty yard-lands, and these men of the town (*homines villae*) had nine ploughs and ploughed once a week in the autumn for the lord. The market by then was worth £4. 3s. and the mill forty shillings and 200 eels.[28] The market place is triangular

[28] T. Stapleton (ed.), *Chronicon Petroburgense*, Camden Society (1849), p. 158.

in shape, swelling out at the junction of West Street and North Street. Henry III granted the monks a yearly fair in 1208. The handsome late-medieval church with its slender pale yellow stone tower and needle spire dominates the little town and suggests a good deal of prosperity in the middle Nene valley in the fourteenth and fifteenth centuries.

Leland spoke with approval of Oundle in 1540: "The town standeth on the further ripe [bank] as I came to it: the bridge over Avon (Nene) is of five great arches and two small . . . the town hath a very good market and is all builded of stone. The parish church is very fair." A survey of 1562 confirms that the basic street pattern has scarcely altered in the last 400 years, only the names have been changed; what was High Street in Elizabeth I's reign is now West Street and North Street; Bury Street has become New Street.[29] Leland mentioned: "on the south side of the churchyard a pretty almshouse of squared stone, and a goodly large hall over it for the brotherhood of that church". This was replaced by a grammar school and alms-house by Sir William Laxton, grocer of London in 1556. The present town hall and market house which stands in the middle of the market place is currently threatened by hostile shopkeepers who want it demolished. It was erected in 1826, the year in which the market cross which stood at the top of St Osyth Lane was destroyed. While architecturally not remarkable when considered separately, its contribution to the setting of a stone town of great character is vital.

The famous school of Laxton's foundation remained obscure and modest in size until the remarkable uplift in its fortunes in the mid-nineteenth century when it was changed into a public (i.e. private) boarding school. Its effect on the townscape is far from prominent owing to its well-mannered, mostly neo-Tudor buildings which harmonise with the many seventeenth- and eighteenth-century houses of the little town. They have introduced an architectural

[29] *V.C.H. Northants.*, Vol. III, pp. 87–88.

quality into the town; and the chapel, Great Hall, boarding houses, playing fields and avenues have prevented the town from sprawling to the north. There is a mushroom growth of development now in the 1970s along the Glapthorn road, but to the west and south the flood plain of the Nene is an inhibiting factor.

5. The later medieval landscape

Deserted villages. Parks. The medieval building-stone industry

Deserted villages

AS IN OTHER counties in midland and eastern England one of the most characteristic features of the landscape of Northamptonshire in the fourteenth and fifteenth centuries was the desertion or contraction of many of the settlements which had existed in 1300.[1] The earthworks on the sites of these abandoned villages form now our best evidence for reconstructing the appearance of the medieval village. Unfortunately they are being destroyed at an alarming rate by deep ploughing, draining and other modern agricultural practices, frequently before they are even surveyed or recorded. Aerial photographs taken at intervals since the 1940s chart the gradual elimination of these interesting sites from the landscape.[2]

Their existence was first noticed in the early eighteenth century by the county's zealous historian, John Bridges, whose account of Nobold focusses attention on a set of one of the best-preserved deserted village earthworks in the county.

[1] K. J. Allison, M. W. Beresford, J. G. Hurst, *The Deserted Villages of Northamptonshire* (Leicester, 1966).

[2] Dr J. K. St Joseph recently published a telling example at Downtown, Northants., where a complete set of earthworks of this village, deserted in the seventeenth century, was levelled by ploughing between 1958 and 1965. Hedges and trees were uprooted, closes and paddocks round the margins of the village were thrown into larger fields. This is happening all over the county, *Antiquity*, Vol. XLV (December 1971), pp. 298–9.

Fig. 13. Deserted Villages of Northamptonshire

This map covers the approximate number (82 +) gazetteered in K. J.
Allison, M. W. Beresford and J. G. Hurst's pioneer work (1966). The
date range is from *c.* 1086, until the twentieth century, but according
to the authors, 4 (five per cent) were deserted soon after 1086; 1 (one
per cent) between *c.* 1100 and *c.* 1350; 10 (twelve per cent) between
c. 1350 and *c.* 1450, and 34 (forty-one per cent) between *c.* 1450 and *c.*
1700. The empty area in the soke had few medieval villages and each
was large and economically sound enough to survive recurrent agricultural crises. The forested areas were lightly settled and the small fields
attached to the villages unlikely to excite grazier's greed. The Northampton Heights have depopulated sites "as close packed as anywhere in
England", but it is difficult to say why this was so vulnerable a region.

Throughout the whole close are many irregular banks and hollows, such as are usual in ruinous places, about which have been turned up walling stones, and old hearth stones, as supposed from the marks they bore of fire. Round these heaps and hollows are partition banks and ditches, inclosing such extents of ground as are commonly allotted to the homesteads of cottages and farmhouses. Nearly the length of the close along the middle of it is a list or tract of ground, lower than the ground on both sides, which appears to have been raised by rubbish, supposed to have been the principal street of the town. Upon boring into it in several places, the stick was checked as by a stone-causey about three inches below the surface. In one part is a plot of ground immemorially called the church-yard, and a large old tree growing in it, lately cut down, always called the church-yard tree. Human skulls and bones have been dug up here. There are also fords, and tracts of roads still remaining which led here from other towns.[3]

Aerial photographs of Nobold show a simple plan of one central, slightly winding east–west village street with eight roughly rectangular enclosures—the house platforms on each side: behind them, parallel to one another and divided by deep ditches, the crofts lead up to the Clipston–Sibbertoft road on the north and to a stream crossed by fords to the south (Plate 17).

This essentially linear plan is found elsewhere. At Kirby, for instance, the sunken line of the long main street of the medieval village scars the side of the hill south of the pale yellow fretted shell of the Elizabethan hall. In *The Survaye of the mannor of Kyrby*, dated 1587, a few houses remained on the west of the hall, but the street mentioned was already empty (Fig. 14). The field on the east was labelled 'Kyrby Crofte' and the still-unenclosed block of open-field arable to

---

[3] J. Bridges, *History*, Vol. II, pp. 23, 314, 315.

the west was called 'the furlonge by the Townes side'. From
the air the complexes of farm buildings with their masonry
foundations can be made out under the grass. Where ploughing has encroached there is a thick litter of limestone rubble
and a scatter of medieval pottery in the ploughsoil. Bridges
in 1721 wrote: "some scattered houses are remembered to
have stood in a close South west of the house", and states,
"where the mount now is, a cart load of bones was dug up
about twenty years since".

A nucleated village plan is found in other deserted sites.
Sulby, which had thirteen people recorded in Domesday
Book and eighty-nine in 1377, was completely lost from the
sixteenth century onwards. The name survived in Sulby
Hall, Sulby Lodge, Sulby Covert and Sulby Grange, but the
village was on none of these sites. It was discovered by Dr
J. K. St Joseph in one of his aerial sorties. In the remote
upland area on the edge of the county which borders
Leicestershire the hollow-ways of the streets zigzag and
converge among house plots in an irregular-shaped field of
permanent pasture corrugated with the ridge-and-furrow
of the medieval field system. In one corner the right-angle
of a more formidable earthwork suggests a manorial moat.
Medieval potsherds can be picked up among the cowscrapes,
especially under the trees.

Sulby is in fields unconnected now with the road system.
Other deserted villages can be located by the convergence
of green lanes or footpaths in what is otherwise 'open
country'. Glassthorpe, for instance, marked now by only
one farm building, is on a green track that leads over the
fields between Little Brington and Upper Heyford. The
earthworks of the houses and their crofts are strung out
along a sinuous hollow-way which is flooded during the
winter: the crofts are long and rectangular and separated by
straight ditches which extend to the beginning of the open
field system. Faxton, similarly, although not completely
deserted until the beginning of the twentieth century, was

163

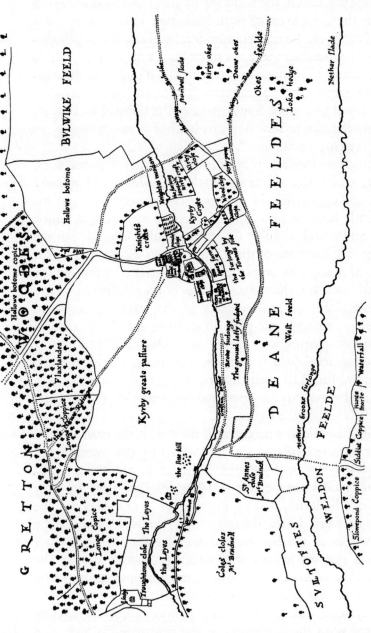

Fig. 14. 'The Survaye of the mannor of Kyrby as it is now in Anno 1587'

Northamptonshire Record Office, Finch Hatton MSS. 272. The site of the deserted village lies between 'Kyrby Crofte' and 'the furlonge by the Townes side'.

never connected with the metalled roads of the motor age and the site with its deserted church, lately destroyed, is approached by a confluence of field paths.

Stuchbury, between Sulgrave and Helmdon, is another deserted village whose existence is recalled by the name of a Stuchbury Manor Farm, cottages, hall, lodge and house. But the site is at none of these. Swelling earthworks, a string of fishponds and a dam are found in two neighbouring fields separated by a deep hedged hollow-way which connected the settlement with Greatworth, two miles to the south. Other footpaths also converge from Helmdon, Thorpe Mandeville and Sulgrave. There was a population of ten mentioned in Domesday Book; this had increased to fifty-nine by 1377. St Andrew's Priory, Northampton, held it from 1084 until the Dissolution and by that date it had become depopulated. Two closes called 'Westfyld' and 'Townefyld' were let for twenty-three pounds but no houses or tenants remained. Bridges, who realised that "there were here both a Manor and a town, or the remains of a town, several centuries after the Danes were expelled", recalls that there was still remaining a piece of ground called the churchyard where the long-demolished church of St John formerly stood. He also mentions a little hill in *Gallows Field* where, according to tradition, the hundred court of Sutton hundred was held.

Occasionally the presence of industrial debris betrays the location of a pottery-producing or an iron-smelting settlement, such as at Lyveden in the remote valley between Brigstock and Oundle. Here tremendous concentrations of potsherds and burned limestone on the ploughsoil noticed by Kettering Grammar School boys led to their series of excavations of the pottery-making site from 1965 to 1973. We can picture the activity in the thirteenth century on this site: the smoking kilns fed by huge quantities of brushwood and timber which made ever deeper inroads into the woods surrounding; overlapping claypits, great mounds of wasters forming the pot banks around the kilns; low rectangular thatched buildings, the workshops, store sheds and drying sheds. A century before the start of the pottery-making (in fact *c.* 1100) there was iron-smelting here—the roasting and smelting furnaces, together with pits full of charcoal, have been found associated with over 6000 sherds of creamy Stamford ware imported from kilns twenty miles to the north.

The types of houses and farm complexes found by excavation of deserted medieval villages at Faxton, Wythemail and Lyveden help to fill in an essential part of the late medieval landscape pattern.[4] At Faxton, where a group of four crofts was examined, the sequence of events was for the first rectangular houses to be of timber with post-hole construction and mud walls: these were followed by timber-framed buildings with horizontal sill beams: the later stages superimposed showed houses standing on foundations of boulders, pebbles and limestone. Since the date ranges were quite short, *c.* 1150 to 1300 or at the most 1350, it seems that the houses only lasted about fifty years before being rebuilt. Clay-lined water troughs and a stone oven for drying corn, peas and seeds were found in the yard of one of the farm crofts. The village street was cobbled and led to the neigh-bouring village of Old.

At Wythemail a similar structural sequence occurred. A timber building within a ditched enclosure came first, perhaps in the twelfth century. This was replaced by a stone longhouse of period II (the late thirteenth century), thirty-seven feet by sixteen internal dimensions, with dwarf walls built of limestone slabs. Its upper room with a central

[4] For Lyveden see J. M. Steane, 'Excavations at Lyveden 1965–7', *Journal of Northampton Museum*, 2 (December 1967), G. F. Bryant and J. M. Steane, 'Excavations at Lyveden 1968', *Journal*, 5 (June 1969), G. F. Bryant and J. M. Steane, 'Excavations at Lyveden 1969–70', *Journal*, 9 (June 1971). For Faxton see L. Butler, *Current Archaeology*, 6 (January 1968), pp. 163–4 (September 1969), pp. 144–8. Also *B.N.F.A.S.*, 2 (November 1967), pp. 23–24. For Wythemail see D. G. Hurst and J. G. Hurst, 'Excavations at the Medieval Village of Wythemail', *Medieval Archaeology*, Vol. XIII (1969), pp. 167–203.

hearth was separated by a paved cross-passage from a byre with a drain at the lower end. In the fourteenth century a stone longhouse, fifty-seven feet by thirteen internally, was set at right-angles to the earlier building. Both the main and the inner room had hearths; there was a sunken cross-passage with two lower rooms for animals and farm use. To the south-east was a cobbled yard, and byres and ovens bordered this. There were signs of the complete replanning of the complex on several occasions: the period II longhouse had been rebuilt at right-angles and over the earlier one; it also cut across the earlier property boundary ditch; in period III again there was a change of alignment through an angle of ninety degrees. Also a cobbled road had been driven over the yard at a later stage, separating the house area from the outbuildings which went out of use.

Complete and frequent replanning such as this was noticed at Faxton, where one house in the first phase was placed roughly parallel to the village street but seventy feet south of it; only in the thirteenth century was it brought close to the street and set more exactly parallel to it. The croft boundaries also moved with amalgamation of holdings and the rerouting of village roads. Moreover, there was a tendency for the barns, store sheds, byres, and corn-drying kilns to change from temporary structures to permanent stone-built sheds fixed in relation to the house and enclosing roughly rectangular courtyards. At Lyveden, for instance, a rectangular barn abuts at right-angles to a mid-fifteenth-century longhouse with byre and living ends. A paved yard divides the farmhouse from the next toft which belonged to a tiler.

The tendency to replace timber buildings by stone is connected with the fact that wood available for house repair was restricted from the thirteenth century onwards because, as we have seen, the clearance of tree cover was far advanced, while the forest fines of the reigns of John and Henry III deterred further encroachment without licence. Moreover, rebuilding on better-drained foundations was advisable in view of the deterioration of the climate. Evidence from sources such as tree-ring study indicates that summers of the period 1150 to 1300 were appreciably drier than during the later Middle Ages. A run of very wet years followed between 1316 and 1320 and there was a particularly high frequency of wet autumns in the first half of the fourteenth century.

This is borne out in the documents and in the archaeological record. At Higham Ferrers we know that in 1313–14 vines were still being grown out of doors, which implies a freedom from late spring frosts and sufficient sunshine and warmth in the summer. The accounts for that year state: "And 60s. for the wages of a vine dresser [*vineatoris*] for the year. And 4s. 5d. for the wages of 38 men gathering grapes, as it were for one day, and making green must, [*viridis succi*— or young wine] with salt bought for the same."[5]

Prolonged bad weather is likely to be responsible for the appearance of complex drainage systems and paved surfaces at Wythemail and at Lyveden in the later phases of that thirteenth- to fourteenth-century industrial site. Another pointer to this is the presence of corn-drying kilns, which are more usual in wetter western Britain. These have been found at Faxton, Stamford Castle and Brixworth, where three can be seen as excavated to the south of the churchyard. An entry in the 1266 Patent Rolls tells us that the corn of the king's enemy, Simon, was kept "in the churchyard of Brixworth".[6]

How far climatic deterioration was a factor leading to the desertion of settlements is difficult to determine. Certainly there is a suggestion that those villages on the cold upland Boulder Clays had a higher rate of desertion. There was in

---

[5] D. Justin Schove and A. W. G. Lowther, 'Tree Rings and Medieval Archaeology', *Medieval Archaeology*, Vol. I (1957), pp. 78–95, and H. H. Lamb, 'The Early Medieval Warm Epoch and its Sequel', *Palaeogeography, Palaeoclimatology, Palaeoecology*, Vol. I (1965), pp. 13–37, W. J. B. Kerr, *Higham Ferrers and its Ducal and Royal Castle and Park*, p. 56.

[6] *Cal. Patent Rolls*, 1258–66, p. 600. I owe this reference to the excavator, P. J. Woods.

fact a retreat from marginal land as holdings became available by the deaths of villagers on more easily worked and more rewarding soils.

This immediately connects bad weather, depopulation and plague. Doubtless years of famine produced chronic malnutrition, which in turn reduced resistance to disease. It is more difficult, however, to point to a documentary basis for assigning a desertion of a village to the period 1350–1450 when the Black Death was particularly virulent. Occasionally there is an explicit statement, as that made to the Pope in 1412 that pestilences had robbed Elkington of all its parishioners except three or four servants of Pipewell Abbey. A catastrophe of this kind possibly had occurred at Sulby where the population dropped from eighty-nine taxpayers in 1377 to a mere four households in 1428. We know from a study of the appointments of beneficed clergy by the Bishop of Lincoln made to vacant benefices in the county that there were 131 changes out of a possible 281 in 1349, which suggests a mortality of crippling proportions. Before May and after October 1349 there were thirty-four institutions: in May, eight; June, fifteen; July, twenty-five; August, thirty-six; September, ten; October, seven. All the monks with William de Shelton their prior, were said to have died at Luffield, that secluded spot in the forest of Whittlewood. A group of charters (nos. 137–40) of various dates in May 1349, however, imply a community in being and have no reference to a crisis, and another (no. 86) of 30th May is a licence of Edward III to acquire land in mortmain sufficient to support an additional brother in the house. At Wothorpe near Burghley "the convent being poorly endowed was by the pestilence which lately prevails reduced to such poverty that all the nuns but one on account of their penury have dispersed".[7]

---

[7] 'The Black Death in Northamptonshire', *Northants. Notes and Queries*, Vol. VI (1896), p. 115. D. David Knowles in a review, *English Historical Review 1*, Vol. XXV (1970), p. 606.

The first impact of the Black Death would no doubt have produced some abandoned holdings everywhere the disease struck, but within a short time the easily worked soils in the more fertile areas would have filled up with people from the more difficult and marginal lands of the upland areas of the county. Here fields fell right out of cultivation causing the abandonment of some villages.

A third and perhaps more potent cause for depopulation was the massive revolution of land use which occurred in the later Middle Ages in many parts of midland England. Landlords and tenants decided to make a complete transition from arable to grass, from growing corn to rearing sheep. The advantages were twofold. Firstly, they met the needs of the still-growing home market and the traditional overseas market for raw wool. A cloth trade had been firmly established as early as the twelfth century in the county and we find Henry II buying cloth at Northampton. A few years later John equipped his wardrobe with cloth bought at Northampton and Stamford. English cloth was exported directly from Stamford by the Welland and the ports of the Wash, mainly to Flanders, but some went to Lombardy. Secondly, they cut labour costs which were rising because of plague mortality; only a few shepherds with their dogs were needed to look after thousands of sheep.[8]

The effect on the landscape was to reduce the area of arable land, to quicken the process of enclosure, and to depopulate and even destroy some settlements. Instances may be cited of an early changeover from arable to pasture, one from the centre and the others from the south of the county.

As one travels south from Kettering along the A43, the

---

[8] E. Miller, 'The Fortunes of the English Textile Industry during the Thirteenth Century', *Econ. H.R.*, 2nd Series, Vol. XVIII (1965), pp. 65–66. E. Carus-Wilson, 'The Medieval Trade of the Ports of the Wash', *Medieval Archaeology*, Vols. VI-VII (1962–3), pp. 182–202. *V.C.H. Northants.*, Vol III, p. 27. A. Rogers (ed.), *The Making of Stamford* (Leicester, 1965), pp. 43–45.

1819 turnpike road to Northampton, there is a gap in the settlement pattern with no villages for about ten miles between Broughton and Moulton. In the early Middle Ages, however, there were two additional settlements in this area. Wythemail, we have noticed already. Badsaddle in Orlingbury, 'Baetti's hazel' or 'hazel clump' was colonised late in the Anglo-Saxon period from Orlingbury. Pottery picked up from the ploughsoil gives a date range for occupation between the eleventh and fourteenth centuries. Henry Green, one of a family of lawyers, bought the manor in the early fourteenth century and Sir Thomas Green died in 1392 seised of it. It consisted in this year of twenty acres of meadow, 200 acres of pasture and twenty acres of wood. No arable or tenants are mentioned. On the 400-foot contour mark where the land is rather cold and exposed we find a set of village earthworks surrounded by ridge-and-furrow. Bridges describes a lone house, formerly surrounded with a moat, now filled up. George Clarke, the schoolmaster artist, came here in 1840 and recorded the single house and moat in one of his painstaking watercolours. Hedges have now gone and the prairie-sized fields stretch down over the hills towards Orlingbury. Badsaddle in fact lasted a bare half-millennium.

In the valley of the Tove, two miles north-west of Towcester, is the parish of Greens Norton. The name recalls that the 'north farm' was held by Henry Green, knight, in 1369. To the north of the village is a farm called Field Burcote, first mentioned in documents *c.* 1200. The name means 'Peasants' cottages in the open country'. Sir Thomas Green destroyed four houses here in 1499, converting 200 acres to pasture. In 1551 the 'lands, meadows and pastures' were occupied by John Hickling's flock of 2000 sheep. The neighbouring hamlet of Caswell, 'Cress spring', a mile to the west was also first recorded *c.* 1200. It was similarly eliminated in 1509 when 300 acres were enclosed, converted to pasture, and five houses, perhaps the whole hamlet, were

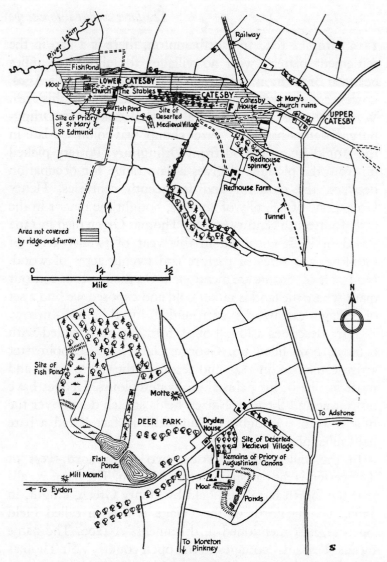

Fig. 15. *Catesby and Canons Ashby.* Two deserted medieval villages and monastic sites

Catesby was the site of a Cistercian house of ten nuns set up *c.* 1175 and endowed with the whole village. In 1495 the prioress destroyed fourteen houses and converted sixteen virgates to pasture, but five houses survived at the Dissolution. In 1536 the priory was dissolved and all the property was granted to the Onley family. The parish church at Upper Catesby was destroyed at the same time and a new church was destroyed by Sir Nicholas Vaux of Harrowden who married Green's heiress.[9]

These late medieval enclosures sometimes converted the original open fields to pasture just as they lay. An example of these huge fields is seen at Silsworth in Watford where one freehold family gradually accumulated holdings in the fifteenth century. These were acquired by William Catesby of Ashby St Ledgers, and were described in 1485 as 300 acres of arable land and 490 acres of pasture and in 1594 as three 'closes or pastures' called Middle Field, High Field and Sharrocks Close. Such enormous fields produced new problems for the Tudor graziers. The difficulties of providing shelter for stock and of achieving close grazing forced farmers to plant new hedges inside the original fences and thus create smaller fields.

The monasteries were deeply involved in this revolution in land use and their activities during the last fifty years

[9] *Deserted Villages of Northamptonshire*, pp. 35, 36, 40.

---

built on the site of the priory. An extensive series of fishponds and a defensive moat on the western side are adjacent to the supposed priory site. No earthworks remain of the village but the extent (shaded on plan) is determined by mapping the area untouched by ridge-and-furrow in aerial photographs of the 1940s.

Canons Ashby. The place-name ('Ashtree village') is the most southerly place-name ending in *by* in the Midlands, an isolated Danish outpost in English Mercia. The centre of the manor of the Norman landowner, Walter de Flanders, is probably the motte to the north-west of the Augustinian priory which was founded 1147–51. The sole surviving fragment of this is the church of St Mary. The village, according to Bridges, "was formerly very considerable", but in 1489 the prior enclosed and converted 100 acres to pasture and destroyed three houses. Only nine tenants paid rent in 1535. The manor, already wholly enclosed, came at the Dissolution to Sir John Cope who made a house of the priory buildings to the south of the church. The Dryden family succeeded Cope and built the house to the west of the priory. Elaborate fishponds were dug to the west of the deer park which adjoins the Dryden house. A medieval mill mound is by the side of the road leading to Eydon.

before the Dissolution put them in the ranks of the improving landlords. They thus aroused great odium and envy which doubtless contributed to the movement leading to their downfall. The Cistercian nunnery of Catesby, founded *c.* 1175, had been endowed with the church of Catesby and chapel at Hellidon and most of the lands, tenements and mills in the village. We know from the early-fifteenth-century accounts that certain lands were untilled ("and for xxv*s.* x*d.* received for the pasture of untilled *Grounds* in Catesby and Newbold this year, let to divers tenants"). It also appears that the nunnery practised sheep-farming in a substantial way ("and for vi*l.* xvi*s.* for one sack and eight weigh of wool, price of the sack civ*s.* . . . and for vi*s.* ix*d.* received for 18 wool Pells sold before shearing. And for ix*s.* vi*d.* received for 38 pells sold after shearing"). In 1495 the prioress destroyed fourteen houses and enclosed and converted sixteen virgates to pasture. Sixty people were reported in 1517–18 as being evicted. Twenty years later at the Dissolution the parish church of St Mary at Upper Catesby was destroyed; Tillemans' drawing in Bridges' *History* shows the remains of a tower among a tumbled heap of masonry. Only a brambly churchyard and a tree-grown mound now remain. Even the earthworks of the village have largely disappeared; but the bounds can be traced by the ridge-and-furrow; a moat and fishponds lie at the end of a long avenue near the site of the priory at Lower Catesby (Fig. 15).[10]

The death of the settlement at Thrupp in Norton, half a mile west of the M1 at Long Buckby wharf, may also be ascribed to the 'improving' activities of a monastery. Here the prior of Daventry was the landlord. In 1498, 100 persons were expelled from Thrupp and in 1518 the church was said to be '*in desolacionem*'. A survey of the possessions of the priory made in *c.* 1532 described Thrupp Grounds, "which

[10] G. Baker, *History*, Vol. I, pp. 278–9. *Deserted Villages*, p. 37. J. Bridges, *History*, Vol. I, pp. 32, 35.

sometimes was a Town & in tillage & now converted into pasture". No discernible traces of the village remain, apart from concentrations of medieval pottery and building stone in the fields around Thrupps Lodge and in *Briery* (corrupted from Priory) orchard, the reputed site of the chapel.[11]

The field-name *Grounds* recurs many times in west Northamptonshire. The term is used for 'a large grazing field' and the plural is used of an 'outlying grazing farm'. The earliest use is *Grundes* in Eydon (1281). The name is also found at Newbold, part of which was held by Catesby Priory and here 'Newboldefeld' in 1535 had been converted into pasture (now called Newbold *Grounds* farm).

Parks

The countryside was rapidly being tamed towards the end of the Middle Ages: areas of natural woodland were shrinking with the advance of assarting and the increase of upland grazing pastures. As disafforestation took place, kings, bishops and great feudal lords safeguarded their reduced forest rights in creating parks.

Medieval parks were not primarily for pleasure but were enclosures for storing live meat in the form of deer and other animals; they were also a source of timber for building purposes and for fuel. When Edward III granted his queen, Philippa, licence to make a park at Brigstock, he appointed Walter de Wyght "to have the enclosure finished, make dykes there and deer leaps [*saltus*] and lodges [*lugeas*], to have the palings of the park repaired with the timber of the park . . . and to make trenches [?clearings] in the park, taking care that the wood cut down in such trenches be sold or made into charcoal as shall be most to the Queen's profit".[12] The remains of the earthen bank originally enclosing

[11] G. Baker, *History*, Vol. I, pp. 316, 425. M. W. Beresford, *Lost Villages*, p. 368.
[12] *Cal. Pat. Rolls, 1348–1350*, p. 552.

Brigstock Park can be traced in the fields between the village and Geddington chase. The southern tongue is coterminous with the parish boundaries adjoining Grafton Underwood and Sudborough.

Some parks were attached to castles. Moulton Park, three miles north of Northampton Castle, was already in existence at the beginning of the thirteenth century, and Simon *de Parco* held land there in 1202. In Henry III's reign, Robert de Marisco was ordered to slaughter thirty deer there and to send them salted to Westminster for the feast of St Edward. Parks did not simply serve as preserves for deer but were also used to pasture cattle. The sheriff of Northampton in 1229 was told to turn out of Moulton Park all beasts except those belonging to the king, keeping enough pasture to fatten the oxen and beasts for the royal household in winter. To keep the stock from straying required expensive fencing. The sheriff again was ordered in 1223, 1251 and 1257 to see that the park at Northampton was enclosed by those who ought to contribute to such an undertaking. This task was shared by several townships and periodically individuals defaulted and were arraigned before the hundred court. Sir Nicholas Lilling was appointed keeper in Richard II's reign and in 1393 the walls were thoroughly overhauled and extensive repairs made. Two carts were employed for carrying stones to the faulty places and at tenpence a day cost thirty shillings for thirty-six days and four masons with three assistants were employed for forty-five days. By the sixteenth century there was a wall on the north side of the park which had the names of contributing townships inscribed on the stones. Parts of this still stand between Moulton Park Farm and Moulton Park House. Moulton Park is now being swallowed up in the expansion of Northampton. The Lyons group plan an enormous factory where Angevin kings formerly hunted.

Higham Park has been studied in detail by Beresford. Castle, borough and park were part of a complex of estates

Plate 17 The deserted medieval village of Nobold. The hollow-way of the medieval street is bounded on both sides by squarish tofts with crofts lying behind. The road between Clipston and Sibbertoft runs along the right side.

Plate 18 Barnwell. The Norman motte-and-bailey hidden in the trees was succeeded c. 1266 by the castle of Berengar le Moyne which shows a close understanding of all-round defence. The strongest point is the gatehouse. Beyond is the stone terrace constructed by Thomas Drew in 1613. Below is the renovated Tudor manor house (seat of H.R.H. the Duke of Gloucester). Both are screened by eighteenth-century tree plantings from the Blisworth–Peterborough line of 1845 (not visible in this photograph).

held by the Earl of Derby in the thirteenth century. The park lies three miles to the south of the castle and borough on the Bedfordshire border. Since it was some way from the castle it needed resident keepers who lived at a 'Great Lodge' near the north-west corner. The moats surrounding this can be found near the farmhouse known as Higham Park. There was a smaller lodge on the south side which no longer remains. A short section of the earthen bank which formerly carried three and a half miles of dead hedge-pale on the south-west side of the park can be seen where the Rushden boundary runs. It seems that pieces have been taken from the Rushden and Newton Bromswold parishes to make its rectangular shape and a third addition, a piece of Knotting parish, takes the boundary of the park beyond the old ridge road in a curving arc over the former county boundary. In this way Northamptonshire has taken a bite out of Bedfordshire. Henry III helped the earl to restock his park with several grants of animals. In 1234, five bucks and twenty-five does were sent from Weybridge in Surrey and in 1244, fifteen does and five bucks were sent from King's Cliffe near Peterborough.[13]

The growth of parks within the forest was an indication that the days of unrestricted hunting were numbered. The beasts of the chase needed to be managed much the same as domesticated cattle and sheep. We know that a park existed at Rockingham at least as early as 1258 because Hugh of Goldingham was ordered to hand over to William of Swineford six oaks that were "in the forest of the king at Rockingham outside the park" (*extra parcum*).[14]

There were also royal parks at King's Cliffe, Brigstock and Grafton. The park at Cliffe is first mentioned in Henry III's reign when grants of deer were frequently made to

---

[13] For Moulton Park, *Cal. Close Rolls*, 40 Henry III, pp. 245, 363. *V.C.H. Northants.*, Vol. IV, p. 94. For Higham Park, M. W. Beresford, *History on the Ground*, pp. 216–19, and *V.C.H. Northants.*, Vol. III, pp. 279–80.
[14] *Cal. Close Rolls*, 40 Henry III, p. 290.

various lords. Again the problem constantly recorded is the fencing. About 1339 two parts of the park were enclosed by the tenants of King's Cliffe and Woodnewton who petitioned that this action might not be taken as a precedent. In the next reign carpenters and other men were arrested to fence Queen Anne's park at Cliffe. Leland, a Tudor observer, reported that "Cliffe Park was partly waullid with stone and partly palid."

Magnates in their turn sought the privilege to enclose land for parks; this was granted somewhat more frequently than licences to crenellate (fortify). Fotheringhay was probably first imparked by John, Earl of Huntingdon, who in 1230 was given permission to make two deer-leaps there, and twice in the next few years he was granted does and bucks from Rockingham to stock his park at Fotheringhay. The park which now surrounds the house at Overstone originated in the licence given to Gilbert de Millers by Henry III "to inclose with a dike and hedge or with a wall, his wood of *Oviston* and to make a park thereof". Stoke Park similarly goes back to this reign when in 1270 Pagan de Chaworth had license to enclose his wood.

Simon de Drayton obtained in 1328 a licence to crenellate together with the right to impark thirty acres in the manor of Drayton. Two years later he was allowed to enclose "Eldesale, Newsale and Lappe containing sixty-two acres and Winecrosse and adjoining ground of twenty acres lying within the limits of Rockingham Forest".[15]

Recent fieldwork by Dr Peterken of Monks Wood Nature Conservancy Station has established the boundaries of the successive park circuits here. The first enclosed was Round Lown Wood which lies between Slipton Lodge and New Lodge half a mile north of Drayton House. Further extensions of this are seen to the north where the great bank of the medieval park boundary can be traced running

[15] For Fotheringhay see *V.C.H. Northants.*, Vol. II, p. 572. For Overstone see *V.C.H. Northants.*, Vol. IV, p. 97. For Stoke, G. Baker, *History*, Vol. II, p. 241, Drayton, *V.C.H. Northants.*, Vol. III, p. 237.

diagonally across the rides cut in the eighteenth century through the woods. It runs along the western boundary of Snapes Wood and Long Lown Wood thirty feet across and up to four of five feet high with an internal ditch. It was ploughed out in the early 1940s north of New Lodge but the position of the clay bank can be clearly seen as a yellow soil mark turning a right-angle 200 yards east of Round Lown Wood. A splendid stretch runs parallel with the road for 100 yards east of Slipton Lodge. Just behind the farm here are the moated earthworks of the park-keeper's house, known to the locals as 'The Nunnery'. It can be realised that the imparking activities of the gentry and nobility of Tudor and Stuart Northamptonshire merely carried on a process well under way in the later Middle Ages, though the parks they made had a different purpose—chiefly that of setting off their handsome new houses.

Another privilege sought from the crown was the right of free warren and the remains of rabbit-warrens form a distinctive if occasional feature in the landscape from the later Middle Ages into the sixteenth and seventeenth centuries. The site of the castle of the Dukes of Lancaster to the north side of the church at Higham Ferrers is distinguished by a monumental L-shaped moat, recently saved from an unhistorical if hygienic filling, and a shapeless mound now overgrown with bushes. There is little doubt that this mound is the *cunicularia* or rabbit-warren which is mentioned as early as 1314. This was enclosed by walls and a gate and constantly figures in the ministers' accounts of the fourteenth and fifteenth centuries, being a temptation to poachers and wall-breakers. In 1372 it was alleged that a certain Stephen Bailly of Rothwell with eleven other persons named had broken into the Duke's park of Higham Ferrers, entered his free warren there, hunted in his park and warren without licence, taken away deer from the park, and hares, conies, pheasants and partridges from the warren. This high-spirited poacher also "had chased 3 oxen and 300 sheep with dogs at Rothwell inciting the dogs to bite them so that the oxen and 200 sheep died (worth £40) and the others were greatly deteriorated". John Ryder was fined in 1452 for making a common way for himself over the wall of the king's *cunicularia* by means of a ladder.

Animal protein food was sufficiently hard to come by for doves to be bred in dovehouses. The ruins of one of the two formerly in the outer ward of the castle at Higham may be seen. Further dovehouses were at Rushden and in the park. In 1313–14 £6 18s. 1d. was spent for re-roofing the last, and included in the account was "50s. 8d. for 4000 tiles called *sclat stone*" and "15d. for 260 large nails, 2s. 4d. for 2000 nails called *lathnayl*: 16s. to William *Sclatyer* for roofing the said dovehouse".[16]

The medieval building-stone industry

This problem of roofing the ducal dovehouses reminds us of Morton's words: "even the meanest Houses of the Towns and Villages thereabouts are slated. A safe, strong, and durable Covering it is, and so white and fine when new especially, that in a bright Day it very pleasingly affects the Eye of a Traveller that has one of the Towns thus slated in his view."[17] Whenever one is along the stone belt the sight of grey stone slate roofs providing a proper complement to the stone building beneath them gladdens the eye.

The source within the county for this fissile material is the bed of slate stone which lies under the village of Colly-weston, three miles south-west of Stamford. Stone slates from this source have been found at Roman sites such as Irchester and Apethorpe; and in Edward III's reign, in view of a visit from the king to hunt in the forest, seventy-six

---

[16] 'Court Rolls of Higham Ferrers'. *Architectural Societies Reports and Papers,* Vol. XXXIII (1915–16), pp. 134–5, and W. J. B. Kerr, *Higham Ferrers and its Ducal and Royal Castle and Park* (1925), p. 154.

[17] J. Morton, *Natural History*, p. 109.

shillings was paid for 9500 stone slates and their carriage from 'Colyn Weston' to Rockingham castle cost twenty-eight shillings and sixpence at three shillings the thousand. References in exchequer accounts in the fourteenth, fifteenth and sixteenth centuries show that there was a great demand for them in the royal building programme.[18] The quarries today are found in long narrow stone-walled slaters' plots to the west of the village. They are entered by means of 'foxholes' and one clambers down to see the slate 'log' which varies from three feet to a few inches in thickness, lying over a bed of Northampton Sand. This is picked out with a 'foxing pick' during December and January so that the slate stone can be barrowed out to the surface. Here it is laid out and watered to allow the winter frosts to help the natural cleavage. Then the 'logs' are ready for splitting—called locally 'cliving'—which is done by tapping them gently round the edges with a chisel-ended 'cliving hammer'. Next they are dressed into suitable shapes and sides with a 'dressing hammer' which has one axe-like cutting edge, a broad claw at the opposite end and two flat sides with which to beat the edges of the slates to straighten them. A bill is used to peck nail holes near the head of the slates which are then sorted into sizes and stacked in heaps—each containing 840, or a slater's thousand. During the rest of the year the slaters who quarry and dress the slates fix them to roofs. Individual slates can be renewed with the help of a long iron instrument called the slater's 'rip' which slides under the slates until it finds the faulty one. The slates are laid in diminishing courses from eaves to ridge and the widths are random. The traditional method was to hang them by wooden pegs on riven laths, but now copper or composition nails are used. Between the roughly tapering heads of the larger slates and covering the nail holes small pieces called 'shales' are bedded in lime mortar. This gives a more even bedding all over.

[18] *V.C.H. Northants.*, Vol. II, p. 296.

While every village on the Jurassic belt had its stone pit, some quarries early acquired prominence.[19] We have seen how Barnack had provided the stone which went to build Ely and Norwich Cathedrals, Thorney, Ramsey and Sawtry Abbeys and dozens of other churches. Stanion (from *Stanere*, 'a collection of stone buildings') had quarries worked during the Roman period and furnished the foundations of the Roman villa at Great Weldon in the Chapel Field. Morton claimed that the parish churches of Stanion, Weldon, Geddington, Twywell, Deene, Weekley, Corby, Brigstock and Little Oakley were built of Stanion stone.[20]

"On the south side of Welledon (Weldon) a little without it, hard by the highe way, ys a goodly quarre of stone, where appere great Diggyns." So remarked Leland. The stone has been worked since the thirteenth century and is said to have provided the material for Geddington Cross. In the Rockingham Castle accounts for 1275 Edward Geoffrey, the quarryman, was paid 8s. 2d. for cutting 700 freestones at 'Welledon'. Master Thomas of Weldon not only sold stone but also provided skilled stone-cutters and layers (*cissores* et *cubitores*) with a certain number of unskilled labourers, and he personally directed their work. Bridges established a tradition that Weldon stone was used extensively in old St Paul's and it was certainly recorded from 1480 to 1483 in the building at King's College, and again by Bishop Alcock at Jesus College, Cambridge.[21] The workings, although largely grassed over, as at Barnack, extend over a considerable area and deserted underground quarries are a mile or so to the south-west of the present cutting. In 1966 quarrying began again and the ledges of warm honey-coloured stone can be seen just below the level of the A43 trunk road to the south of the village. A working platform

[19] J. M. Steane, 'Building Materials used in Northamptonshire and the area around', *Northants. Past and Present*, Vol. IV, No. 2 (1967-8), pp. 71-83.
[20] J. Morton, *Natural History*, p. 110.
[21] D. Purcell, *Cambridge Stone* (London, 1967), pp. 39-40.

is made by the removal of the overburden. A series of holes are drilled to the full depth of the bed. Into each of these is placed a pair of long narrow steel plates called 'feathers' and between these are put steel 'plugs' which are then gently and evenly tapped down with a sledge hammer until the stone splits along the line. Long steel crowbars inserted laterally prise the block free and lift it so that a chain from a derrick can be passed beneath it. The blocks are roughly squared up on the quarry floor. Recently the stone has gone to Chichester and Ely Cathedrals for repair work and it is in demand at Oxford and Cambridge colleges.

As one passes into central Northamptonshire the colour and nature of the stone buildings change: from the cream and greys of Weldon and Barnack to the ginger tones and dark browns of the iron-impregnated Northamptonshire Sandstone. At times a curious polychrome effect is achieved by mixing the two in alternating bands of grey and dark brown, as can be seen at Finedon church and many buildings in the village of Blisworth. Again local stone pits were the source of much ironstone rubble. The Norman round church of St Sepulchre's, Northampton, is wholly built of this orange material. In some churches such as twelfth- and thirteenth-century Pytchley All Saints the quoins and dressings are of ironstone blocks and the walling of limestone rubble. At Braybrooke an early medieval building of ironstone has had a splendid perpendicular chapel built of Weldon stone tacked on to the south side of the chancel. On Earl Spencer's estate at Harlestone a sandstone freestone quarry is still being worked. Brilliant emerald pools of water stand in the workings which look like a vast gingerbread stepped and slabbed. With its strong ferruginous streaks which wore out tools this stone was known as 'the mason's bankrupter'. Formerly there was a market for it in the north when it was used by housewives for sanding steps.

6. Tudor and Stuart landscapes

Early enclosures. The forests. The great rebuilding.
Tudor and early Stuart parks. The great rebuilding—
lesser houses. Schools and almshouses

Early enclosures

LELAND, THAT 'omniverous topographer-antiquary' who
travelled England in the reign of Henry VIII collecting
monastic books for the king's library, has left the first connected description of the landscape of the county. Between
Wellingborough and Northampton "al be *champaine* corne
and pasture ground, but little wood or none, even as it is
betwixt Oundale and Welingborow ... Towcester is 7 miles
from Wedon, and as much from Northampton, al by playne
corne ground and pasture ... Thens by champayne ground,
being good grasse and corne, a 9 miles to Ketering."[1]

Despite the close settlement of the county, and the relative fertility of the soil for corn-growing, there was a strong
tendency from the beginning of the Tudor period for tillage
to be converted to pasture. As we have seen, some Northamptonshire pastures were already enclosed in the fifteenth
century, and the possibilities for sheep-farming on a large
scale perhaps more than other amenities "allured nobilitie
to plante themselves" in the county.

The advantages of sheep-farming included low labour
costs. Only five shepherds were responsible for 10,000 sheep

[1] L. T. Smith (ed.), *The Itinerary of John Leland* (London, 1967), pp. 7, 11, 12.
Champaine is unenclosed or common land.

and lambs in the pastures of the Wormleighton group of Spencer manors in 1577. Marketing difficulties could also be reduced. The market for wool was an ebullient one, with rising prices at least until 1550, the time of the collapse of the Antwerp market. Thereafter, there were greater profits to be made by supplying mutton and beef for the London market, and men like the Spencers of Althorp who sold their breed "when it was fatt, to the Citie of London, and other places yerely" stood to gain greatly.

The repercussions of all this on the landscape were considerable. The most obvious one was a spur to enclosure and consolidation in those parts of the county where open-field villages were dominated by improving squires. If enclosure could be carried through on a grand scale, it would facilitate the movement of stock between pastures, "and the oft changing of pasture shall amend all kind of cattel in shorter time than to remain long in one pasture". Four examples from different parts in the county show the interaction between the rise of family fortunes and their relative success in shaping the landscape to suit economic considerations.

John Isham, mercer and merchant adventurer (1525-90), bought the manor of Lamport from Sir William Cecil and his wife in January 1560 for £610. Lamport is on the upland country between Northampton and Market Harborough. His motive was clearly to adapt it to the needs of sheep-farming and thus convert it to a profitable business concern. He was already operating as a wool-dealer and it seemed a suitable place for raising stock. There was much good meadow and pasture to hand and opposition to enclosure was likely to be weak, owing to the small number of copyhold tenants.

The first two enclosures, Pond Close and Colcott Closes (now Corkcutt Close on both sides of the Brampton branch of the Nene), were made in 1570, two years before John Isham settled in Lamport. The land involved was taken from the holdings in the common fields which involved

Isham in a series of complicated exchanges, and he continued in the late 1570s to put hedges round *Holbeck, Dinges, Bluebarrow, Redgrass* and *Parkes*. Nineteenth-century field names roughly locate his enclosures. Side by side, he pursued a policy of buying up land in Lamport, no matter how small a portion, aiming at consolidating his property. Miss Finch has demonstrated the effects of this in the size of his flocks and sales. In August 1583 he had 1572 sheep; his wool sales varied from £219 in 1572 to £73 19s. in 1587. His sheep sales averaged £74 per annum and he was paid £443 from the butchers between 1582 and 1587.[2]

He used some of his profits to improve the appearance of his estate. "Here he aplyed himselfe to plantinge, buildinge, making of pooles, includeing of grounds and all other woorks of good husbandry, as though he had been brought up in them from his infancy." Lamport Hall is still basically an Elizabethan manor house built round a courtyard, dating from John Isham's time. Extensive Jacobean additions and a splendid south-west front, built in 1655 to the designs of John Webb, have changed its appearance, and the Ishams went on through the seventeenth century improving their property. Thomas Isham recorded in his diary, referring to the recent acquisition of Hanging Houghton, 18th November, 1671: "Father and I went into the fields to determine where ditches should be dug and hedges planted." On the 21st: "Thomas Nuns measured the fields near Haybrig, and, near the spring commonly called Rodewell." This survey has survived and shows that the total of the common field was 246a–3r–16p at Houghton with two closes Rowell (Rodewell) and 'Little Close' making 284a–0r–5p in all. Lamport field contained *inter alia* 'Hay bridge meadow' (Haybrig).[3] The map accompanying the survey shows these encroach-

[2] M. E. Finch, *The Wealth of Five Northamptonshire Families, 1540–1640.* Northamptonshire Record Society, Vol. XIX (1956), pp. 18–19.

[3] N. Marlow, G. Isham (eds.), *The Diary of Thomas Isham* (London, 1971), p. 63.

ments on the open fields which otherwise continued at Lamport and Hanging Houghton until 1795 when the enclosure award was made.

In the central part of the county, five miles to the north-west of Northampton, another great sheep-farming family was rising to fame and wealth during the sixteenth century. The Spencers are first heard of as graziers in the fifteenth century in Warwickshire. Sir John Spencer (d. 1522) founded the fortunes of his family with the profits of cattle- and sheep-farming. He bought the manor of Althorp in 1508 for £800. In 1510 he added a manor in Hinton in the parish of Woodford and the manors of Upper and Lower Bodding-ton; in the following year he acquired the manors of Wicken and Nobottle. As an experienced grazier in this district he had especially selected his land because it was ideal for sheep pasture. Much had been enclosed and converted to pasture before Sir John bought it and by the mid-sixteenth century the great sheep farm of the Spencers was organised round two centres, Wormleighton and Althorp. The latter group included four main closes, Chinkwell, Mill Field, Lucas Field, and Langland Field; there were also feedings in the common field of Brington, Nortoft Field in Guilsborough and Misterton and Elkington. The total count of Sir John Spencer's flocks was between 13,000 and 14,000 and the profits from the wood and sheep formed the foundation of the Spencers' great wealth.[4] They paid for the magnificent house and park which arose at Althorp after the civil war in the seventeenth century.

During the fifteenth century the Tresham family had already begun to acquire a large but scattered estate in Northamptonshire through some twenty-five different manors. John Tresham (d. 1521) built the main part of Rushton Hall, presumably from the profits of the estate, but it was Prior Tresham who embarked on a policy of selling outlying properties and acquiring in their stead lands "of

[4] M. E. Finch, *Wealth of Five Families*, pp. 39, 41.

moche more yearly value than those sold". He turned his
attention to the Lyveden valley, an area in which much
assarting had gone on in Rockingham forest during the
Middle Ages. In 1538 he bought the assart lands called
Luscottes (O.E. *hlose and cot(e)*—hence 'pigstye' cottages)
first mentioned in Edward I's reign, and added eight closes
containing about 170 acres of pasture. Further along the
Harley Way in 1540 he received licence to impark 120 acres
of wood, 250 acres of pasture and fifty acres of meadow to
form Lyveden Park (Plate 21). Lyveden had been a site of a
village and pottery but the last documentary reference to
people living there had been 1403 when a manor court was
held. Recent excavations have demonstrated that at least
one farm and an adjoining tilery were functioning in the
third quarter of the fifteenth century. In 1544 Tresham
bought Somersailes, a pasture in this area sufficient for 300
sheep, and eleven years later he added another small Lyveden close. Leland estimated that Lyveden with its 'godely
meadows' was worth 300 marks a year. Recent large-scale
removals of hedgerows have changed the enclosed appearance of the valley, which is now lonely and remote, with
huge arable fields on the Boulder Clay on which crawl the
powerful double tractors preparing the land for potatoes
and barley.

Grand Prior Tresham, by one of the ironies of history,
both profited from the Dissolution of the monasteries and
became the short-lived prior of the restored Order of St
John of Jerusalem in England. In 1554 he secured from
Mary's government long leases of the site of the Cistercian
monastery of Pipewell and of the East and West Granges
there with the lands that went with them. Pipewell had once
been a great sheep-farming house and these lands were to
afford valuable pasture.

His grandson, Sir Thomas Tresham, embarked on an
enclosing policy at Rushton before 1581, and in that year he
enclosed about eighty acres of his demesne and converted it

from tillage to pasture. By 1590 a further eighty acres of demesne had probably been enclosed and converted. To this he added 110 acres of tenant land, enclosed and taken from farms in the 1580s. In the other area of his interest the pastures of Lyveden were increased by the purchase of two small closes in Luscottes in 1583 and of Great and Little Northoe pastures, containing 140 acres in 1588. As Miss Finch remarks, "So, by resumptions, inclosures and purchases, Tresham built up a great sheep farm."[5]

From these two centres, the rented pastures at Pipewell with the adjacent closes at Rushton and the assarts and pastures in and around the manors of Lyveden and Churchfield, Tresham managed his ranchlike estates. At this date he estimated his total flock at 3000 head. Some fifteen years later it had nearly doubled, for a record of 1597 gives a total of 6780. As well as his profits from sheep which brought in about £1000 per annum in 1600 he also sold horses at Market Harborough, hogs at Kettering and oxen at Coventry and Banbury. He sold corn, hops, cheeses, pigeons, hides, timber and lime. A profitable sideline was the sale of rabbits and rabbit skins, for the warren in Rushton contained 300 acres and there was also a 'connegerie' at Pipewell. Ferrets were kept for bolting rabbits and three times every week his carriers made the journey between London and Rushton with boxes of rabbits and skins. Tresham had to compensate the holders of lands adjoining his warren for the depredations of his rabbits. The site of the warren, largely replaced by eighteenth-century landscape gardens and overgrown, can be seen to the north of the house.

During the last ten years of his life Tresham became increasingly oppressed by debts arising mainly out of enormous fines for recusancy levied on his estate. He responded by borrowing and by modernising the antiquated methods of estate management, including new and sweeping

[5] M. E. Finch, *Wealth of Five Families*, p. 74.

projects for enclosure which aroused great resentment. The results of his consolidation, enclosure and conversion to pasture of his lands in Haselbech was that he had taken away 700 acres from seven houses or barns and his consequent policy of raised rents resulted in the virtual eviction of his tenants who would not, or could not, pay the new rents for the great pastures. Some sixty persons thus lost their livelihood, excluding those dispossessed by the other freeholders. At Rushton too he severed 540 acres from nine farms, but at Orton he forbore to enforce his schemes of exploitation for fear of popular outcry and disturbance; and similarly Francis Tresham was prevented from advocating the decay of the whole village at Great Houghton, "you could not remove all the tennantes without much clamour and especiallie when itt is so neare Northampton, whose affectiones are well knowen to you". In this way the financial exigencies of the Tresham family fomented the levellers' risings of 1607.[6]

In the far north of the county, the Fitzwilliam family were building up another great congery of estates on the edge of the fens. A village had existed in the early Middle Ages at Milton with twelve households recorded in 1086 and fifteen in 1301. Sir William Fitzwilliam, an opulent London alderman, warden of the Merchant Taylors and Mayor of the Staple, invested his profits in land and in 1502 bought the manors of Milton and Marholm. Many of the fields had been already enclosed at the time of his purchase. Wolsey's commissioners of 1517 had attributed to Fitzwilliam the conversion of pasture of forty-five acres of arable in Castor in 1495 and the decay of two messuages and the engrossment of 100 acres of arable in 1500. This is more likely to have been the work of Robert Wittelbury who had made a hedge on part of the manor of Thorpe "for the close keepyng and defence of hys pasture of Mylton".

[6] W. E. Tate, 'Inclosure Movements in Northamptonshire', *Northants. Past and Present*, Vol. I, 2 (1949), pp. 19–33.

It seems highly probable that Sir William I chose the
Milton pastures because of their suitability for sheep. The
fact that he was a stapler and traded in wool implies that he
was also interested in growing it. His eldest son, Sir William
II, was left with a group of manors with rich possibilities
because these lands between the Welland and the Nene,
sloping down towards Peterborough, became famed for
their rich meadows owing to the frequent overflowing of
the river. Pitt wrote of them in 1813: "the spreading of the
water of these rivers and the filtering of sediment from the
upland, had formed an immense bed of even surface: this
bed was sown by the natural process of seeds of grasses and
upland herbage being wafted down by autumnal floods and
deposited upon this sediment by the gradual subsidence of
these waters".[7] They only required draining to become rich
grazings. The surviving fields at Milton were enclosed
before 1576.

Sir William Fitzwilliam III supplemented his landed
income from numerous court offices, becoming Treasurer
at War in Ireland and finally Lord Deputy. Despite his
constant cries of ruin he went on making purchases of land
in the county and is found buying up land where there had
been deserted villages, at Woodcroft and Helpston (the
village of Torpel) and at Etton. All these properties consolidated the Milton estate.

The Fitzwilliams experienced difficulties in the way of
consolidation and enclosure. In a single set of village fields
several manorial interests might be involved, for it was
usual for the open-field holdings of the tenants of several
manors to be intermixed. Groups of villages also intercom-
moned in the fen that they surrounded or adjoined, and one
piece of marsh thus served as common pasture for the cattle
and sheep of a number of villages.[8] Some of the richest

---

[7] W. Pitt, *General View of the Agriculture of the County of Northampton*
(London, 1813), pp. 168–9.
[8] H. C. Darby, *The Medieval Fenland* (Cambridge, 1940), pp. 67–82.

meadowland was divided up by the inhabitants of a number of manors. Westings meadow was shared between Helpston, Elton, Woodcroft and Marholm, Peakirk and Maxey. Further rights of common after the hay had been gathered impeded unrestricted enclosure. These conflicting rights caused fierce disputes between Lady Fitzwilliam and Robert Wingfield in 1557 which resulted in the latter breaking into new enclosed pasture by force of arms, consuming Lady Fitzwilliam's herbage there with his stock.

Such changes involved casualties. We have noticed that some settlements were destroyed in the fifteenth and early sixteenth centuries to facilitate the changeover from arable to pasture. When the search for evidence against grazing and enclosing landlords was conducted in 1517–18 and again in 1548–9, Northamptonshire and Oxfordshire between them account for thirty-one per cent of the prosecutions brought before the exchequer in these years. Authentic cases, however, of total depopulation are few in the sixteenth century. The troubles of 1548–9 and 1607 made it clear that public opinion and the government were hostile to the complete removal of villages.

What happened instead is that houses disappeared one by one in a village overshadowed by a great house, and were not replaced. At Easton Neston, for instance, a small park was created *c.* 1500 by Sir Richard Empson by the enclosure of sixty-four acres of arable and pasture; he also converted twenty-four acres of arable to pasture. Richard Fermor, a London merchant, bought the manor in 1531 and ten years later the manor house in the park, meadow and pasture were mentioned, but no villagers. Today the superb Queen Anne period house stands within the park next door to the medieval church which is the sole survivor of the village (Plate 23).

At Fawsley, the manor was bought by the Knightley family in 1415. They began to evict their reluctant tenants at the end of the fifteenth century. The results may be seen

Plate 19 Newton near Geddington. St Faith's church stands alone in the fields, the sole relic of the deserted medieval village of Great Newton. Above it the winding embankment of the medieval mill leat leads from right to left, the convolutions of the river Ise just beyond it. In the centre is the site of the sixteenth-century house of the Treshams with terraced gardens and a two-bay dovecote. The ironstone quarry face of the twentieth century cuts diagonally across medieval ridge-and-furrow.

Plate 20 Wakerley. The manor house of the Cecils with its elaborate garden layout of sunken lawns, terracing and arbours, lies under permanent pasture in the centre. The ruined dovecote is the only upstanding building. To the left of the Georgian enclosure road is a fishpond complex with inlet channels running down the slope. The Peterborough and Market Harborough section of the London and North Western railway slices across the earlier features.

Plate 21 Lyveden. In the centre at the top medieval field roads converge on a thirteenth-century moated site, whose extent is marked by the area free from ridge-and-furrow. Across this earlier landscape was imposed the imparking of the Tresham family (1540), and from 1595 the ambitious complex of L-shaped water features and mounts of the gardens joining the Old Building (far right) to the cruciform and roofless ruin of the New Building. Most of the hedges have now gone and the earlier moat has been bulldozed.

when one walks across the park (there is no road) to the church today. It stands amidst grass-grown mounds—a few hundred yards away is the Tudor mansion, a glorious oriel window looking out over the lake which lies on top of the site of the village. Until six years ago the whine of a sawmill replaced the bleating of the 2500 sheep which grazed on the site in the mid-sixteenth century.

The most celebrated contemporary critic at the end of the fifteenth century, John Rous the chantry priest, provides us with another example. He was aware that villages were being destroyed in neighbouring Warwickshire and drew on Northamptonshire to cite the case of Upper Charwelton (which had recovered) and to warn that Lower Charwelton was in mortal danger. The trouble started in the late fifteenth century when Thomas Andrew leased lands here from Biddlesden and Thorney Abbeys. His son kept 1200 sheep here in 1547; the Knightleys of Fawsley maintained another 500 and a third freeholder, 300. Four hundred years later the landscape still bears the marks of these transactions. I walked over the ridge-and-furrow to the lonely Decorated towered church and single farm at Lower Charwelton. Around lie the earthwork platforms and hollow-ways of the village depopulated by sheep-farming. On the floor of the north aisle is Thomas's armoured effigy in brass; his left foot rests complacently on the diminutive figure of a sheep chewing clover.

The forests

Recent study of the royal forests has produced the best-documented topographical study of this important aspect of the history of the landscape to date.[9] Dr Pettit makes it clear that at the beginning of the reign of Elizabeth I, the forest

[9] P. A. J. Pettit, 'The Royal Forests of Northamptonshire, 1558–1714', *Northants. Record Society*, Vol. XXIII (1968), on which the following paragraphs are based.

still covered extensive tracts of the county despite the considerable inroads made by the medieval process of assarting. In the far north of Rockingham forest in Cliffe Bailiwick, the crown's demesne woods were concentrated in the three hays of Morehay, Westhay and Sulehaye ('hay'—an enclosure used to denote part of a forest fenced off for hunting). Morehay was a royal hunting ground and course for horse-racing enjoyed by both James I and Charles I. Westhay straggled between the open fields of King's Cliffe and those of Duddington on the Welland. Twelve forest villages—King's Cliffe, Apethorpe, Duddington, Fotheringhay, Nassington, Woodnewton, Yarwell, Benefield, Bulwick, Deenethorpe, Glapthorn, Southwick—all shared rights of common in the forest. Rockingham forest was described by Morton in 1712 as "one of the largest and richest in the whole kingdom". Its undulating fields and pastures interspersed with wedges of woodland stretched over an area at its maximum eighteen miles by eight miles. Salcey forest was on rather a smaller scale and here, only 1100 acres of coppices surrounded Salcey Lawn, with its ancient ornamental oaks. Six forest villages, Ashton, Hackleton, Hartwell, Piddington, Quinton and the large Buckinghamshire village of Hanslope, shared rights of common in Salcey. The other remnant of the ancient *Bruneswald* was larger and more important as a royal hunting ground; Whittlewood or Whittlebury forest consisted of 6000 acres, of which 4500 were woodland in 1608. Wakefield Lawn, enlarged *c*. 1600, was totally encircled by woods and was overlooked by Wakefield Great Lodge. This was a royal hunting lodge under the Angevins and still stands as restored in 1745 by the Dukes of Grafton, wardens of Whittlewood. The king lavished money on his house at Grafton, described in 1635 as "the bravest" and "best seat in the kingdom, a seat for a prince, and not a subject". Within the honour was a series of parks which the crown had enlarged or newly imparked.

All the nucleated forest villages had open fields which

were normally retained until the era of parliamentary enclosure. One difference Pettit notes is that they were often relatively smaller than those of the non-forest villages and in 1600 open fields comprised only about a third of the total forest landscape. The villages paradoxically tended to be large and populous but none exceeded 1000 inhabitants.

The woodland in places was sufficiently wild to provide a cover for criminals. In 1576 Mary Queen of Scots was robbed and her horses and jewels were taken to Geddington woods. A lantern on Weldon church, according to local tradition, guided forest travellers and fires were lit through Hazelborough to lead villagers from St Andrew's Fair at Brackley so that they might "be in safety from robbing".

The principal developments taking place in the royal forests arose from the changing emphasis of Tudor and Stuart government policy. The improvement of revenue from forest woodland and the preservation of oaks for the navy began to transcend the importance of the forests as royal hunting grounds. This happened because of the decline of interest in hunting of Edward VI, Mary and Elizabeth I and partly from a desire to extract a fuller economic return in an inflationary period when governments were finding it hard to make ends meet. As long as forests were thought of as hunting preserves there were serious restrictions placed on their economic development. Crops in adjacent fields were damaged by deer; underwood and saplings were spoilt; fine timber oaks were ruined by keepers seeking browsewood; the cyclical cutting of coppices was restricted since only a third could be enclosed at any one time.

Hence there were powerful incentives to extract more crown revenue from the forests. This was done by extraordinary wood sales; £1410 was raised in Northamptonshire in 1609 and 1132 trees felled, and £3739 in 1617 from a total of 3190 trees felled. Disafforestation was also tried. Elizabeth I disposed of some of Rockingham forest when she granted Sir Christopher Hatton Cottingham and Middleton woods in 1572, and Gretton and Little Weldon woods in 1581. In 1592 she granted Cliffe Park to the Earl of Essex and this subsequently passed to Lord Burghley. In 1602 Sir Robert Cecil acquired Brigstock Parks. The woodland was largely cleared and the parks were converted to agricultural use. Charles I intensified the process. He granted 863 acres of Handley Walk to the Earl of Northampton with power over the game and covert and permission to convert the woods to arable. Pipewell woods, which since the Dissolution of the monasteries had been leased out for years or lives, were now sold to Sir Christopher Hatton for £1500. After the Restoration the majority of the forests still remained—at least in name. Geddington woods became a private chase in 1676 and the underwood of Whittlewood and Salcey passed to the Dukes of Grafton, but disafforestation came much later in the era of parliamentary enclosure.

The Stuart kings made determined attempts to recover their rights at forest law but this is of more interest to the legal than the landscape historian. It is significant however to notice how far assarting had gone by the beginning of the seventeenth century. Otto Nicholson was granted in 1600 assart lands in Northamptonshire, Buckinghamshire and Huntingdonshire on lease for twenty years and in 1605 he was appointed receiver of all money accruing from the improvement of assarts. The total sum raised in the county from this source, 1605–16, was £10,460 in fines. George Lynn of Southwick held 500 acres as part of William Kirkham's estates but the king claimed them as part of Rockingham forest. In 1613 an inquisition held at Oundle showed that 1300 acres of land in Southwick were assarts and purprestures from Rockingham forest, belonging to the king.[10] Charles I's government also attempted to extend the boundaries of the forests and revived old courts such as

[10] P. A. J. Pettit, *Royal Forests*, p. 77.

Swanimotes. One held in Salcey produced 123 offenders, including those accused of destroying or carrying away wood, commoning sheep, grazing unringed pigs and making small enclosures. Enquiries resulted in forest courts fining such local potentates as Mountjoy, Earl of Newport, £20 for having a 'deer leap' in Fotheringhay Park and several villages were fined £5 for stealing timber trees for maypoles. The maintainers of rabbit-warrens and the potters of Potterspury who were accused of digging pits—for clay —in the forest waste, were also fined. The heaviest penalties, however, bore on the grantees of forest land. Robert, Earl of Salisbury, was convicted of assarting 2200 acres of Brigstock Parks in 1604, destroying the greenwood and 1000 deer and converting the parks into twenty-four separate closes. His heir was fined £20,000. Sir Christopher Hatton, similarly, was alleged to be fined £12,000. The curious thing is that those fined most heavily were in fact royalists during the Civil War.

The Tudor assault on the crown woodlands has been exaggerated in Dr Pettit's view, and, in Northamptonshire at least, "the erratic management of the forests under Elizabeth, marked an advance rather than a recession in their exploitation".[11] The silvicultural methods employed in the county followed the south midland norm 'coppice with standards'.[12] Under this system occasional trees, commonly oak and ash, are allowed to grow up to their full timber height. They developed large, much-branched and bushy crowns which provided plenty of 'knee pieces' for ship-building and braces for timber roofs. The *coppice* (O.Fr. 'to cut') or underwood grows in clumps of brushwood and small poles useful as fuel, making hurdles for folds and wattle panels for house walls. Since shoots readily spring from the base or stump of most deciduous species they can be cut every twenty years on a rotational system.

[11] P. A. J. Pettit, *Royal Forests*, p. 111.
[12] H. L. Edlin, *Trees, Woods and Man* (London, 1970), p. 101.

Extensive surveys of woodland were launched by the Elizabethan government and the surprising fact emerges that the number of oaks in the crown forests in the county actually appears to have increased from 85,000 in 1565 to about 130,000 in 1608. It may be that the Act for the Preservation of Timber (1543) decreeing that twelve timber saplings should be left to an acre was taking effect by 1600. Between 1610 and 1665, however, there was a relaxation of government vigilance in the systematic preservation of timber, and timber reserves dropped as the naval tonnage increased from 17,000 tons in 1603 to 104,000 tons in 1685.

By the end of the seventeenth century, planting on great private estates, with the gentle urging of John Evelyn's classic, *Sylva or a Discourse on Forest Trees*, became a patriotic and gentlemanly activity. The Dukes of Montagu attempted to improve Geddington woods by systematic planting and 'Planter John', as we shall see, distinguished his other estates round Boughton with impressive avenues mostly of elm. The royal forests, however, continued to decline and no new plantations were made in Whittlewood or Salcey owing to their remoteness from naval dockyards and the unfortunate clash of interest between the commoners, the enclosers of coppices and the Dukes of Grafton.

An entertaining example of the high passions roused in the forests occurred in June 1727 when the coronation of George II triggered off extensive timber-stealing riots involving forty-five places. Country people and even the gentry in the neighbourhood of the forests had the idea that they had a right to go into the forests and cut down and carry away what timber they pleased; the trees they so carried off were termed 'coronation poles'. Mr Thomas Herbert, the bailiff of the Duke of Grafton who was woodward in Whittlebury forest, was beset with the problem of seeing his master's trees disappear in an orgy of patriotic arboricultural destruction.[13]

[13] *Northants. Notes and Queries*, Vol I (1866), pp. 123-7.

Nevertheless, it is obvious that the royal forests in Northamptonshire still existed in the eighteenth century and the assertion that an expanding seventeenth-century agriculture was responsible for huge inroads into the nation's forests is quite mythical as far as this county is concerned. They were not left completely stripped or transformed into stretches of heathy moor and barren waste, for after 1660 Whittlewood and Salcey could still produce unprecedented supplies of timber.

The great rebuilding

In 1591 Norden found the county "adorned both with salutarie and profitable seates, manie and notable sheepe pastures; rich feedings for cattle, firtile corne groundes and lardge fields greatly inrichinge the industrious husbandman". There were a number of advantages persuading the nobility and gentry to invest in land and buildings in Northamptonshire during the sixteenth century. We have noticed that its pastures were one attraction. The county was also near enough the capital, to cater for the demands of an expanding London market. Moreover, seventy miles from London put the county into what might be termed the courtiers' commuting belt. When one goes a little further from London into the neighbouring county of Leicester, there is a singular lack of great Tudor houses on the scale of Burghley, Castle Ashby, Holdenby or Kirby. The forests had drawn the court to the county in the early Middle Ages; the hospitality of great aristocratic houses continued to act as a magnet to royal company in the age of Elizabeth I.

The acquisition of a great estate with a sufficiently strong economic base founded on large-scale sheep- and cattle-farming led naturally to the next step in lordly advancement, the building of an elaborate and fashionably up-to-date home. Building great houses was one of the extravagances of the time. "Oh many have broke their backs with laying manors on 'em" (*Henry VIII*, I. i. 83).

What is remarkable is that medieval traditions of planning and style in house-building continued far into the sixteenth century and the Renaissance as an architectural fashion was not received in this part of the Midlands until the mid-fifties. We find that these houses of the gentry had a great hall, often open to the roof, with a wing used for private bedrooms and withdrawing rooms at one end and a kitchen block or wing at the other. In general they presented a picturesque and rambling appearance with an irregular skyline recalling the embattled and turreted mansion of the Draytons of an earlier period.

Apethorpe Hall is a good example of the continuing medieval tradition. It belonged to Sir Guy Wolston in 1491 and early in the sixteenth century to his son-in-law Thomas Empson; in 1515 Henry Keble, grocer of London, acquired the manor and his grandson, Lord Mountjoy, sold the manor and hall to Henry VIII in 1543. In 1550 the property came into the possession of Sir Walter Mildmay. The house of *c.* 1500 had as its core the hall range, originally open to the roof, approached through screens from a north-east and north-west porch. On the north side is a cross wing which is pierced by the north gateway. The four-centred arched doorway, the canted bay window, the oriel in the gateway, are all early sixteenth-century features. The side of the hall facing west was given a new even frontage *c.* 1530–50 when wings on the western and northern sides were added. The eastern front of Apethorpe is "the most stately and coherent Jacobean piece in the county" and really is an elaborate screen with three big, shaped gables, two big chimney breasts and stacks and an array of two-storeyed mullioned and transomed windows.

On a much smaller scale, but containing the same original elements, is Brigstock manor house. This was occupied in the 1520s by Sir William Parr, keeper of Brigstock Parks,

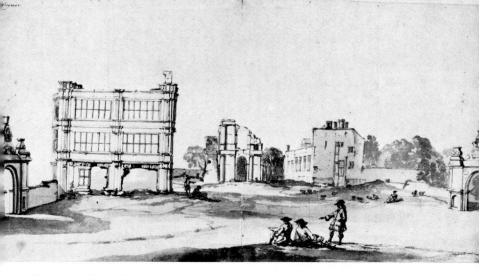

Plate 22 Holdenby House. T. Eayre's view, *c.* 1721, shows some Georgian gentlemen sketching the ruins of Sir Christopher Hatton's Elizabethan house. The two triumphal arches leading to the terraced garden still remain but the house was reconstructed in the nineteenth century.

Plate 23 Easton Neston. One of the finest and most elegant Queen Anne period houses in the country, seen next to the medieval church and behind a formal, geometrically laid-out garden with topiary. This sketch by Eayre must have been done within eighteen years of the completion of Lord Lempster's house.

Prospect of the Lord Lempsters house taken in the Garden

A View of Northampton from Queen's Cross on the London Road

Plate 24 Northampton by T. Eayre, 1721. Forty-five years before, the town had suffered a disastrous fire (1676) from which virtually only the medieval churches of the Holy Sepulchre (spire to left) and St Giles (tower to right) survived. All Saints was rebuilt in provincial classical style. An early Georgian travelling coach bumps over the execrable rutted surface of the London road past a post-mill and Edward I's memorial to his wife Queen Eleanor. Her body had lain at Delapre Abbey (below right) on its way to burial at Westminster Abbey.

Plate 25 Peterborough. T. Eayre's companion view, 1721, shows the great length of the monastic church, dominating the little borough. Five boats are moored below the rickety trestle bridge, where there is still a fine Georgian customs house. The steeple (now tower only) of the parish church and the high gable of the Guildhall show the position of the Market Place in front of the Minster Gate. The town had not yet spread south of the Nene.

View of Langdyke Bush & Country Adjacent taken upon Helpston Heath near the Bridge. 29 Aug. 1721

Plate 26 'View of Langdyke Bush and Country Adjacent taken upon Helpston Heath near the hedge.' J. Clare knew every tree and bank of Helpston Heath and deeply regretted the inroads made by enclosure on its wild state, seen here in T. Eayre's sketch, 1721. It is near the hundred meeting place of Nassaborough (see p. 86).

Plate 27 T. Eayre's view of Oundle, 1721. The fifteenth-century spire of the medieval church pushes a finger up from the low ridges above the Nene occupied by the town. Its single-storeyed thatched cottages have now been replaced by stone houses making it the most perfect Georgian town in the county. Leland wrote of the bridge in the sixteenth century: "It is cawllid the Northe Bridge, being of a great length, by cawse men may passe when the river overflowith, the medowes lying on even side on a great leavel thereaboute."

View of the Town Church and Bridge of Oundle taken in Ashton Field to the North

sheriff and M.P. in the Reformation parliaments. It consists of a one-storeyed hall with chambers over, and on the garden side is the original buttressed porch. There are Jacobean extensions to the north and south.

From the mid-sixteenth century onwards new improvements of living standards began to be demanded and new ideas in design became fashionable. There was, firstly, a growing desire for symmetrical elevations, especially to the front of a building; the rambling functionalism of medieval planning was giving way to the stricter Renaissance symmetry. Secondly, there was a change from the one main living room, the great hall, to a multiplicity of smaller rooms for special purposes, and thirdly, a much higher standard of comfort in the shape of more glass windows, a greater use of plaster ceilings, wooden panelling and tapestried hangings. Lastly, there was the necessity to build very big houses. "Partly this was because their owners needed to keep up a certain 'port' and have their suites of gentlemen and pages; partly because the one essential condition for retaining their wealth and standing was to continue in royal favour, in office, in possession of patents and monopolies; and to do this it was wisdom to entertain and accommodate the court."[14] Northamptonshire furnishes some splendid examples.

Kirby had been a village mentioned in Domesday. We have already noticed that to the south of Kirby Hall a strip of unploughed grass winding for half a mile up the hill preserves the sunken hollow-way of the village street; on either side are the mounded platforms of the vanished houses. Sir Humphrey Stafford chose the secluded hollow to the north for his house (begun *c.* 1570) which is built about an axial plan running north–south and afforded an uninterrupted vista across the forecourt, the inner court, and through the doorways of the great hall to the privy garden. Inside, the exigencies of symmetry demand windows

[14] E. Mercer, *English Art 1553–1625* (Oxford, 1962), p. 13.

where no windows need be and the influence of Italy produces an arcaded loggia, the use of a giant order, the classic pilaster applied to the full height of the two-storeyed building and the fantastic 'frontispiece' of the porch— enriched by a rather over-powering and flamboyant rendering of the classical orders, piled columns and pilasters rising above the main elevation. Kirby Hall was bought by a wealthy courtier, Sir Christopher Hatton, captain of Queen Elizabeth's bodyguard and afterwards Lord Chancellor.

About this time Sir Christopher Hatton began to build a vast new house at Holdenby, with the deliberate idea of being able there to entertain the Queen lavishly and with splendour (Plate 22). Burghley put their common motives in a nutshell in 1579 when he wrote to Hatton: "God send us both long to enjoy Her, for whom we both mean to exceed our purses in these buildings." The palace built round three courtyards was on a truly princely scale, comparable with Blenheim; its fronts were 360 feet and 224 feet long as against 320 feet and 270 feet at Blenheim. It has gone through some notable vicissitudes. The parliamentarian, Adam Baynes, demolished some of it and converted a part of 'the offices' into a big farmhouse. Some roofless fragments survived to inspire early-eighteenth-century water-colourists. The nucleus was incorporated into R. Carpentier's new 'Holdenby House' in the Victorian period.

A parallel process occurred at Steane Park near Brackley. Tillemans' drawing of 1719 shows the large house of the Crewe family flanked by two Tudor towers with an arcade linking them and the house behind. On the death of Nathaniel, third Lord Crewe, Bishop of Durham, in 1721, it was bought by Sarah, Duchess of Marlborough, who gave it to her grandson, John Spencer of Althorp. The Spencers pulled down the big house and converted 'the offices' into a farmhouse. This in turn was upgraded into a Victorian manor by the Norris family at the end of the nineteenth century.

Kirby, Holdenby, Steane, were all formerly medieval villages. Burghley House, near Stamford, begun by William Cecil in the 1550s and completed by Lord High Treasurer William Burghley between 1577 and 1587, stands also on the site of a deserted village in the heart of a park created to take it. This monstrous and yet magnificent palace with its astonishing skyline of obelisks, pillared chimneys, stone balls, turrets and pinnacles, and its profusion of rich ornament, underlines the element of vulgarity to be found in the ebullience of the Elizabethan court.

Althorp has been the home of the Spencers since the early years of the sixteenth century. Extensive dry rot trouble recently revealed that in the core of the house is a late-medieval courtyard, well hidden by an almost complete recasing in the seventeenth century after the Civil War. Count Lorenzo Magalotti described the sumptuous entertainment given his master, the Prince of Tuscany, in the newly fashioned house of the Sunderlands.

The whole of the edifice is regularly built both as to its exterior and interior, and is richly ornamented with stone of a white colour, worked in the most exquisite manner, which is dug from a quarry at Weldon, fourteen miles distant . . . and it may be said to be the best planned and best arranged country seat in the kingdom . . . none are superior to it in symmetrical arrangement.[15]

The strange washed-out appearance of the house is explained by the refacing in white 'mathematical' tiles by Henry Holland in the late eighteenth century.

The Spencers are interred magnificently in their chapel attached to the medieval church of Great Brington, and the Fitzwilliams lie in the splendid outsize chancel rebuilt as a mausoleum by Sir William Fitzwilliam I at Marholm in the 1530s.

[15] N. Marlow and G. Isham, *Diary of Thomas Isham,* pp. 24–25.

It frequently happens that the church survives from a village deserted in the medieval or Tudor period because it is annexed to the country house, becoming virtually a private chapel for the landowner's family and servants. William Winstanley's drawing of Rushton Hall in 1741 shows the church of St Peter's, hard by the house of the Treshams; the village was a quarter of a mile away and in any case had its own church. St Peter's was demolished *c.* 1790. Deene church, neglected and falling into ruin, was practically the only vestige of the former village, swallowed up in the park of the Brudenells. When the family transferred its allegiance to the Anglican Church in the middle of the eighteenth century they refurbished St Peter's, and the seventh countess built an ornately uxorious monument to the hero of Balaklava. Side by side with the great house at Easton Neston, dating from Queen Anne's reign, is the medieval church (Plate 23). The village has been banished outside the park.

The most curious sequence has occurred at Newton, now in Geddington parish. There were two settlements, Great and Little Newton, both with churches. The parish church in Great Newton was allowed to decay and until recently when foundations and burials were found under a barn to the south of the village, its site was unknown. The chapel of St Faith only a few hundred yards away became the parish church (Plate 19). It houses the memorials of the Treshams, a branch of whom built a mansion in the sixteenth century complete with terracing, an island water feature and gardens. This house is now no more than a scatter of brick rubble, clay pipe fragments and post-medieval potsherds in the ploughsoil below the bank on which perches a splendid rectangular dovecote dating from *c.* 1600. The church stands forlorn in the fields, a victim for vandals, although its future may be assured if it attracts sufficient finance to become a study centre for the countryside.

Church-building practically ceased after the Reformation

although the exquisite building at Whiston on the scarp overlooking the middle Nene valley, the work of the masons of St Margaret's, Westminster, at the expense of the Catesbys, shows that craftsmanship and patronage of the highest order was still to be found in the county in the 1530s. Occasionally a great family gave architectural expression to their pride of lineage by building a chapel or extending a chancel. Such is the late Gothic structure standing in the park at Steane, built by the Crewe family, *c.* 1620. Kelmarsh church has a chapel dating from the reign of Charles I in 'Brasenose gothic' style, added by the Hanbury family. The Ishams rebuilt the chancel at Lamport church in 1651–2 and added a chapel in the classical style to serve as a mausoleum twenty years later. In general, however, such buildings are rare.

Despite the radical decline in church-building after 1540, religious passions continued to dominate men's minds and Northamptonshire furnishes a striking example of the way one man's religious views could leave a lasting impression on the landscape. Sir Thomas Tresham's main buildings were the Rothwell market house, constructed in the 1570s, and in the 1590s the triangular lodge at Rushton, the tiny Hawkfield lodge, and additions and alterations at Rushton Hall. Work on the old house at Lyveden and at the New Building also belonged to the nineties. The warrener's lodge at Rushton, "grotesque in its triangularity, a curious riddle in stone with its mystical numbers and monograms . . . symbolised Tresham's favourite doctrine, the Trinity". The Rothwell market house, peppered with coats of arms, is a tribute "to his sweet fatherland and County of Northampton but chiefly to this town his near neighbour. Nothing but the common weal did he seek: nothing but the perpetual honor of his friends." The New Building at Lyveden, designed as a lodge to the manor house, is now remote, roofless and a ruin (Plate 21), whose superb ashlar masonry is some of the finest in the country; but the fantastic ingenuity of its didactic sculptured decoration recalls its builder's dedication to the themes of the Passion of Christ and, linked with this, the Mother of Christ, Mater Dolorosa, Our Lady of Sorrows.

For all its apparent extravagance, this impressive building programme exerted remarkably little strain on Sir Thomas's resources. Nearly all the materials came from his own estate. Some stone came by ox team from Weldon and King's Cliffe: most of the limestone and ironstone came from pits at Rushton, Pipewell and from Tresham's quarry at Pilton. The timber, sand and lime also came from his own lands. Most of the workmen employed were his own tenants—of the freemasons old Tyrrol and his three sons lived on the Rushton estate while William Grumbold, who was paid £60 for his work on the Rothwell market house (built mainly of Weldon stone), and his relatives were largely employed at Lyveden. The most delicate carving was entrusted to a skilled freemason named Parris. The total expenditure for five years seven months was £971 0s. 11d. (1594–1600). The total for all the building was about £2000. The Treshams were ruined not by extravagance of building but by the combined political pressures of recusancy with its accompanying crushing fines and the treasonable folly of Francis Tresham, the Gunpowder Plot conspirator.

All these houses were meant to be seen in a setting. They were surrounded by gardens, and considerable changes in layout and design took place during the period. Sir Thomas Tresham, for instance, meant Lyveden to have elaborate grounds. Bridges mentions "to the east is a pretty high mount, encompassed with a broad deep moat with one entrance, and near it are other smaller mounts, with several walks pointing from the house planted with sycamores and elms". Although ploughing has damaged the site one can still trace the mounts. There are two of truncated pyramid design at one end and two circular ones with ramps spiralling up the conical sides. The banks built to dam the water in

the moats are terraced with steps to give access to the top.
Apparently eight large arbours were to be made, and beyond
the outermost fence a deep alley to be constructed "which
shall serve to walk round about in". There was to be a
bowling green, well-gravelled walks and a raised 'terass' as
well as orchards, roses, damask and red 'perynles' (perennials), strawberries 'or the like'. There were to be fishponds
for 'congers'.[16]

Similarly at Lamport in the seventeenth century there was
a *Mount*, mentioned in the diary of Thomas Isham. In the
orchards here "the trees were planted in rows . . . in the form
of a quincunx". There was a series of stepped fishponds
made by John Isham, and the quiet sport of angling seems
to have been a favourite recreation at Lamport. "We sent
some boys into the pond to drive the fish out of the rushes
and by this method we took seventeen carp" (2nd July,
1672).[17]

Bridges had a discerning eye for an earthwork as we have
noticed before. At Wakerley—"Here was an antient seat
belonging to the family of Cecil at a small distance from the
church, demolished about thirty years ago. The remains of the
terras are yet visible in the garden." From the air we can see
the mounds of the ruins of the house, to the south are the
straight lines of formal gardens, probably of the seventeenth
century, to the east a huge sunken lawn with raised terraces
on two sides (Plate 20).

A very similar layout existed at Harrington. Here the
manor house of the Earls of Dysart lies under a confusion
of mounds, to the south of which lies a rectangular sunken
garden, 200 feet by 255 feet, and to the east, rising by steps
which are cut diagonally, a series of immense terraces with
small rectangular sunken features which may be ponds.
Certainly water was involved in the garden since a spring

[16] G. Isham, 'Sir Thomas Tresham and his Buildings', *Northamptonshire
Antiquarian Society*, Vol. LXV (1964–5), p. 28.
[17] N. Marlow and G. Isham, *Diary of Thomas Isham,* pp. 31, 115.

rises halfway up the terraces. The date is uncertain but close parallels can be seen in the Elizabethan environs of Hold-enby. Here, wrote Norden:

> And above the rest is especially to be noted with what industrye and toyle of man, the garden hath here raised, levelled and formed out of a most craggye and unsitable Grounds, now framed a most pleasant sweete and princely Place with divers walks, manie ascendings and descendings, replenished also with manie delightful trees of Fruite, artificially composed Arbors and a Destiling House on the west end of the same Garden, over which is a Ponde of Water brought by Conduite Pypes out of the Feyld adjoyninge on the west $\frac{1}{4}$ of a myle from the same house. To conclude the state of the same house is such and so beautifull that it may well delight a prince.[18]

The terraces of the Elizabethan palace remain but they are now grassy steps to the south of the present nineteenth-century house. Two great triumphal arches standing in isolation in a field adjoining are all that is left upstanding of this vast monument to courtly ambition (Plate 22).

Tudor and early Stuart parks

We saw how in the Middle Ages there was a sprinkling through the county of deer parks belonging to the magnates and the crown. Christopher Saxton's County Atlas, published in 1579, was the first to show parks by a separate symbol so that we are no longer dependent on the chance survival of documents for listing parks (Fig. 16). These circular and oval shapes surrounded by paled fences show that Tudor Northamptonshire had twenty parks—well might Norden say: "No shire within this lande is so plenti-

[18] J. N. Norden, *Speculum Britanniae Pars Altera or a Delineation of North-amptonshire* (1720), pp. 50, 51.

fully stored with Gentry, in regard whereof this shire may seeme worthy to be termed the Herralds Garden." For, as Beresford pointed out, the Elizabethan park was as much a demonstration of social rank as the pedigree and the coat of arms.[19] Hence the Brudenells were not content with building up a profitable estate of consolidated sheep pastures but raised an impressive house which they surrounded by a park. Deene Hall is mostly the work of Sir Edmund Brudenell and was completed about 1570. The park was being enlarged in 1586 as land was exchanged with Sir Christopher Hatton. Enclosures in Deene in 1612 enabled Lord Brudenell to expand his park from 183 to 280 acres. Further extensions were gradually made until in 1642 it contained 350 acres. The Treshams similarly received licence to impark 120 acres of wood, 250 acres of pasture and 50 acres of meadow to form Lyveden Park.

There is no doubt in fact that parks were on the increase in the Tudor and early Stuart period. Speed's map of 1610 marked twenty-seven. Prestige, a sign of enhanced social status, was one motive behind imparking; hunting was another. The Elizabethan deer parks could be anything up to three square miles of pasture and meadow, pieces of forest and coppice, scraps of former open fields. Among these oaks and grassland was room to course—"deer both red and fallow, both in parks, forests and chases as no shire yieldeth the like". This of course meant mounding with stone or wood. The estate survey of Holdenby drawn in 1587 after the park had been made by Sir Christopher Hatton at the expense of a large expanse of 'Fareham Meadowe', 'Parke Feelde' and 'Longlande feelde' shows the five-mile circuit of the timber fence, tall and pointed to discourage the deer from escaping. It also shows the new inhabitants; two huntsmen, each with a hawk; walking, leaping and feeding deer; rabbits sitting up in alarm and running. Part of the deer leap can still be seen on the eastern

[19] M. W. Beresford, *History on the Ground* (London, 1957), p. 211.

Fig. 16. Part of Saxton's map of Northamptonshire, 1576

The parks are oval, circular or kidney-shaped, and ringed with little pales. Note the way Higham Park juts into Bedfordshire. Holdenby did not acquire a park until 1587 so it is not drawn by Saxton.

side. The hedge and trees which have replaced the palings are growing on an artificial bank made by throwing up soil from an inner ditch.

Parks were a natural place for tree-planting. John Evelyn wrote: "I have often wished, that Gentlemen were more curious of transmitting to Posterity, such records, by noting the Years when they begin any considerable Plantation." Such records are found in profusion in the nineteenth-century Grafton and Montagu estate papers, but successive tree-plantings can be traced from as early as 1567 in a remarkable series of inscribed stones in the Spencers' park at Althorp. The oldest trees in the park are the oaks on the western side, running in part parallel with the wall nearest to Brington church. Some scattered trees about the parish were probably planted long before the estate was purchased by the first John Spencer of Wormleighton in 1512. His grandson, Sir John, planted a belt of oaks on the north-west side of the park in 1567-8 and this experiment was commemorated by a stone tablet with his coat of arms and an inscription. The next wood lies to the west and was planted by his eldest son, another Sir John, in 1589, as a further stone records. Sir Robert Spencer, created Baron Spencer of Wormleighton, made a third planting midway between Althorp House and the East Lodge on the North-ampton and Rugby road in 1602-3 and more plantings in the park were made and similarly recorded in 1625, 1798, 1800 and 1901.[20] The deer move quietly under the trees of Althorp. The house lies low, its chimneys being the only visible feature from many places in the park. It is sad that many of these magnificent oaks are nothing more than hollow and crevassed shells, their mighty girth reminding us that formerly Nelson's battleships were constructed from their like.

A parallel process of imparking is seen among the crown

[20] 'Datestones in Althorp Park', *Northamptonshire Notes and Queries*, N.S., Vol. III (1910-11), pp. 65-76.

lands in the sixteenth century. To enhance his pleasure when hunting at Grafton on his annual progress Henry VIII included within the honour of Grafton, which was created in 1541, a system of parks which he had enlarged or newly imparked. They included the swollen Grafton Park to which Henry had added seventy-six acres from the fields of Grafton and seventy acres from Alderton; Paulerspury Park, alienated to the crown in 1541; Potterspury Park of which 150 acres were imparked in 1537; Stoke Bruerne Park wholly imparked in 1541. Pettit has followed the bounds of Grafton Park and reckons that a modern hedge-row, punctuated by the decaying stumps of great oaks, follows its north-west boundary. A mound survives at times, three to four feet high for several hundred yards. Within the park the long curving sweep of an existing hedgerow arouses suspicion of a pre-enclosure origin—here is apparently part of the park's medieval boundary.[21] One can imagine the king riding through the Grafton Park enjoying the pleasures of the chase. We find payments for arrows, for greyhounds and falcons in the accounts of the Privy Purse. He also paused to touch for the king's evil: "The same day paied to ii pouer women that were heled of their sikenes XV'S"; "the same day paied to a pouer woman that gave the kings grace peres and nutts in the forest iiii*s.* viii*d*".[22]

There are some signs that disparking was also a feature of the Tudor landscape. The reasons were that the pressure of population on land began to increase and as agriculture revived men planning parks found themselves competing with others. Burghley bought the old royal park of King's Cliffe and, according to Bridges, disparked it. Sir Robert Cecil was granted Brigstock Parks in 1602 and began to dis-park them, depriving the villagers of Brigstock of the rights of gathering fuel and pasturing cattle. The wood and timber

[21] P. A. J. Pettit, *Royal Forests*, pp. 14–15.
[22] G. Baker, *History*, Vol. II, pp. 174–5.

were systematically cleared from the Great Park except for fifty acres and shortly after the wood from the Little Park went. Cecil realised a total of £1082. Finally the deer were driven into the forest and the parks were disafforested in 1612; on the eve of the Civil War we find that the parks had been divided into twenty lots and let to thirty-nine persons.[23] Moulton Park in the meantime was crumbling and in 1560 its state was lamentable. The two lodges were in such decay that one could not be repaired under £20 and the other under £10, while the park was enclosed with a wall so low "that neither deer nor other beasts can be kept there" and in many parts the wall "lyeth wyde open, the dere thereof daylye and nightlye go oute and fede of the corne and grase growinge in the fieldes nexte abowte adjoyninge".

The great rebuilding
Lesser houses, farmhouses of yeomen, husbandmen, labourers

As one descends the social scale it is apparent that the great rebuilding was equally widespread among the houses of the yeomen and the parochial clergy, the husbandmen and the labourers. The building traditions of the area were adapted to climatic, agrarian and social conditions and there is some evidence for a regional style in the Banbury area which includes the south-western part of the county.[24] To judge from the few surviving examples, the typical farmhouse of the late Middle Ages in this area consisted of a single-storey hall with an open hearth or brazier, which precluded the introduction of upper floors. Chinnery Farm, Chacombe, serves as an example. The earliest part of this house comprises a three-bay hall measuring thirty-five feet by eighteen feet and containing two pairs of crucks which are built into rubble walls. Another example of such a hall house is 'the

[23] P. A. J. Pettit, *Royal Forests*, pp. 175–6.
[24] R. B. Wood-Jones, *Traditional Domestic Architecture in the Banbury Region* (Manchester, 1963).

monastery', Shutlanger, whose soot-caked, massive, arched roof-timbers dramatically display the former existence of an open central fire. In this case the hall is approached by a fourteenth-century porch of ecclesiastical dimensions with groined and embossed vault.

There was an extensive time-lag, perhaps fifty years or more between the beginning of the movement for rebuilding the houses of the gentry and the general extension of this to the dwellings of lesser men. Though there is virtually no documentary evidence, the Renaissance practice of dating buildings reflects the increasing importance of the yeoman and the husbandman. Frequently we find his initials coupled with those of his wife on a stone with the date of the erection or the extension of the building. The first example of this in the south-west of the county is 1579.

By 1550 the single-storey hall had been superseded by multiple-room houses in most parts of the country in the upper classes of building, and within fifty years the yeoman dwellings followed this improvement. The introduction of the wall fire-place made possible the insertion of upper floors which were at first built partly within the roof space as a loft or attic. These were lit by dormer windows or windows in the gables and in many cases the floor was over part of the building only. These 'one and a half storey' houses when associated with early forms of roof structure are generally among the earliest examples of the great rebuilding.

The plan and layout is of greater significance. The through entrance passage with service room and hall becomes general with the hall fireplace being placed on the end wall against the passage. This two-unit version was seen in two cottages now demolished at King's Sutton and there are a number of others just over the border in Oxfordshire as at Grange Farm, Balscott and Bluegates, Bloxham. A further innovation was the addition of a third apartment, the ground-floor parlour serving both as a bedroom and a

withdrawing room which is added to the larger houses—
Beech Tree House, Lower Middleton Cheney, shows the
planning characteristics of these small early yeoman
houses. The central chimney stack, three-room plan,
through passage and stud partition dividing parlour from
hall and the full two-storey height except for the service bay
show the way these houses were being improved in the first
half of the seventeenth century. Haunt House, Weldon,
built *c.* 1636 by a local master mason, Humphrey Frisbey,
has a chimney stack on the axis of the house with back to
back fireplaces but it combines an additional quality,
symmetry of design, with all its convenient simplicity of
arrangement. For here the four principal rooms on the two
main floors were later subdivided.

Symmetry, as we saw when reviewing the houses of the
gentry and nobility, was one of the prevailing ideologies of
the Renaissance and signs of its influence in diluted form are
found among the lesser houses in their increased formality
and balance of design in the principal elevation. Windows
increase in size and number, four or five light openings
being employed, the lights being divided by ovolo section
mullions. They are inserted in tiers in the end walls which
are given more prominence by their gables being finished by
parapets with decorative kneelers. More houses are found
placed at right-angles to the road to gain a southern aspect
for their principal apartment. An increased desire for privacy
and convenience results in a change of emphasis in the use
of rooms, with a reduction in the importance of the hall and
an increase in the size of the parlour and the kitchen. In
addition there is an increase in height to two full storeys
with attics above or cock-lofts lit from the gable. The
Poplars Farm, Chacombe, bearing the date 1654, illustrates
many of these tendencies, the hall here has been eliminated
and Renaissance influence is revealed in the principal front
elevation and the ovolo mullioned ground-floor windows.
Workworth Farm, dated 1639; Mill Farm, Overthorpe, *c.*

1675–90; Farley's Farm, Lower Middleton Cheney, all incorporate similar features.

By the beginning of the seventeenth century village populations, particularly in the forest areas, began to increase rapidly. Most houses of the farming community had grown up within the villages, along the village street, their sites long and narrow with strips stretching out to the open fields behind. The earliest houses were almost invariably parallel to the street. Behind them had lain the farmyards, flanked by farm buildings, and behind these again the croft or enclosed pasture and an orchard.

The swollen populations were housed in various ways. Some houses were planted at right-angles to the road, an arrangement which gave greater privacy. Others were placed in line, skirting a common entrance passage. Such are rows of almshouses as at Kettering in 1688 and King's Cliffe in 1668 which, as Seabourne hazards, may have suggested a model for the rows of cottages providing one room up and one room down for labourers and their families so characteristic of the nineteenth century. Another method of housing increased numbers was for dwellings to be contrived in any open spaces within the built-up area. They encroached at times on the green itself, or on the street, and thus produced a more compact grouping. Further houses were contrived from outbuildings: stables and barns. "There are besides these certain others that inhabit shops very dangerous to dwell in because of the casualty of fire," complains an Elizabethan note in the parish chest at Brigstock. Small cottages were being built as well. In the royal forests such cottages, when they were erected on the waste, were regarded as purprestures. In 1619, a survey in Grafton, Hartwell and Roade, mentioned twelve cottages newly erected from the waste, so this phenomenon was not confined to the forest. In 1637 twenty-three were presented as being built in Geddington in the previous thirty years.

Not many of these smaller village houses have survived

from a period earlier than the sixteenth century. Of five of this date described by Seabourne at Brigstock, Corby, Gretton, King's Cliffe and Wilbarston only one, at Wilbarston, still remains.[25] They were relatively small structures, with average floor areas of about thirty by twenty feet; they all had rubble stone walls and thatched roofs supported on cruck blades inserted midway in the walls. Each pair of crucks had been made by splitting a single oak tree. Originally these houses had open, centrally-placed hearths with smoke rising into the roof space. They were all considerably altered, probably in the seventeenth century, when the desire for greater privacy and for upstairs bedrooms became usual among lesser as well as more important people. A one-room house at King's Cliffe, for instance, was later converted into a cross-passage house with three rooms on the ground floor and bedrooms above. Staircases, fireplaces and internal partition walls were usually later features. This sub-division of houses doubtless absorbed numbers of the increased population. "Of late years, by evil permission and sufferance, divers and many poor people are crept into forest towns, videlicet two or three tenants in one house wherein one only tenant was wont to dwell," stated Sir Thomas Tresham and Sir Edward Watson in their articles for the better preservation of the coppices in Rockingham forest in 1577.[26]

As one crosses the county the building materials change. The western and northern half has buildings of brown ironstone or ferruginous limestone; this can vary in colour from orange to dark brown or purple. The northern and eastern half of the county, as we have seen, was plentifully supplied with good limestone which ranges in colour from near white through greys and yellows to medium brown. Where the two stone types meet there is a pleasing attempt to

[25] M. V. J. Seabourne, 'Small Stone Houses in Northamptonshire', *Northants. Past and Present*, Vol. IV, 6 (1971–2), pp. 366–9.
[26] P. A. J. Pettit, *Royal Forests*, pp. 143, 170.

create a polychromatic decoration. The main walls are of brown stone; grey limestone is used for window mullions, roof copings and chimneys. Bands of stone are sometimes used with alternating colours (Blisworth had several good examples), occasionally a limestone building has ironstone quoins.

The houses of the labouring poor, being of poorer workmanship, inferior materials, meaner size and lesser convenience, have not survived in large numbers from before the end of the eighteenth century. It is likely that they continued to be built of timber, plaster, and mud or cob long after the houses of the yeomen and gentry had turned to stone and consequently they needed to be replaced at more frequent intervals.

Cob is a mixture of local soil with chopped straw, grass and cow dung added to improve its adhesive quality. Walls of this material have to be built on a solid rubble stone plinth and topped with some kind of coping, usually a thatched roof. The technique was widespread and the surviving buildings suggest a distribution mainly along the edge and to the west of the limestone belt of good building stone. There are twenty-nine villages in the county where buildings of cob are to be found and the main concentration of mud cottages is in north-west Northamptonshire. They date mainly from the seventeenth and eighteenth centuries and were frequently only of one or two rooms downstairs with the same upstairs. At times, as at Clipston and Scaldwell, the front walls of the cottages were stone with rear walls of mud. Good examples can be seen at Spratton, Ravensthorpe and Rothersthorpe, Braybrooke, Guilsborough and Nether Heyford.[27]

William Pitt remarked: "I observed, in various parts of the county, particularly in the open parishes, a great number of tenements built with mud and covered with thatch. It is

[27] M. V. J. Seabourne, 'Cob cottages in Northamptonshire', *Northants. Past and Present*, Vol. III, 5, pp. 215–28, 6, pp. 283–4.

very possible that sufficient shelter and warmth may be afforded by these materials and that they may afford health and comfort to the humble inhabitant, but they certainly have a miserable appearance and are hardly consistent with the dignity of a rich county." On reflection, however, he comments: "The old cottages seem to have had very little design, respecting either convenience or comfort; shelter from the weather and room to sit or sleep in, rather in a promiscuous manner, seems to have been the whole extent of the object in view of their construction."[28] From 1800 onwards the material was regarded as rather plebian and tended to decline in use, and the mass production of bricks and the development of railways allowing them to be distributed cheaply led to the decline of cob walling as a form of construction.

These more humble dwellings were set amidst gardens. Lawns were unknown, but flowers vied with herbs and vegetables and a record has been preserved of the flowers in bloom in the garden of Goodwife Cautray, a Northamptonshire yeoman's wife, in 1658. Amongst the plants listed are larkspur, sweet william, spiderwort, lupins in four colours, "the great blew, the little blew, the yellow and white", scabious, marigolds, London pride and hollyhocks. Such practical additions as double fennel flower, camomile and white lilies, used for medicinal purposes, were also included.[29]

Schools and almshouses[30]

The oldest school building in the county is at Higham Ferrers where Henry Chichele, Archbishop of Canterbury, founded a college in 1422. Fragments of the college stand

[28] W. Pitt, *General View*, pp. 29–30.
[29] M. Campbell, *The English Yeoman* (Yale, 1942), p. 241.
[30] M. V. J. Seabourne, *The English School; Its Architecture and Organisation, 1370–1870* (London, 1971).

in the High Street; the parish church was used as the chapel for the college and the school building, looking like a chapel in the Perpendicular style, measuring thirty-seven by sixteen feet may be found in the churchyard to the west. To the south is a magnificent early-fifteenth-century almshouse in polychrome masonry, now used as a parish hall. Only one Tudor school building survives in the county, that built in 1595 north of the church at Finedon. There is usually a close geographical connexion between church and school, and often between school and almshouses. A sprinkling of seventeenth-century schools remains in towns like Daventry (1600) and Wellingborough (1617)—where a former Grammar and English School on the north side of the churchyard still stands. At Burton Latimer (1622) the old grammar school in Church Street is now closed; it has lately been bought by a doctor and will be saved (Plate 31). Cottesbrooke School, erected by Sir John Langham in 1651, is linked with almshouses recently restored. Probably the most impressive seventeenth-century school building in the county was Guilsborough, founded by Sir John Langham, a Turkey Company grocer; the master's house and school accommodation for fifty pupils were placed next to one another and it used to cater for pupils from Guilsborough, Cottesbrooke, Cold Ashby and other parishes within four miles.

During the eighteenth century, elementary schools for the poor of the neighbourhood were added to a number of Northamptonshire villages. In Church Street, Finedon, for instance, about twenty girls were educated, maintained and clothed in a subscription school of 1714 which is now a private house of seven bays and two storeys. Educational purposes were often allied to charitable, as in the interesting complex of buildings in Bridge Street (formerly School Hill) at King's Cliffe. Here on the north side there are groups of widows' almshouses, boys' school and master's house, and, on the south, spinsters' almshouses and the mistress's house. This is the joint foundation of Mrs Elizabeth Hutcheson and the Rev. William Law (in 1749 and 1752).

These early school buildings all seem more like large houses than purpose-built educational establishments: they consisted usually of one large schoolroom with a house for the schoolmaster often attached. There were two such buildings in Kettering. The former national school in Market Street built in 1820 is now occupied by the Weights and Measures Department of the County Council; its original schoolroom can be made out and there is a teacher's house facing the London Road. Less fortunate was the handsome ironstone Victorian Gothic building of the Kettering Grammar School, with master's house attached, which stood in Gold Street from 1856 until it was demolished to the great regret of the townspeople and replaced by the utilitarian façade of a supermarket in 1964.

7. Georgian and Victorian landscapes: the countryside

The sources. The pre-enclosure landscape. The process of enclosure. Drainage and reclamation from the fen. New farmsteads. Country houses, parks, hunting

The sources

TOWARDS THE END of the seventeenth century the sources for the historian of the landscape multiply. For the first time we begin to receive visual glimpses of the ordinary countryside apart from the formal views of great houses and their gardens which usually creep in as mere backgrounds to seventeenth-century portraits. The county is fortunate in that its most noteworthy historian, John Bridges, 1666–1724, commissioned Thomas Eayre, the Kettering bell-founder, draughtsman and designer of ironwork, and Peter Tillemans, the Flemish artist, to produce a series of topographical drawings designed to illustrate his projected History of the county. Two hundred and sixty-eight drawings, many dated 1719 or 1721, survive, and among the pictures of churches, monuments and houses beloved of eighteenth-century antiquaries are a few of stretches of countryside, remarkable because they give us our first views of a pre-enclosure landscape.[1]

During this period, landowners employed surveyors to

---

[1] B.M. Add. MSS. 32467. A selection is being edited by G. Isham and will be published by the Northants. Record Society. For T. Eayre see P. King, 'Thomas Eayre of Kettering', *Northants. Past and Present*, Vol. 1, 5 (1952), pp. 11–23.

make large-scale maps of villages and estate plans which enable us to reconstruct lost landscapes in every detail. Such is the superb series of the Montagu estates, now hanging in the corridors of Boughton House, drawn and tinted by John Booth, George Nunns and William Brasier, 1714–48 (Plates 28 and 29).

Literary evidence comes from the diaries of zestful travellers such as Celia Fiennes and Viscount Torrington, and descriptions emerge of the growing market towns, the appalling roads and, particularly, the dreadful state of the inns. The lively interest of the eighteenth-century nobility and squirearchy in their estates, which contrasts markedly with the neglectful absentee landlordism of their contemporaries across the English Channel, is reflected in correspondence of families such as the Ishams of Lamport, the Comptons of Castle Ashby and the Brudenells of Deene. Almost every aspect of the landscape in the great estate of the Brudenells is touched on, for instance, in the recently published letters of Daniel Eaton to the third Earl of Cardigan, 1725–32.[2]

With this enlightened self-interest on the part of landowners went the growth of a rural professional class of lawyers, surveyors, estate agents, valuers and intelligent tenant farmers who patronised the agricultural writers—such as Arthur Young who wrote his *Farmer's Tour through the East of England* 1771, James Donaldson, the author of the first *General View* of Northamptonshire (1794) and William Pitt whose *General View* first appeared in 1809.

Central Government records also proliferate during the period with a succession of acts improving river navigation, setting up turnpike trusts, licensing the cutting of canals and, above all, the 203 Enclosure Acts (1727–1841) which affected half the total area of the county during these years. Lamenting the loss of well-loved unenclosed heath,

[2] J. Wake and D. C. Webster (eds.), *The Letters of Daniel Eaton 1725–32*, Northants Record Society, Vol. XXIV (1971).

commons and open field around the village he had known during his boyhood, John Clare, a rural poet of more than local stature, spans the two worlds: the unplanned pre-enclosure midlands and the essentially linear, opened out and explained landscape of Victorian England. The water-colour drawings of George Clarke, schoolmaster of Lamport and itinerant artist, produced between 1819 and 1868, provide "the finest record of Northamptonshire's buildings as they appeared during the middle years of the nineteenth century".[3] It is with such materials that the historian can attempt to reconstruct the landscapes of Georgian and Victorian Northamptonshire.

The pre-enclosure landscape

The most characteristic feature of the early-eighteenth-century Northamptonshire landscape was its open nature. Morton, writing in 1712, confirms that in his time there were three main tracts of heath in the county. In the far south-west there was an area called *Bayard's Green*, "a heathy Ground of perhaps several Hundred Acres within the Lordships of Croughton, Imley (Evenley) and Hinton". In the centre were Harlestone, Duston, Dallington and Church Brampton heaths on the west side of the Brampton Nene, as well as areas in Northampton, Kingsthorpe, Boughton, Pitsford, Moulton, Sywell and Overstone Lings on the east side. "These are a hollow, springy, or rippling Ground, that resounds to the Strokes of the Horses Feet when they are ridden upon it, as having naturally many little cavities within it, and having never been open'd and disturbed by Plowing." Morton noted that the Northamptonshire heaths "are not without their Commodities and Use; as affording not only a Fewel for the poorer Sort of People, that is, the Sod or Turf with the Heath or Ling upon it . . . but also

[3] B. Bailey, *George Clarke of Scaldwell*, a catalogue of an exhibition held in Northampton Museum, 1972.

Furze, and Broom in some Places, and Fern or Brakes, a
very good sort of Firing for the Bakers, and very proper for
the burning of Lime . . . It yields a sweet and cleanly Herbage, which feeds a breed of small sheep, whose flesh is
usually much commended and esteemed." He also observed
that "these also are the Places for Warrens: as consisting of
such a lax and dry Earth as the Rabbets delight to burrow in,
and affording an Herbage peculiarly fit for them".[4] In the
north on the edge of the fen were Wittering heath, Easton-
on-the-Hill, Barnack, Helpston, Thornhaugh and Ufford
heaths. Eayre's drawing shows a great expanse dotted with
isolated trees and bushes (Plate 26). This is the limestone
heath country over which Clare wandered.

> In thy wild garb of other times
> I find thee lingering still;
> Furze o'er each lazy summit climbs,
> At nature's easy will.
> Grasses that never knew a scythe
> Wave all the summer long;
> And wild weed blossoms waken blithe,
> That ploughmen never wrong.[5]

It was also known as 'Emmonsailes' or 'Ailsworth' heath
and some common grazing was still permitted at the time of
the enclosure (1809) although, as Barrell points out, the
larger part of the heath land which lay within the parish
boundary had been taken over and fenced by the Earls
Fitzwilliam of Milton, the lords of the manor, as early as
1772.[6]

It is still possible, however, to recapture a glimpse of
Clare's world when walking through Castor Hanglands, a

[4] J. Morton, *Natural History*, pp. 9–10.
[5] J. W. Tibble (ed.), *The Poems of John Clare* (London, 1935), Vol. I, p. 382.
[6] J. Barrell, *The Idea of Landscape and the Sense of Place, 1730–1840* (Cambridge, 1972), p. 101.

221-acre National Nature Reserve since 1945, five miles north-west of Peterborough.[7] Approaching it via the Ufford–Marholm road from the north we scrambled, one September afternoon, along overgrown quarry bottoms and walked through the dense oak-ash woodland, a valuable relict of the old midland limy-soil plant community, and emerged across a wide stretch of grass heath where rare butterflies flourish. The wind rippled through the tall seeding grasses and the sun shone on ripening blackberries. Looking north we could see the beginning of the level fen. Clare again records his sense of unrestricted freedom in the open expanse of the landscape before draining and enclosure:

> Far spread the moory ground, a level scene
> Bespread with rush and one eternal green,
> That never felt the rage of blundering plough,
> Though centuries wreathed spring blossoms on its brow.
> Autumn met plains that stretched them far away
> In unchecked shadows of green, brown, and grey.
> Unbounded freedom ruled the wandering scene;
> No fence of ownership crept in between
> To hide the prospect from the gazing eye;
> Its only bondage was the circling sky.
> A mighty flat, undwarfed by bush and tree,
> Spread its faint shadow of immensity,
> And lost itself, which seemed to eke it bounds,
> In the blue mist the horizon's edge surrounds.[8]

Eayre and Tillemans did not venture with their drawing books into the forests of Rockingham, Salcey and Whittlewood, or what shreds remained of them in the 1720s. When, however, they came to the valley of the middle Nene the

---

[7] Dudley Stamp, *Nature Conservation in Britain* (London, 1969), pp. 149, 232.

[8] *Poems of John Clare*, p. 419.

widespread open aspects of the county were again apparent. The *View of the County about Northampton taken from the Road between Northampton and Kingsthorpe September 1721*, shows the willow-lined river running through unenclosed meadows stretching as far as the eye can see to the low undulating hills corrugated with the ridge-and-furrow of the open fields of Duston, Dallington, Holdenby and Brington. On the eastern side of Northampton the *View of Cliffords Hill and Country adjacent taken in Houghton Pva Feild* [*sic*] *8 August 1721* shows the strips curving down towards the river and the wooded Norman motte over a prairie-like stretch of country (Plate 8). North of the county town, the *View of Buckton* [*sic*, Boughton] *Church now in Ruines with a View of the Town, September 1721*, shows a hedgeless scene where now there is a chequerboard pattern of small fields. The bare and unenclosed fields lap up to the outskirts in Eayre's drawings of Northampton, Kettering, Wellingborough and Oundle. The only scene among these drawings which shows a partially enclosed landscape is the *View of Brackley to the South, 12 July 1721*, and even here, in the far south of the county, the eye is led over a broad stretch of open land before it lights on the hedged and consolidated fields in the environs of the town.

The process of enclosure

Considerable areas had been enclosed by private agreement during the sixteenth and seventeenth centuries and in some places the parliamentary award merely polished off a job already almost completed. Three examples—one from the western uplands, one from the Ise valley and one from the forest area of the north—illustrate this. A parish like Sibbertoft was never the subject of an enclosure Act but its upland pastures seem nevertheless to have been divided up by agreement at an early date, since the 1841 Tithe Award map shows the process complete. The non-tithable meadow land

on both sides of the young Welland, which rises in the centre
of the parish, is arranged in eight long narrow blocks—
evidently enclosed from the common meadow. The bridle
roads which have now mostly disappeared from the modern
map, bend in a series of right-angled corners to avoid the
furlong blocks of the former open fields, dimly visible in the
north-western corner of the parish from air-photographs
taken in 1969. In the undulating uplands to the south of the
village where the Royalist forces massed for the battle of
Naseby, the fields have been laid out in neat rectangular
holdings each of approximately ten acres. Prince Rupert
Farm, a nineteenth-century creation, recalls the traditional
site of the Royalist battle headquarters.

At Pytchley, on the low hilly country overlooking the Ise
valley, the fortunate survival of a 1662 map shows the
process of enclosure by agreement well advanced in the
area to the north of the village.[9] *Stanbury Hill* (now Tambury
Hill) appears as heathland and rough pasture but it is already
enclosed by a ring fence. A substantial slice of the medieval
open field has also been enclosed and is marked on the map
as *New Corn Field* (60a, 0r, 0p) and *The Corn Field* (48a, 3r,
16p). The 1841 Tithe Award shows that these fields had
been further subdivided during the previous 180 years.
Stanbury Hill had been replaced by *New Grounds* and
Tambery Hill. Upper Cow Pasture (20a, 1r, 0p) had been split
into two, and Corn Fields had been further split into four
(two are called *Limekiln 1* and *Limekiln 2*).

Daniel Eaton's correspondence with the third Earl of
Cardigan[10] exemplifies the tortuous negotiations involved
in enclosure by agreement. In December 1725 we find him
meeting the copyholders of Corby to discuss with them a
proposition to exchange their rights of common and so

[9] *A Mapp of Pychley Farne lying and being in the parish of Pychley,* by John
Fiske (1662). Original in Peterborough Museum, copy in N.R.O. I owe
this reference to Mrs Rosemary Eady of Pytchley.
[10] *Letters of Daniel Eaton,* pp. xxxvii, 42, 44, 113, 115

increase the earl's woods. They were at length prevailed upon to resign their right of common in the two "*Sow woods and Bandy Slade*," on the understanding that *Thachley Green* was enclosed for their use and that they were to become possessed "of the houses upon your Lordships wast, none of which ever paid any rent". They were also prepared to give up their rights of common in "*Upper Shrub and Neither Shrub*" if the earl agreed to clear them to make a cow pasture, for which they would be willing to pay rent. The signatures dribbled in and by May 1727 the opposition had dwindled to four.

The motive for enclosure was clearly economic. Pitt explains that the advantages of enclosure would be "an immense saving in the labour of occupiers by concentrating their business, now so dispersed"; a cleaner tillage which would result in greater productivity; an increase in pasture food for sheep, "by sowing clover and other seeds, now omitted"; and, above all, "by improving the quality and healthiness of their flocks (now injured by folding and promiscuous assemblage, and from these causes, subject to rot, scab and other fatal complaints)".[11]

Certainly experiment was now possible in agricultural methods to a far greater degree. Daniel Eaton reports that he had ploughed land by the plantation in the park at Deene to grow turnips; this was as early as 1731. By the end of the century they were a common crop in the county, "generally eaten off by sheep and lambs, being hurdled off in small plots". Morton, writing in 1712, reckoned that rye-grass was best for woodland in enclosures ("I say enclosures, because there is no practising this or any other improvements in the open fields"). Sainfoin, too, was grown for mowing and Charles Kirkham of Fineshade wrote half a little book about its virtues in 1726. One of the pieces of land enclosed from the waste outside the orbit of the open fields at Warkton was called Sainfoin Close. Daniel Eaton's

[11] W. Pitt, *General View*, p. 69.

opinion of trefoil was that it would increase the value of land sown in the first year from a mark (13s. 4d.) to a pound an acre.[12]

Pitt was emphatic on the increase of profits which followed enclosure:

> Kettering Common field, lately enclosed, about two thousand acres; rent, when open £1 to £1 10s. per acre, but since enclosed, worth from £2 to £3 15s. per acre; but some of the richest land near the town thrown to grass, or intended for it, the breadth of corn grown here will, in consequence be lessened, but the quantity grown per acre doubtless increased.

He goes on to analyse the system of cultivation practised in the three great fields of about 800 acres each in the neighbouring township of Rothwell, and claims that the present rent (in 1806) of the open field is less than a pound per acre; when enclosed and relieved of tithe, its value would not be less than thirty to thirty-four shillings per acre.

With such incentives it is not surprising that improving landlords used the machinery of the law to quicken the process of enclosure by parliamentary Act in the eighteenth and nineteenth centuries. Tate reckons that at the beginning of the eighteenth century "some four-fifths or at least three-quarters of Northamptonshire was still open".[13] Gonner calculated that the process of enclosure under Act of Parliament reached a climax in the decade 1771–80 when 17·1 per cent of the total area of the county was involved. There was a second, smaller impetus during the Napoleonic wars, linked with the agricultural boom coinciding with the embargo on foreign corn. From his tables it seems that

[12] *Letters of Daniel Eaton*, pp. xxxviii, 6.
[13] W. Tate, 'Inclosure Movements in Northamptonshire', *Northants. Past and Present*, Vols. 1, 2 (1949), p. 30.

Northamptonshire was second in the league after Huntingdonshire with no less than 51·4 per cent of its total area
being enclosed from common fields between 1760 and
1870.[14] Tate puts the figure slightly higher, making the
total parliamentary enclosure in the county 368,000 acres,
raising the percentage to 59. In addition 2·9 per cent of the
total area was inclosed during the period from the wild
state.

The historical geography of the enclosure movement in
the county has scarcely begun to be written. Only a handful
of studies of the way enclosure was accomplished in
individual cases have been published.[15] It seems clear,
however, from preliminary mapping that the areas most
heavily affected in the first fifty years from 1727 to 1774
were the south-west and centre, the middle Nene and
Welland valleys. By the turn of the century, a band of
Enclosure Acts had spread right across the middle of
the county. In the forest area to the north, Corby was
enclosed in 1829; Rockingham and Gretton in 1832;
Salcey forest and Hartwell in the south-east were enclosed
in 1825.

Enclosure by agreement produced a landscape virtually
indistinguishable from the effects of a parliamentary
enclosure award. In both cases the result was long-lasting
and it can be fairly claimed that in large parts of the county,
especially in the south and west, we are looking in 1972 at a
Georgian enclosed landscape. Where before there had been
what the Reverend James Tyley referred to as "unbroken
tracts that strained and tortured the sight", the fields were
now parcelled out and fenced in. Their size varied from 100

[14] E. C. K. Gonner, *Common Land and Inclosure* (London, 1912), pp. 280,
285.
[15] See W. E. Tate, 'Inclosure Movements', for Ailsworth and Castor; for
Finedon see S. Ranson, *Northants. Past and Present*, Vol. III, 6 (1965–6), pp.
285–8; for West Haddon see J. W. Anscombe, *Northants. Past and Present*,
Vol. IV, 3 (1968–9), pp. 175–81. Mr Anscombe has generously allowed me to
consult his annotated county list of Enclosure Acts and his maps.

acres down to fragments of five acres and less, as anyone who has looked at an enclosure award map will know, but the average aimed at, or at any rate achieved by the latter part of the nineteenth century, was ten acres.

In the north of the county round the slate-producing villages of Collyweston and Easton-on-the-Hill, the new field boundaries were drystone walls of flaggy limestone, similar to those found further south along the Jurassic ridge in the Cotswolds. Far more usual in other parts was the planting of hedges.

The award for Potterspury and Yardley Gobion (1775), for instance, specifies that the boundary fences of the fields were to be made of quickset hedges with post and three rails on one side and post and two rails on the other. Such hedges needed additional protection and a frequent direction of the commissioners was that no lambs or cattle were to be allowed in the fields for a specified period, sometimes four years (as at Syresham 1765), but it could be up to ten, a drastic decision. A good and substantial fence against (the deer in) Rockingham forest was ordered to be made in the award for Nassington, Yarwell, Apethorpe and Woodnewton (1777). Fencing the new fields was very expensive as can be seen in the case of West Haddon where there was a riot in 1765, the crowd setting fire to the stacks of posts and rails; the damage caused was calculated by the *Mercury* of 9th September as being about £1500, very nearly the cost of the award. Clare hated fencing:

> Dire nakedness o'er all prevails;
> Yon fallows bare and brown
> Are all beset with posts and rails
> And turnèd upside down.

And again when he speaks of enclosure he sees it as a restriction on freedom which he relates to the openness of the old landscape:

Fence meeting fence in owners little bounds
Of field and meadow, large as garden-grounds,
In little parcels little minds to please,
With men and flocks imprisoned, ill at ease.[16]

Now that the modern economic climate is forcing farmers to be obsessed with cost-effectiveness, hedges are being grubbed out by the mile and we are suddenly realising that a valued element in the landscape is rapidly disappearing. Early-nineteenth-century drawings of hunting in Northamptonshire show the intensely linear criss-cross of these incipient hedgelines; they must have made hunting a good deal more thrilling than in the previous century. Pitt mentions the cost, in 1813, "of which is about 7s. 6d. the perch of five yards and a half, including every expense; till the quicksets are grown to a fence, but gates not included; but some fences have been raised at a less expense, by raising mounds, or banks of earth, on each side the quicksets, instead of post and rails". The hedgerow plant most favoured was the white hawthorn and a parliamentary enclosure hedge can be recognised by the dominance of this species. Arthur Young remarked that in a grazing county particular methods were found necessary to strengthen hedges:

for the bullocks destroy everything with their horns that is not very strong; they, therefore, instead of the common method, plash down the largest branches the hedge yields, with all the spray, so large and broad as to spread five or six feet thick; but where many cattle go, the only secure way is to leave very good and strong rows of white thorn uncut.[17]

The second new element brought by the enclosure commissioners was the great alteration made to the old road

[16] *Poems of John Clare*, Vol. I, pp. 72, 420.
[17] Quoted by W. Pitt, *General View*, pp. 56–57.

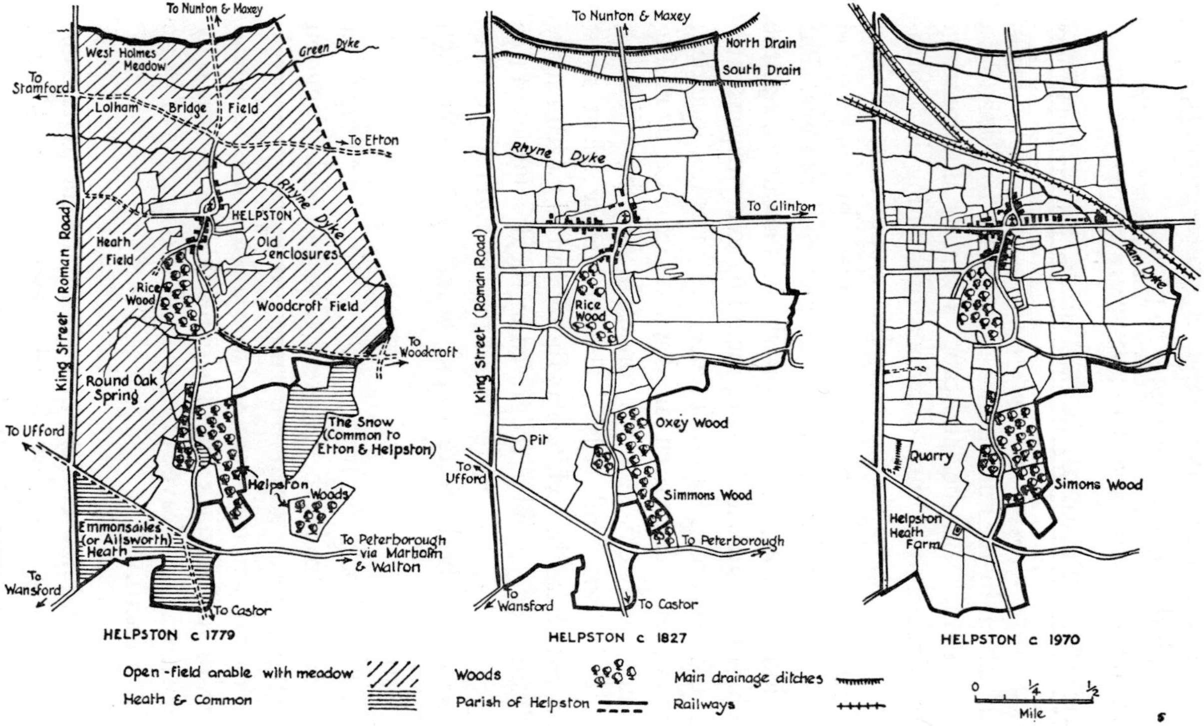

Fig. 17. Helpston

HELPSTON c 1770

Open-field arable with meadow

Heath & Common

To Nunton & Maxey

Green Dyke

To Etton

To Woodcroft

West Holmes Meadow

Lolham Bridge Field

Rhyne Dyke

HELPSTON

Old Enclosures

Woodcroft Field

King Street (Roman Road)

Rice Wood

Heath Field

Round Oak Spring

Emmonsales (or Ailsworth) Heath

To Stamford

To Ufford

To Wansford

The Snow (Common to Etton & Helpston)

Helpston Woods

To Peterborough via Marholm & Walton

To Castor

HELPSTON c 1827

To Nunton & Maxey

North Drain

South Drain

To Glinton

Rhyne Dyke

King Street (Roman Road)

Rice Wood

Pit

Oxey Wood

Simmons Wood

To Ufford

To Wansford

To Peterborough

To Castor

Woods

Parish of Helpston

Main drainage ditches

Railways

HELPSTON c 1970

Main Dyke

Simmons Wood

Quarry

Helpston Heath Farm

0   ¼   ½

Mile

system of the townships. The width of each public and
private road, bridleway and footpath was specified in the
award. At Braybrooke in 1778, the public roads were to be
forty feet in width between the ditches but later with the
improvement of road surfaces this was often reduced to
thirty feet. The commissioners were enjoined not "to divert,
change or alter the Course or Direction of the present
Turnpike-Road, leading from Market Harborough . . .
through and over part of the Said open and Common
Fields . . . to the Town of Kettering." In Moreton Pinkney
the roads were not to be 'laned' (that is fenced or hedged on
both sides) until they were made or repaired and certified as
such by the two justices of the peace.

The commissioners could say whether or not gates could
be erected across public roads; at Syresham (1765) they
decreed that the gates were to be made to swing both ways
to describe a half circle round the hinge or axis. Some
parishes such as Earls Barton and Potterspury forbade the
planting of trees nearer than thirty yards to each other on
public roads. It was usual to allot some land in the parish for
gravel or stone for the upkeep of the roads; about three
acres was usual but often it was less, sometimes in one plot,

Fig. 17. Helpston.

(a) *c. 1779* This shows the nucleated village surrounded by irregularly
shaped fields, which are old enclosures. The shaded area is open-field
arable and leads towards the flat meadows of the Welland in the north
and extensive heaths and woods in the south.

(b) *c. 1827* The regimented parliamentary enclosure field pattern has
been imposed, straight and improved roads built, and large-scale
drainage systems dug in the north of the parish.

(c) *c. 1970* Some further sub-division of the fields has taken place, the
railway has sliced across the parish, and the new outlying farm,
Helpston Heath Farm, has been added in the south.

These plans are a compilation from T. Eayre's 1779 map, A. Bryant's
1827 map and two excellent sketch maps in J. Barrell's *The Idea of
Landscape and the Sense of Place 1730–1840*, with details from the 1960
edition of the two-and-a-half inches to one mile Ordnance Survey map.

sometimes in three. The grass growing on these plots and by the roadside verges was frequently awarded to the Surveyor of the Highways for the upkeep of the public roads, but at Helmdon it went to the parish constable.

These enclosure roads can be easily recognised as one drives across the country. They run straight from village to village, "with none of that apparently aimless wandering in short stretches, punctuated by frequent bends, going half-way round the compass to reach the next hamlet or village",[18] the mark of roads in country never in open field or long since enclosed. At Helpston, John Clare's village, for instance, the 1809 Act was a very comprehensive one and provided for the enclosure of Maxey to the north and of Peakirk, Northborough, Glinton and Etton to the east. The commissioners planned a new system of roads linking the six parishes as a unit. A long straight road was laid out, linking Glinton and Helpston and the Peterborough–Market Deeping turnpike road (Fig. 17). A further road was driven westwards to King Street, taking out the kinks in the old field road which had formerly picked its way round the furlong blocks of Heath Field. Heath Field was further dissected with two roads running east–west to King Street. The ancient roads running north to Nunton and Maxey and south to Castor were not re-aligned but were now to be widened and properly hedged. Clare mentions that a considerable number of footpaths through the old arable fields were 'discontinued' at the enclosure.

Drainage and reclamation from the fen

The mid-nineteenth century was a golden period for English farming and high capital investment made possible elaborate drainage schemes. Bearn describes the different draining methods current in the county in the 1850s, traces of which

---

[18] W. G. Hoskins, *The Making of the English Landscape* (London, 1955), p. 154.

can be discerned in the landscape today.[19] Furrow drains were made by a draining plough drawn by four or six horses penetrating eighteen to twenty inches into the soil. The furrows were then filled with stones or blackthorn wood. More expensive but more long-lasting methods were to use turf to create cavity drains, or stones placed in a V or a Λ at the bottom of the drain, or by using inverted U-shaped tiles. It was the invention of pipe tile-making machines, on show at the Great Exhibition of 1851, however, that revolutionised Victorian arable farming. Bearn commends landowners such as Lord Southampton whom he describes as improving his estate in Astwell by employing 100 to 120 men to dig drains. Parallel lines ran either across or up to the furlong into main drains laid out according to the natural fall; the ditches were deeply dug out to give a good fall for the water to run speedily away. The pipes used varied from two to five or six inches in diameter. Naturally, these drains are not generally working 120 years later but their widespread application is appreciated by the archaeologically minded fieldwalker who will be familiar with the presence of the shattered remnants of the evenly fired red fabric of Victorian mass-produced field-drain pipes brought to the surface by modern deep ploughing.

The prime example of the revolutionary effect of large-scale drainage schemes on the landscape is seen in the north of the county and in the Soke of Peterborough. Helpston again furnishes a good instance. Across the northern boundary of the parish a long drain called Maxey Cut or the North Drain was dug: approximately parallel with it was the South Drain, and between them they stretch from Lolham bridges on King Street in the west to the river Welland at Peakirk Moor in the east[20] (Fig. 17).

East of Glinton and Peakirk stretch the level fenlands of Peakirk Moor and Newborough Fen. In 1812 the appraising

[19] W. Bearn, *Prize Essay on the Farming of Northamptonshire* (London, 1852), pp. 49–54.   [20] J. Barrell, *The Idea of Landscape*, p. 108.

eyes of the enclosure commissioners were focussed on this area which until now had defeated successive generations of would-be drainers since the early seventeenth century. The sixty-five pages of the Enclosure Act for Newborough empowered them to repair mills or engines, scour out, repair and widen all drains, ditches, watercourses, tunnels, watergates, sluices, banks and bridges, and they were to set out a foreland on the east side of Carr Dyke Bank.

I walked along the great grass-grown gravel embankments running parallel with the Welland 300 yards away, on a raw February day in the drizzle with a stiff wind blowing from the north-east. The emerald turf between *the washes* contrasted with the dense black peaty soils of Peakirk Moor stretching as far as the eye could see into the grey, misty distance. Silver lines of full drainage ditches cut the land into rectilinear blocks. The farms lay low, slate roofs, shallow-pitched, sheltered by clumps of trees on the north side. The road to Decoy Farm was causewayed and lined with the rotting trunks of ancient willows leaning drunkenly into water-filled ditches. The Decoy itself, in plan like an undershot water wheel with netted funnel-shaped tributaries leading off the main central pond, is now owned by the Peakirk Wild Fowl Trust.

Newborough itself did not exist when the first edition of the one-inch Ordnance Survey map was printed in 1824; it is an early-nineteenth-century colonial settlement on the fen (Plate 46). It is now approached by straight causewayed roads across the treeless fen. The houses are laid out in neat blocks like their model counterparts in 'Monopoly'; yellow brick facing, pink and orange brick behind; iron rods and stays betray the soggy and insecure foundations. The queer little neo-Gothic church with a castellated tower and large lancets was built to serve the new parish which was created in 1830 (Plate 47). The commissioners of 1812 had ordered that a new church was to be built at the expense of the proprietors.

New farmsteads

We have seen that the basic settlement pattern of nucleated villages every mile or two, distributed uniformly throughout the county except in the areas of forest and fen, was established before the Norman Conquest. Little change in this pattern took place during the next 700 years; a few villages, about forty in number, were added before the mid-fourteenth century, and about eighty went out of existence and became deserted before the beginning of the nineteenth century. With the increased momentum of the parliamentary enclosure acts towards the end of the eighteenth century a new element appeared which began to alter the distribution of rural settlement within the county. This was the outlying farmstead.

Pitt had noted that farmhouses in the county "are very generally most inconveniently placed: instead of being in the middle of the farm or occupation, they are, almost universally, pent up in villages, and are, consequently, either on one side of the farm or totally detached and off from it".[21] Bearn writing fifty years later reckoned that "in some villages you will not see a good farm homestead; the houses are low, with small barns and stabling, ill contrived yards, with miserable accommodation for cattle and pigs; all the buildings covered with thatch, and often very dilapidated".

Nevertheless, from the late eighteenth century there was a movement afoot to build farms on the outskirts of the newly enclosed fields of townships. The double advantage was that here they could be constructed on more spacious and convenient plans, and they were sited in the centre of the fields they served. Bearn records the construction of "lodge farms", many of them the property of the occupier, "who has erected some convenient outbuildings, to which is attached a comfortable residence; some of them may be

[21] W. Pitt, *General View*, p. 25.

ranked among the most commodious and pleasant occupations in the county, being often situated on the side or top of a hill, and commanding a wide and beautiful prospect".[22]

The exact year of their building is sometimes seen in date stones; more often an approximate date must be derived from map evidence. Eayre's map of 1779, for instance, shows the nucleated village of Pytchley with no outlying settlements in the township. By the time the surveyors for the first Ordnance map came round (1817), Pytchley Lodge East, Pytchley Grange and a cottage on the site of Spencer Lodge had been built. Pytchley Lodge, now known as Top Lodge, is mentioned in an 1808 indenture as "lately erected and built by John Brown and John Cole". In the next twenty years further improvements and extensions were made and a dwelling house was built at Spencer Lodge; barns and stables were added on the north and west round a stock yard and a cart hovel lined the straight enclosure road which had been driven out from the crossroads connecting the Broughton–Orlingbury road with the Pytchley–Walgrave road. This cart hovel is a replica of the one at Sywell Lodge Farm, both built by the Overstone estate in the second half of the nineteenth century.

This reminds us that the great estates were responsible for much development in rural housing and improvement in farm building in the Victorian age. Immediately on the right of the road, as one passes under the impressive bridge built by Stephenson for the London–Birmingham railway at Blisworth, is a well-built double-fronted Victorian house in ironstone. This was put up under the management of the Duke of Grafton's agent, John Gardner, as is recorded in his disbursements for "*erecting a new Double cottage at the railway station, Blisworth and 4 New Houses and Farm buildings at Charlock (Farm) Abthorpe, Caswell, Burcote, Greens Norton and Seywell*" [sic].[23] These model farms built in 1839–44 are

[22] W. Bearn, *Prize Essay*, p. 43.
[23] Account Book in the *Grafton Papers*, N.R.O. G 3901.

Plate 28 Geddington, 1717. A map by John Booth, surveyor, in the Duke of Buccleuch's collection, Boughton House. The village is on the edge of Geddington Chase in Rockingham forest—hence the large enclosures at the expense of the woodland, top right. Castle Close, centre, is the site of the royal hunting lodge north of the church which has Saxon masonry. The triangular space in the centre of the village street has the Eleanor Cross set up by Edward I in the 1290s. The meadows on either side of the river Ise are enclosed, but the three great open fields, with many of their furlong blocks showing a pronounced aratral curve, are still there.

Plate 29 Barnwell. Another map from the Duke of Buccleuch's collection. These Nene valley pastures have been completely enclosed by the early eighteenth century. Notice the recurring field name 'ground'—a large upland grazing field.

Plate 30 Boughton Park. The remnants of John, 2nd Duke of Montagu's seventy miles of elm avenues criss-cross the Buccleuch estate with its untouched villages of Warkton, Weekley and Grafton Underwood. In the centre is the 'Versailles of the Midlands': Boughton House. Vestiges of huge seventeenth-century formal gardens and canals are seen to the left of the house. Between them and the smoke clouds of the iron and steel town of Corby remain considerable tracts of Rockingham forest.

singular because of their rational and formal layout: the three-bay houses and lower wings continuing in line or recessed or at right-angles, have low slate roofs; the farm buildings are grouped in a planned relationship to them. The Althorp estate also erected substantial gabled neo-Tudor housing dated 1848 at Church Brampton, Chapel Brampton and Harlestone.[24] Lady Carbery, a little before 1800, had rebuilt the village of Laxton and raised pairs of gabled stone cottages, with bargeboards which Pitt considered "both comfortable and ornamental", a great improvement on tenements built with mud and covered with thatch. He welcomed "a display of neat and decent cottages, built with economy, but with lasting materials".

Country houses, parks, hunting

The enterprise shown in agriculture brought prosperity to the great landed families, and was reflected in their ambitious programmes for rebuilding and enlarging many of their country houses. Much has been written about these houses and their place in the mainstream of national architecture is well known. Their setting in the landscape which was often altered to receive them has been less studied.

Sir Edward Montagu, Lord Chief Justice in Henry VIII's reign, purchased an estate at Boughton in 1528 and altered the late-medieval house, whose grounds stood over the site of the deserted medieval village. This Tudor complex surrounds three courts and is masked by the magnificent north façade added by Ralph, first Duke of Montagu (1683–1709). He had been Charles II's ambassador to France and "Here it was that his Grace found his Ideas in his own mind, both of Buildings and Gardening."[25] The influence of St Cloud and Versailles is still strong on the landscape. Ralph

[24] N. Pevsner, *Buildings of England, Northamptonshire* (1961), pp. 63, 65.
[25] J. Cornforth, 'Boughton House, Northamptonshire', *Country Life*, 3rd, 10th, 17th September, 1970; 28th February, 4th, 11th March, 1971.

Montagu employed a Dutch gardener called Leonard Van de Meulen to create his formalised layout of canals, fountains and parterres to the west and north of the house. The highest pool to the south of the house, which is still there, provided the head of water piped to the four fountains in the parterre which Stukeley shows in a drawing of 1706. Another source of water was the Grand Étang, now seen in outline to the north-east of the house, and a stream was canalised to frame the west end of the parterre, finally supplying the cascade before resuming its normal course. John, the second Duke, modified the layout from 1720 onwards, adding a great court and a large pond in the place of the parterres and fountains. He also added a network of elm avenues and rides which intersect and border the estate, reputedly of the same mileage as separates Kettering from London (Plate 30). Although the bomber aerodrome of Grafton Underwood made inroads into John the Planter's elm avenues in the Second World War, they are still a distinctive feature of the landscape as soon as one leaves Kettering along the Stamford road.

On an equally magnificent scale were Capability Brown's alterations and additions to the buildings and grounds of Burghley.[26] He began shortly after 1756 and designed the stables, greenhouse and bathhouse. The principal part of the house, facing north, had been approached round a large pond which Brown filled up and replaced with turf. He swept away the endless array of straight alleys and avenues shown on an estate map of 1735 and completely remodelled the grounds of the park. The countryside came right up to the house. Four acres of kitchen garden discreetly screened by trees were added. Small groups were planted near the house which was encircled by *hahas* (sunken ditches providing a barrier to cattle but not interrupting the vista). A thirty-two-acre lake was created south of the house with a handsome stone bridge spanning it, and plantations of

[26] D. Stroud, *Capability Brown* (London, 1957), pp. 51–52.

beech, fir and chestnut were set in more distant parts of the seven-mile enceinte of the park.

A similar revolution was accomplished in the grounds of Castle Ashby. Here were seventeenth-century formal gardens lying to the east of the house and four avenues radiating to the four points of the compass. Brown made a contract in 1761 with Charles, seventh Earl of Northampton, for extensive alterations. These were carried out in the next few years and included the removal of the north and west avenues. The southern one, which leads to Yardley Chase, was retained, but the eastern one was broken into groups of trees. A series of small ponds at the foot of the hill was changed into the Park Pond and the Menagerie Pond. Across the latter, the plantation walk was carried by a delicate iron-balustraded bridge. As at Burghley, only a haha bounds the gardens so that there was an uninterrupted sweep of lawn down to the edge of the lake. Brown retained many of the ancient oaks in the park and planted chiefly chestnut and beech, with cedars at intervals to provide contrasting foliage.[27]

The aristocratic impact on the Georgian landscape was not confined to buildings and parks. Horse-racing was mentioned in the diary of Thomas Isham as taking place at Harleston, Rothwell and Irthlingborough in Charles II's reign, but it is curious that there is only one mention of fox-hunting and that not in Northamptonshire, but in Buckinghamshire.[28] Nevertheless, we know that from the early years of the eighteenth century it was customary among Northamptonshire squires to keep a few hounds and unite them to form a pack to hunt over their estates. Kennels were built at Deene by 1710 and Lord Cardigan had a hunters' stable as well as a coach-horse stable here in 1725. With the process of enclosure, hunting became more difficult since it

[27] D. Stroud, *Capability Brown*, pp. 72–74.
[28] G. Isham (ed.), *The Diary of Thomas Isham of Lamport* (London, 1971), p. 30.

demanded more skill in jumping.[29] Sir Charles Knightley, who was master of the Pytchley in 1818–19, used to say that "it was the duty of every man to take care of his health for the sake of riding to hounds". 'Sir Charles' Leap', a large hedge and brook on the left of the road leading from Brixworth station to Creaton, used to be pointed out.

There were three main hunts operating in the county in the nineteenth century. The Pytchley covered Rockingham forest, the deep pastures separated by large ox-fences near Market Harborough, the large grass fields and double hedgerows of Fawsley and the smaller arable fields near Northampton. To the south was the Grafton country, consisting of Whittlewood and Salcey forest and the area round Towcester; it included tracts of thick wood, deep grass, light plough and many large fences. The Fitzwilliam ran from Stamford to Huntingdon from the Welland to the Nene north of the Pytchley.

One has only to read extracts from the hunt diaries of the time to realise that the aristocracy and gentry adapted the landscape to their sporting requirements. Sir Justinian Isham recorded on 4th August, 1718: "This year being remarkable for an early Harvest, we were a Hunting in ye open field."[30] What was required was plenty of spinneys and gorse coverts where foxes could breed. Lord Fitzwilliam recorded, 9th November, 1789:

Threw off at Ashton Wold, found many foxes, ran well in covert $\frac{1}{2}$ of an hour; went off at the Polbrook Corner to Kingsthorp Coppice, ran very hard to the further corner of the Coppice, . . . then bore back downwind into the Hemmington inclosures, and through the back of the village and past the farm house, and through the elm nursery, then crossed the inclosures and past the patch of

[29] *Letters of Daniel Eaton*, pp. xlvii, xlix.
[30] *Architectural Societies Reports and Papers*, Vol. XXIX (1907–8), p. 97.

furze in the open field, and then again into Ashton Wold (always going upon a tolerable scent) killed in five minutes after it.[31]

With the enclosure of heaths and commons the area of natural gorse cover where foxes could hide and breed diminished. Coverts and spinneys were therefore deliberately planted by hunting landlords in order to encourage foxes and to distribute them more evenly across the county. In the Pytchley country many of the coverts are of moderate size, not less than two acres and rarely more than twenty. The oldest artificial covert in Northamptonshire was planted in Yelvertoft field by Lord Spencer and called after him. Crick covert dates from 1817 and Waterloo covert was planted at the same time and named after the battlefield. Blue covert had a military origin, being planted by the Regiment of Blues when they were stationed in Northampton. A covert was established near Church Brampton in 1854 by Lord Spencer who wished to call it 'Balaklava', but this was not a popular name and it has always been known as Sanders Gorse.[32]

These artificial coverts can be distinguished from ancient woodland by their small size, regular shape and the fact that they are usually tucked into odd pieces of commonland. They are particularly noticeable as patches of green on the one-inch Ordnance Survey map in the largely open upland country between Northampton and Market Harborough.

The aristocratic influence on the Georgian and Victorian countryside was deep. At times concern for agricultural improvement allied to domestic opulence was seasoned by a dash of downright eccentricity. At Lilford, for instance, the medieval church which stood a short distance to the southeast of the hall, was taken down by the fourth Thomas Powys of Lilford in 1778. Three arches from the nave

[31] Quoted in *V.C.H. Northants.*, Vol. II, p. 373.
[32] *V.C.H. Northants.*, Vol. II, pp. 368, 369.

arcade were set up in the Lynch below Achurch. The second Earl of Strafford, a friend of Horace Walpole, spent his time in the 1760s and 1770s building medieval follies round his house at Boughton Park near Northampton. A gate lodge known as the Hawking Tower, an obelisk erected in 1764, a heavily castellated Bunkers Hill Farm, several triumphal arches and a gatehouse called the Spectacles are among his gothic follies. As the motorist grinds to a halt at the Finedon crossroads and regards the road ahead with its rash of red-brick terrace houses on either side, he will spy a remarkable pyramidal obelisk with directions and mileages recorded on it. An entry in Sir English Dolben's diary runs thus: "This day I laid the first stone of the Fineden obelisk, at the cross turn pikes East Town End (Sumpter of Irthlingborough, mason) as a Direction Pillar and to record the many blessings of 1789." An odder folly, to be seen not more than two miles away on the Thrapston road, is a circular building, reminding one of a martello tower, raised to commemorate the battle of Waterloo. The story goes that Wellington, staying as a guest at Woodford House and surveying the landscape looking south from the Thrapston road across the Nene valley, remarked that it reminded him of the field of Waterloo. Perhaps the most unusual monument is the little classical pillar in the fields near the great house of Stanford Hall. It records that in these grounds P. S. Pilcher did his flying experiments in the 1890s and was killed in 1899.

8. Georgian and Victorian landscapes: communications and towns

Drove roads and turnpikes. Improvements in river navigation and canals. Railways. Victorian townscapes

Drove roads and turnpikes

THE MEDIEVAL ROAD system of the Midlands was subjected to increasing strains during the Tudor and Stuart periods. The practice of driving large numbers of animals along the drove roads was one of the greatest destructive factors. It dates back to the fourteenth century but the heyday of driving cattle and sheep from Wales and Scotland into England was from the seventeenth to the mid-nineteenth century. The railways put paid to it. A droving track is easily recognisable; animals moving in parallel lines made a number of adjacent paths covering a breadth of sixty to ninety feet; these would be avoided by successive drovers who chose new ground to bypass that already cut up. The mark of such a track on the modern landscape is wide grass verges bordering the narrow macadamised road surface: at times the drove road peters out into a green lane, or simply becomes a grassy corrugation across open country.

Northamptonshire was bisected by two main drovers' routes. It seems that the Welsh drovers crossed Warwickshire in a south-easterly direction to Southam, where on both sides of the town the road is known as the Welsh Road. From Southam the *Welsh Way* (as Bryant marks it in his 1827 map) pursues its course through Priors Hardwick into the county at Upper Boddington, where there was a *Welsh*

Road Barn (marked on the 1834 edition of the one-inch Ordnance Survey map) one mile north of the village. Between Aston Le Walls and Culworth it runs between furlong blocks of ridge-and-furrow bounded by broad grass verges. It crosses the Banbury lane at Culworth and heading for the important market town of Buckingham, passes through Sulgrave, Syresham and Biddlesden.

Both English and Welsh drovers used this route. Mr Richardson, the tutor of Thomas Isham, wrote to Sir Thomas to say that John Chapman "has bought 50 beasts from Wales and will go to York for more, after he has been to London".[1] An entry dating from 1687 in the Helmdon Parish Constables' Accounts records a sum "Given to a poor Welshman who fell sick on his journey driving beasts to London". There are still memories alive in villages in the south of the county such as at Vine Cottage, Syresham, where the loft was used as a resting place for drovers on the Welsh lane, and a field known as *The Meadow* on the Stuchbury Road, south of Sulgrave, was used to keep sheep which were being driven from Wales to be sold to local farmers.

The second drovers' road which is still a pronounced feature on the landscape is the *Banbury Lane,* the prehistoric route running for twenty-two miles between Banbury and Northampton. Drovers from mid-Wales would join it at the famous Rollright Stones near Chipping Norton. It can be clearly followed in the eighteenth-century maps and in the modern road systems all the way from Banbury to Northampton. For the first three miles it is part of the A422 to Brackley. It then becomes the B4525 to Thorpe Mandeville; between Middleton Cheney and Chacombe it serves as the parish boundary; then turns into a narrow grassy lane to Culworth where it meets the Welsh Road. One imagines that Culworth was a halting place since it was at the junction of two of the great drove roads of the Midlands and there is a significant market cross.

[1] G. Isham, *The Diary of Thomas Isham,* p. 21.

This second drovers' road passes over the London and North Eastern railway half a mile east of Barrow Hill (where a tumulus rises ten feet from the road on the top of the hill) and becomes a green lane as it leads north-eastwards. Its extreme antiquity is marked by the fact that it serves as the parish boundary for four miles between Culworth and Adstone and it keeps to the ridge, where its sweeping linear route (dotted with barrows and earthworks) contrasts with the twisting course of the lanes connecting the villages of Culworth, Moreton Pinkney, and Canons Ashby. Then it continues as a minor road to Foster's Booth where it crosses the A5, Watling Street. The grass verges and the surface add up to a total width of between sixty and seventy-five feet. It crosses the Grand Union Canal, goes on through Rothersthorpe, over the M1 and degenerates into a muddy lane for the last mile of its course to reach Hunsbury Hill, the Pre-Roman Iron Age fort on the south-western outskirts of Northampton. There may well have been a large cattle enclosure here. What is certain is that during the springs and summers in the period 1650 to 1850 cattle were sold in the districts round Northampton. As Pitt observed, "for fattening every sort of cattle is brought in: Staffordshire, Shropshire, Herefordshire, Pembrokes, Devon, North Wales, Scots and Irish are met with at different fairs ... and the grazier refuses no sort that looks kindly, handles well, and can be had worth the money." In the early nineteenth century 15,000 cattle were fattened in the county for London's Smithfield Market each year. In the late 1860s a 200-acre farm at Spratton was rented by a dealer for an annual sum of £400 to provide him with fields to rest his cattle after their journey from Wales. He reckoned on moving 2000 beasts each year into England.[2]

The cloven hoofs of large numbers of cattle can have

[2] For the Welsh Road I owe several references to Edward Parry of Magdalen College School, Brackley. For Banbury Lane see K. J. Bonser, *The Drovers* (London, 1970), pp. 194–5.

done the roads little good and complaints began to multiply about their poor state. Samuel Pepys was travelling through the fens and recorded in his diary for 18th September, 1663: "I began a journey through the fens along dikes where sometimes we were ready to have our horses sunk to the belly. We got by night with hard riding to Parsons Drove, a heathen place."[3] Daniel Eaton, writing from Deene in 1725, said: "The roads here are so very bad that I fear we shall not get pit coal at any rate" (this came from Leicestershire and Warwickshire). Two weeks later: "The Surveyor of the roads could not come in a wors time, for they are very bad."[4]

There was in fact a great increase of travellers and freight in the eighteenth century. "The highways . . . have been chiefly spoiled by the Great Number of Carriages and Waggons which are continually passing through the same with heavy Burthens and tearing up the roads." These remarks were among the arguments put forward for a turnpike act for repairing the highways from Brampton Bridge to Welford in 1720. It was realised that the packhorse was being superseded and road surfaces were now imperilled by wheeled traffic, especially since "most part of the soil where the Said Roads lie, consists of clay, and is of such a swampy nature, that it doth suck up all stones cast into them".

A bridge dating from the packhorse era has recently been preserved and restored at Bugbrooke, just south of the church a little upstream. An old sunken trackway leads to it from north of the village; it is of clapper construction and originally consisted of three central slabs of stone resting on piers built of stone.

The first turnpike trust set up to improve roads in the county was that between Old Stratford and Dunchurch in Warwickshire in 1706. During the next 120 years, thirty-six Acts were passed providing the county (including the Soke

---

[3] Quoted in *Fenland Notes and Queries*, Vol. IV (1898–1900), p. 217.
[4] *Letters of Daniel Eaton*, pp. 19, 20, 23.

of Peterborough) with 356 miles 3 furlongs of turnpiked roads, a percentage of 17·5 of the complete network.[5] The last road to be turnpiked was that running from Northampton to Cold Brafield on the way to Bedford in 1826.

The pressure for road improvement came from landowners, nobility and gentry, farmers and merchants. Their names head the subscription lists. The Duchess of Buccleuch, Earl Spencer and Lord Sondes put up £1100 between them for the Kettering–Northampton turnpike scheme of 1819. Among those taking £100 shares was the Kettering shoemaker and entrepreneur John Cooper Gotch who lived in Chesham House, Kettering, a fine eighteenth-century town house, recently saved from destruction by the Kettering Civic Society. Perhaps the most vociferous supporters of further tollhouses on new stretches were other turnpike trustees who clamoured against so-called 'elopers' who avoided tolls by using other routes to short circuit the tollgates. The Act of 1753 to improve the road from Oundle through Barnwell to Alconbury is a case in point. The turnpike trustees of roads from Royston to Wansford bridge and from Market Harborough to Brampton pound were joined in their promotion of this Act by the inhabitants of Oundle and Barnwell. They alleged that it had been the custom for many years "for large droves of beasts, wool waggons and other carriages" to avoid the tollgates on the Royston road by travelling via Oundle, Hamerton, etc. Travellers were hindered by the cutting up of the road by these 'elopers'; farmers were unable to get their grain to market; cornfields and grazing lands were trespassed upon by people forced off the track. The Rev. William Robinson gave evidence that he had given certificates for nearly 20,000 head of cattle a year to be driven on the road by Oundle, cattle which appeared to have come from Stamford. Wool wagons had done the same thing to avoid tolls at

[5] A. Cossons, 'The Turnpike Roads of Northamptonshire', *Northants. Past and Present*, Vol. I, 3 (1950), pp. 28–45.

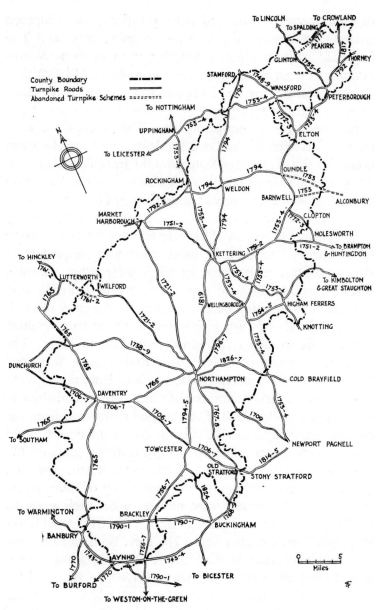

Fig. 18. Turnpike roads of Northamptonshire in 1827

Redrawn from a sketch map in 'Milestones', Northants. Record Office
Archive Teaching Unit, Folder 2.

Godmanchester. It took seven hours for a journey which ought to have taken four. The Act was pushed through.

The subject of these complaints is frequently seen in pictures of the eighteenth-century landscape. Rutted roads of indeterminate breadth weaving their way across unfenced open-field country appear in the Eayre-Tillemans drawings. A turnpiked road would be laned if for no other reason than to make it difficult to cut across country to avoid the tollhouse. Turnpikes opened up some stretches of Northamptonshire not previously provided with roads. A noteworthy example is the Northampton–Kettering turnpike, 1819. Thomas Marshall described the space between the towns as "in the very centre of England, about ten miles in length and eight in breadth, altogether destitute of turnpike roads; this tract including more than twenty villages, which at present communicate only by cross roads that are impassable in winter and at best seasons are unfit for heavy carriages". The new road cut the journey from Northampton to Stamford by five miles in avoiding the circuitous route through Wellingborough, Thrapston and Oundle. It was regretted that its course would not include the villages of Moulton, Holcot and Walgrave. The modern motorist blesses the turnpike trustees for their decision which has resulted in eight miles of trunk road uninterrupted by villages. For most of its length it has the original broad grass verges and tree plantings, now 150 years old. At intervals are earlynineteenth-century brick farms such as Tea Caddy Farm and The Old Red House (now an inn), distinctive elements in the turnpiked roadscape. For the southern half from Broughton Common to Buttocks Booth,[6] the A43 keeps

[6] Recently renamed Boothville in an excess of hypocritical euphemism. Cf. Northampton Cow Meadow renamed Beckets Park allegedly at the instance of the Cow Meadow Ladies' Bowling Club, embarrassed at the bovine connotations of their Society. Also cf. Pisford (spelt as such on map accompanying Morton's *Natural History* and 1777 Militia list) has been bowdlerised into Pitsford; and Shitlanger (*Report of the committee appointed to inspect and consider the Returns made by the Overseers of the Poor*, 1787) has become Shutlanger.

to the course of the prehistoric trackway known as the Jurassic Way.

Tollhouses were built at strategic points to catch traffic. I remember visiting the old lady who lived in the charming grey stone octagonal tollhouse on the hill above Islip on the Wellingborough–Peterborough turnpike of 1753–4. Her grandfather was the last tollkeeper a hundred years before; he used to sit in the projecting porch from which he could espy traffic approaching in both directions. This tollhouse was unnecessarily swept away in January 1969. Only too often road widenings have resulted in their destruction. A water-colour in the saddler's shop in Oundle is the only record of the tollhouse and gate originally situated at Barnwell Mill. Another still survives at Staverton on the former Northampton to Warwick turnpike of 1765 which went via Southam and Daventry.

Some road improvements were the result of the whims of individual landowners. The present course of the A43 between Blisworth and Towcester veers to the west to skirt the grounds of Easton Neston Park. The map accompanying Bridges' History, however, shows it going due south at this point pursuing the course now marked on the two-and-a-half-inch Ordnance Survey map as Old Road Spinney. It wound through the village of Hulcote, past Easton Neston House and so through the park to the present bridge crossing. It was diverted to the west to keep it outside the park wall in the late eighteenth century and had incidentally been straightened and planted with an avenue of trees, shown on the first edition of the one-inch Ordnance Survey map.[7] Hulcote itself was rebuilt by the Hesketh family as an estate village. The houses are all in red brick in a pleasingly fanciful Neo-Gothic style and nestle engagingly round the green.

Despite the improvements, turnpike roads were still

[7] George Freeston of Blisworth in a lecture given to the Kettering Civic Society, March 1972.

heavily criticised. Charles Dibdin in *Observations on a Tour in England* described the Kettering–Market Harborough turnpike in damaging terms: "The danger from this abominable road is the prodigious depths of some of its ruts, which might be remedied with very little labour, for the bottom is perfectly sound." In the space of eleven miles his family and servants had to get out and walk five "over a road the caricature of ploughed ground".[8]

The greatest strides in the technical side of roadmaking were made between 1810 and 1830 and the work of J. L. Macadam and T. Telford made possible the coaching age. Northamptonshire has a fine stretch of Watling Street which was improved by Telford when that great engineer was given the important task of re-grading and re-aligning the route followed by the Irish Mails from Holyhead to London. Most of the work involved embankments across valleys, cuttings through hills and short circuiting of curves. Long stretches were improved at Old Stratford, the Gullet Hills between Potterspury and Paulerspury; Cuttle Mill near Towcester, between Towcester and Fosters' Booth, Stowe Hills and Braunston. In search of easier gradients, Telford occasionally left the route of the Roman road which still carried on as a green lane along the straighter alignment. He paid meticulous attention to detail. He placed little roadside recesses, four to a mile, to hold repair materials. He designed the triangular-headed mile markers of Welsh granite with a cast-iron inset; one recording the seventy-one miles to London and eleven miles to Towcester may be seen just outside Daventry.

The effect of these improvements was a great advance in terms of traffic speed. Mail coach timetables demonstrate this. The average speed for the London–Northampton run was improved from 7·11 mph in 1811 to 9·92 in 1837. Several towns still have plenty of signs of the enlivening effects of the coaching age. Towcester for instance, strung out along

[8] Quoted in Tony Ireson, *Northamptonshire* (London, 1954), pp. 204–5.

Watling Street, a Roman foundation, an Anglo-Saxon burh and a medieval market town, was well placed as a posting station in the seventeenth-century road system. The fine three-storey post office dated 1799, the Talbot Hotel of 1707 and the Saracen's Head Hotel, famous from *The Pickwick Papers,* survive from the coaching era, and there is a good deal of late Georgian town housing on both sides of Watling Street, evidence of the prosperity. Daventry was also a medieval market town and at the junction of four main routes, to Northampton, Oxford, Coventry and London. It was a centre for the unusual industry of whip-making but this declined with the disappearance of the horsedrawn coach.

Up to eighty coaches per day passed through Daventry at the most successful period of coaching travel; they stopped at the Wheatsheaf Hotel and the Saracen's Head (1769). The monumental church, 1732-8, with obelisk spire crowning a broad west front with giant pilasters at the angles completes the impression of Georgian affluence. The High Street of the little town preserves a good deal of its Georgian flavour, recently refurbished by an excellent street improvement scheme, jointly sponsored by the County Council and City of Birmingham who are responsible for planning expansion of the town from 4000 to 48,000 in the next forty years.

Northampton was the travelling centre *par excellence* because it lay at the junction of main routes from the north and west towards London. Consequently it became the greatest horse market in England, and it seems clear that in the eighteenth century there were about sixty inns in the town. These in turn were served by at least 250 people and encouraged the growth of the local coachmaking industry, supported by the presence of saddlers, harness makers and other users of horse hide.[9] There is still a certain Hanoverian

[9] A. Everitt, *Ways and Means in Local History*, National Council of Social Service (1971), pp. 30–31.

Plate 31 Burton Latimer. A single schoolroom measuring forty-four feet by sixteen, bearing the inscription: "This house was built in 1622. The Freeschoole was founded by Thomas Burbanke and Margaret his wife 1587." The names of those who financed the building are carved on the window lintels.

Plate 32 Ashby St Ledgers. A nineteenth-century terrace of farm labourers' cottages. Ironstone rubble, steep-pitched thatched roofs, one up, one down. An estate village.

Plate 33 Watford. The flight of locks which carries the Grand Union Canal through the Watford Gap from Northamptonshire towards Leicester. To avoid a deep cutting and a short tunnel the company had to pay Mrs Bennett of Watford £2000 and £125 per acre for the land they needed. She also demanded (and got) a pleasure boat on the summit level and a say in the appointment of a lock-keeper, whose blue-slated and white-walled cottage is seen on the sky-line.

Plate 34 Weedon barracks. The connecting arm of the Grand Junction Canal enters the cupola-crowned yellow brick fortress gateway under an iron swing bridge and a portcullis, Traitors' Gate pattern.

flavour of a 'county capital' about Northampton; its large and elegant houses which were built in the hundred years following the great fire of 1676 have not been entirely swallowed in the largely tasteless or brutal recent developments.

Improvements in river navigation and canals

Daniel Eaton wrote from Deene in 1725: "As soon as the roads are better, I shall order the sea coal to be brought in by the boon teams." He was referring to the fact that it was cheaper to buy coal which had been shipped by sea from Northumberland and up the river Nene, than pit coal which had to be brought the forty miles by road from pits in Leicestershire or Warwickshire. Since water transport offered such advantages it is not surprising to find that attempts were made to improve the Nene navigation early in the eighteenth century. Acts were passed in 1714 and 1724 to make the river navigable from Peterborough to Northampton. The work had proceeded sufficiently far by 1729 for Lord Cardigan to build his own private wharf at Cotterstock. It was claimed that the construction of the navigation from Thrapston to Northampton would reduce the freight costs of coal from twelve shillings per chaldron to six and eightpence and also that the new route could be used at all times in the year.[10] A number of important local landowners came forward with offers to help. Nunmill lock was given by John Spencer, Rushmill lock by Sir James Langham of Cottesbrooke, Abington lock by Frederick Montagu. Commemorative stones record their munificence which seems to have been partly motivated by a desire to emulate one another in political rivalry for control of the borough representation of Northampton in Parliament.[11] Altogether there were thirty-four locks and twelve staunches

---

[10] *A scheme submitted to the Publick, for bringing the Navigation from Thrapston to Northampton.*

[11] *Minutes of the Commissioners of the Nene Navigation,* 27.4.58; 2.8.60; 8.7.61. Oundle-Nene Catchment Board.

R

or flashlocks. Whereas a pound lock has two sets of gates to pass boats from one level of a waterway, a staunch has but one. The gates normally stood open and only when it was desired to raise the river to pass traffic through were they closed so that the water level could build up. They were all rebuilt in the 1830s by Thomas Atkinson of Peterborough whose initials may be seen on datestones at Perio and Wansford. In 1936–41 the Nene Catchment Board modernised the navigation and eliminated seven of the staunches by deepening the sills of the locks upstream and three were converted into locks.[12]

The official opening of the Nene Navigation took place on 7th August, 1761, at Northampton, when it was declared that traffic could pass from Northampton to King's Lynn. Thirty-seven years later William Pitt reckoned that the navigation of the river was defective and he cited the lack of commerce at Northampton to prove his point: "At the wharfs not a single vessel loading or unloading; a crane stands solitary, and not the least stir of business: a small deposit of coals and a few deals comprize all the visible articles of commerce." Although the reports of the river Nene commissioners do not confirm this dismal account, it is true that the river was being used for a multiplicity of purposes, turning mills, watering meadows *and* navigation. There were at least forty-three watermills along its main stream from the source near Newham as far as Peterborough.[13] Thomas Eayre's 1779 map shows a mill at Billing and the waterwheel and machinery were renewed during the nineteenth century. It was worked up until the Second World War and has recently been restored, being opened in 1968 as a corn-milling museum.

There are only two corn mills working on the Nene in

[12] M. J. T. Lewis, W. N. Slatcher, P. N. Jarvis, 'Flashlocks in English Waterways: a survey', *Industrial Archaeology*, Vol. 6, No. 3 (August 1969).
[13] G. H. Starmer, 'A Check List of Northamptonshire Wind and Water Mills', *Bulletin of Industrial Archaeology in C.B.A. 9*, No. 12 (April 1970).

1972, Whitworths' at Wellingborough and Heygates' at Bugbrooke. The huge concrete rectangular silos of Bugbrooke mill introduce a prairie-like feature to the watermeadows of the middle Nene. There were two mills worth forty shillings (which was a good deal more than most) in 1086. Timber beams set in puddled clay found during reconstruction have been dated to *c.* A.D. 800. The buildings now straddling the Nene include the humble eighteenth-century miller's house at the eastern end. To this was attached a substantial two-bay ironstone house dated 1866. A rubble building containing the remains of the nineteenth-century waterwheel spans the race; to the west is a brick addition of 1941–2 built after a fire. Further silos, dated 1948, 1950 and 1962, and each out-topping its predecessors, were placed on the filled-in course of the Nene which has now been diverted through a new cut to the west of the complex. During the nineteenth century the output of the water-driven machinery was a ton of flour a day. With turbine machinery the scale has increased phenomenally and 120 tons of wheaten flour and 100 tons of animal feeding stuff are now produced per day.

This kind of development has meant that the other forty or so mills have now ceased working. Fieldwork is badly needed to record their sites, to work out the chronology of their structures and to trace the considerable earthworks which compose their embanked leats and drains.

The communications problem was eased for a time by the construction of navigable canals "in different directions, through the county, for the conveyance of vessels of heavy burthen; in the execution of which, hills and valleys are equally disregarded; the one can be perforated and the other filled up".[14] First in order of construction was the Oxford Canal, authorised by an Act of 1769 between the Coventry Canal at Longford and the River Thames at Oxford; it opened in 1790 a route between London and the

[14] W. Pitt, *General View*, p. 233.

Midlands. The Grand Junction Canal was authorised in 1793 to link the River Thames at Brentford with the Oxford Canal at Braunston and thus shorten the route between Birmingham and London. After considerable difficulties encountered in tunnelling at Blisworth the canal was finally opened along its whole length in 1805. A branch was extended from Blisworth Junction to Northampton in 1815. The Grand Union was authorised by an Act of 1810, "its object being to unite the navigation of the Trent and Soar with that of the Grand Junction and Nen"; it opened in 1814 from Norton Junction on the Grand Junction Canal to Foxton, on what was then the Leicestershire and Northamptonshire Union Canal. The Welford arm from a junction near North Kilworth was opened in November of that year. The Old Grand Union Canal was bought by the Grand Junction Canal Company in 1894 and this became the New Grand Union Canal Company in 1929. Finally in 1947 inland waterways were nationalised and the British Waterways Board succeeded in 1963.[15]

Because the county straddles the Jurassic limestone ridge which runs across the county from Yorkshire to Dorset, it was inevitable that the Grand Junction, designed to link Birmingham and London, would need to cut or bore its way through the uplands round Braunston and Blisworth. With the Cornish banker William Praed as promoter, supported by the Marquess of Buckingham, the Duke of Grafton and Earl Spencer on the board, the company employed William Jessop in charge of construction and James Barnes as resident engineer. At Braunston, quicksands caused difficulty and the contractor made a mistake in the direction—persons travelling through the tunnel notice the slight S bend to it. It was opened to Weedon Bec in June 1796 and soon afterwards extended to Blisworth. They encountered considerable difficulties, including excessive water and poor materials, when they came to bore through Blisworth hill

[15] Charles Hadfield, *The Canals of the East Midlands* (Newton Abbot, 1970).

260

and in March 1797 decided to stop work on the tunnel and finish the rest of the canal.

To begin with they built a toll road over the hill to connect the two completed sections of canal, and this was replaced by Northamptonshire's first railway, engineered by Benjamin Outram in 1800.[16] Coal, pig iron, stone, bricks, slates, timber, lime, salt and manufactured goods were hauled up the embanked double tramroad between Blisworth and Stoke Bruerne. The track bed is still visible in the fields and many of the stone sleeper blocks remain. Pieces of rail carrying the initials G. J. (Grand Junction) have been found in old cottages at Blisworth where they had formed the support for fireplace arches. When the tunnel was finally driven through, the railway was taken up and its materials were probably used for the temporary link between Gayton Wharf and Northampton opened in 1805 and lasting ten years. Leggers propelled the boats through the tunnel by lying horizontally on the thwarts and walking them through. The hut where they picked up their candles can be seen on the left of the Blisworth entrance. The use of steam tugs which superseded them caused a bizarre accident in 1861 when two men died overcome by smoke and fumes in mid-tunnel. It caused the company to supplement the four existing ventilation shafts by a fifth; two more were added in 1881. Their grey brick cotton-reel shapes crown the ridge and fragments of early-nineteenth-century pottery and pipes, relics of the navvies, can be picked up from the adjoining grassed-over spoil heaps which demarcate the line of the tunnel between Blisworth and Stoke Bruerne.

For a few years these villages were two of the busiest inland ports in Britain. Blisworth was for a time an industrial village but has reverted to rural pursuits in the middle of this century. It had, Pitt tells us, extensive wharfage and

[16] V. A. Hatley, *Rails over Blisworth Hill*, Northampton Historical Series, No. 2, 2nd edn. (1971).

warehouses for goods, and two new inns on the canal banks. The 1847 Directory lists four: the Sun and Moon, the Navigation, the Royal Oak and the Grafton Arms. What is more interesting is Pitt's mention of 5000 or 6000 tons of coal in stacks on the wharfs. The availability of cheap supplies of coal encouraged brickworks and lime kilns and Bryant's map of 1827 shows them peppering the countryside within a mile or so of the canal in the Blisworth area. There were seven lime kilns at Blisworth, six of which were situated near the canal, two at Knock Lane, two at the north end of the tunnel and two at Blisworth Arm End. In 1821 the Duke of Grafton opened up a limestone quarry in the south-eastern corner of the parish and built Northamptonshire's third railway to carry the limestone (used as a flux for ironstone) to the canal.[17] The great quarry was closed in 1912 and the excavation was soon covered in a luxuriant growth of hawthorn, crab apple bushes and ash trees. The cutting through which the tramway ran has been largely filled in and restored to farm use but its steep gradient is still visible in the fields to the west of the northern tunnel entrance of the canal. The ironstone quarries have now been worked out; canal boats are now no longer made on the stocks; the canal echoes the shouts of summer's holiday-makers on pleasure craft but in winter Blisworth is still.

A short arm, five-eighths of a mile long, was opened in 1804 to connect the Grand Junction to Weedon barracks (Plate 34). The site was chosen as being the farthest point from any coast, the country being threatened by the Napoleonic invasion. The wharf is protected from attack by water by a portcullis and behind it were twelve powder magazines, two barracks for two regiments of the line which have now been destroyed and a Royal suite of three yellow-brick pavilions made for George III to retire to when the

[17] George Freeston discovered the existence of this railway and conducted me round it in 1969. See his *Quarry Line at Blisworth*, Northampton Historical Series, No. 2 (1971).

invasion came.[18] It is difficult to realise that the canal was a main troopship route from London to Ireland. In August 1824, for instance, a single convoy of twenty-eight boats went through with troops from Ireland. The remaining buildings of this once-great military depot are now scheduled for demolition.

The effect of routing the canal in this way was to isolate Northampton, and naturally the town agitated for a connection. When the company built a double-track tramroad, opened in 1805, most of the materials probably came from the disused Blisworth line. This was unsatisfactory, so the Northampton arm, five miles long from Gayton Junction to the junction with the river Nene at Northampton, was opened on 1st May, 1815. Church bells were rung in the town, cannon were fired, and a crowd of people gathered to watch a procession of boats make its way from Blisworth to Northampton.[19] Its course illustrates well the peculiarities and charm which canals brought to the landscape. The insatiable thirst of canal men was served by the public house, The Arm, strategically situated at Gayton Junction. The cottage of the lock-keeper with its broad-eaved blue slate roof and whitewashed brick walls stands next to the top lock of the Rothersthorpe flight of thirteen. They are all narrow, seventy-two feet by seven approximately, with double bottom gates and all single top gates: the gates are of various ages, of both wood and steel: a number date from the 1860s. The pounds are lined with the same pink brick as is used for the humped-backed bridges. The massive blocks with diagonal slots lining the banks under the bridges are re-used sleeper stones originally from the Blisworth cutting of the London–Birmingham railway. The coping stones, the pleasing curves of which lead in from the basins, are of blue brick.

[18] N. Pevsner, *Buildings of England, Northamptonshire*, p. 449.
[19] V. A. Hatley, 'Some Aspects of Northampton's History, 1815–51', *Northants. Past and Present*, Vol. III, 6, p. 243.

The canals eased the transport and distribution of coal used in firing brick, and early-nineteenth-century brick buildings are common in villages, ten miles on either side of the canals. When a farmer's land had to be cut into two, accommodation bridges were built; five of these remain of the original nine, their pivoted drawbridges seeming to come out of a Van Gogh landscape. The company was forced to fence in the towpath to protect stock from entangling with the towing lines and to protect the paved path which was originally the width of a country lane. The hawthorns, no longer cut and grown to tree size, cream with their blossoms in the June sunshine; the towpath has dwindled to a foot or so of crushed brick and ash among the grasses and the knee-high buttercups. The sites of deserted cottages can be traced from the hedgerows of their gardens at the bottom of the flight. The kink in the line of the canal at this point is the result of moving it thirty yards to the west when the Blisworth and Peterborough line came in 1843–5. The original bank of the canal can be seen on the eastern side of the railway opposite the middle lock of the flight. One warehouse remains at Cotton End, Northampton, but Pickford's warehouse at Gayton Junction has been demolished.

The line of the canal after passing Stoke Bruerne follows the Tove valley via Grafton Regis and Yardley Wharf to Cosgrove. Here it runs under a charming neo-Gothic bridge with ogival arch and is joined by the Buckingham arm. It then pursues its way south over the Ouse valley and out of the county by means of a spectacular embankment and iron aqueduct.

Railways

The coming of the railways to Northamptonshire has received some study at the hands of historians.[20] John

[20] C. A. Markham, *The Iron Roads of Northamptonshire* (Northampton, 1904).

Plate 35 Brackley. The broad market street of the medieval new town dominated by the town hall, gift of the Duke of Bridgewater, patron of the rotten borough, in 1706. The Crown Inn, an eighteenth-century coaching inn, is beyond the town hall on the left.

Plate 36 Corby New Town. A landscape in which the pedestrian reigns supreme. Notice the care taken in varying the texture of materials—wood, cobbling, brick, tile—the interest given by the broken silhouette of the buildings and the different window sizes. Maximum privacy has been gained amidst high-density housing. Planting of semi-mature trees softens the harsh angularity of the new town.

Plate 37 Northampton Market Place, *c.* 1900. One of the finest in England with "something of the character of market places in Holland or Belgium" (Pevsner). The mid-Victorian and Edwardian buildings lining the north side have now been torn down, the finest building, the Peacock Hotel, demolished to make way for a brutal and mediocre supermarket; the fine seventeenth-century houses on the left survive precariously. Recently Welsh House has been saved from rocketing development on the east side.

Plate 38 Peterborough Market Place, *c.* 1910. The Old Guildhall of 1671, with steep-lipped roof, overlooks the square which adjoins the monastic precinct to the west. Behind it is the church of St John the Baptist, originally east of the cathedral, and rebuilt on the present site 1402–7.

Plate 39 Braunston. The Anglo-Saxon village runs along a ridge of land overlooking the river Leam. The original length of the crofts on the north side is limited by the back lane which runs parallel to the main street. Ridge-and-furrow covers the landscape and is overrun by the hedgerows of early and piecemeal enclosure, north and south of the village. The 1775 enclosure award resulted in the long straight hedgelines and road going towards the top right. The Grand Union Canal cuts across medieval croft boundaries and the disused line of the Oxford Canal is seen as a dark line snaking up towards it from the bottom left. The former London and North Western railway, Weedon–Daventry line (1895), now disused, with its dramatic cuttings and embankment sweeps through the earlier features.

Plate 40 Weedon. View of the east side of the viaduct carrying Stephenson's London–Birmingham railway, October 1838. Behind to the right, the monumental barrack buildings dating from the Napoleonic War. From John C. Bourne's *Drawings of the London–Birmingham Railway*, 1839.

Plate 41 Blisworth. John C. Bourne's 'View in the deep cutting near Blisworth, looking south, with a train passing', October 1838. The cutting at this point has now been doubled in width and revetted with blue brick. Bourne's view brings out well the immense scale of the works producing this artificial gorge in the early Victorian landscape.

Clare not surprisingly resented railways and wrote in his diary:

> Saturday 4 June 1825. Saw 3 fellows at the end of Royce wood who I found were laying out the plan for an 'Iron railway' from Manchester to London, it is to cross over Round Oak Spring by Royce Wood for Woodcroft Castle. I little thought that fresh intrusions would interrupt and spoil my solitudes. After the Enclosure they will despoil a boggy place that is famous for orchises at Royce Wood end.[21]

It is likely that this entry records a meeting between Northamptonshire's rural poet and the greatest railway engineer of the age, George Stephenson, who, we know, was at this time surveying a route for the Great Northern railway. Nothing came of this for a time.

As early as 1830 a railway joining London to Birmingham was projected running parallel to Watling Street across the county. It was engineered between 1834 and 1838 by George and Robert Stephenson and brought startling changes to the landscape involving the largest earthworks to date the county had yet seen. J. C. Bourne's magnificent lithographs reconstruct the scene during the making (Plates 40 and 41).[22] Along the immense Wolverton embankment advancing over the flat water meadows of the Ouse, a minuscule train with a plume of steam brings materials which are tipped over the end. The artificial gorge of the Blisworth–Roade cutting produces a savage cut through the hedgerowed hills (Plate 41). A high embankment leads to Weedon Bec but before reaching the station the line passes over a branch of the canal leading to the barracks, only two feet above the water level. A swing bridge was fitted. This one has now

---

[21] N. Marlow, 'The Coming of Railways to Northamptonshire', *Northants. Past and Present*, Vol. III, 5 (1964), pp. 203–12. J. W. and A. Tibble (eds.), *The Prose of John Clare* (1951), p. 151.

[22] J. C. Bourne, *Drawings of the London–Birmingham Railway* (London, 1839).

been re-sited a few yards to the west and raised: the cutting is revetted with blue brick.

Robert Stephenson met his greatest difficulties in driving through the quicksands encountered in Kilsby tunnel and was held up for three years, 1835–8. After ten shafts had been sunk and repeatedly flooded and a driftway parallel with the tunnel had been submerged, he had to install thirteen beam engines, whose smoking chimneys and creaking wooden machinery were a temporary feature of the landscape while they pumped 1800 gallons a minute for nineteen months. The line in the meantime had been completed as far as Denbigh Hall where Watling Street passes under the line near Bletchley; passengers were then carried by coach to Rugby. To speed their route, experiments were carried out in road-surfacing, and between Bugbrooke turn and Weedon on the grass verge to the east of the present course of the A5 is a stretch of stone tramway. This was made of flat stones of granite laid in two gutters 3 feet 11½ inches apart, and were designed to reduce resistance to the wheels of coaches and heavy waggons in the uphill pull. The cobbles in between helped horse traffic to gain a footing.

The railways wrought powerful effects on the countryside. Other means of communication shrivelled and died. No longer were cattle driven by road to London; the railway truck largely took over, giving both quicker and less wearing transport. The coming of the railways quickly killed coach traffic and for more than half a century Thomas Telford's great London to Holyhead road fell silent. Turnpike road trusts fell on hard times. The income of some continued to rise for some years where their roads acted as feeders to the railway stations. The decline for most was marked and irreversible. Within the five years 1834 to 1839 the income on the Old Stratford–Dunchurch stretch plummeted 54·2 per cent from £5894 to £2702; the tolls on the Northampton to Newport Pagnell stretch declined by 33·5 per cent from £2260 to £1505.

Cuttings and embankments carrying the lines were the greatest earthworks made by man in the Northamptonshire landscape since hill forts were thrown up in the Pre-Roman Iron Age. Views were blocked and raw wounds were carved in fields and woodlands. The multi-arched viaducts which take the Great Northern line over the river Ouse at Brackley and the eighty-two arches, built between 1874 and 1879, which carry the Kettering–Oakham line over the river Welland at Harringworth, vie with the great Roman aqueducts of the Mediterranean world in dramatic impact.

Villages and towns suddenly sprang into prominence simply because of their proximity to the railway. Woodford Halse, for instance, acquired a station on the Great Central Railway Company's line. Ninety-one acres of marshalling yards and a locomotive depot were laid out, causing the Byfield–Woodford road, shown in A. Bryant's map of 1827, to be re-routed south. Two terraces of artisan housing sprang up to house railway workers. Seventy years later the line is now disused and it has recently been suggested that the cutting and wide embankment which dominates and divides the village of Woodford Halse should be used as a sports area, golf course or for planting deciduous woodland.[23]

There is an intimate connection between the rise of the shoe-making towns of central Northamptonshire in the second part of the nineteenth century and the arrival of the railway.[24] Kettering, Burton Latimer and Desborough all had stations on the main line of the Midland Railway, opened in 1857. Between 1861 and 1901 Kettering rose to second place in the county as a centre of boot and shoe manufacture. The nearby substantial villages of Burton Latimer and Desborough also turned over to the large-scale

---

[23] *Disused Railways of Northamptonshire*, a report by the County Planning Officer (1971).

[24] V. A. Hatley and J. Rajczonek, *Shoe Makers in Northamptonshire, 1762–1911*, Northampton Historical Series, No. 6 (1971).

production of shoes. They grew more rapidly owing to their direct railway connections than the neighbouring small town of Rothwell, which never had a station because the only railways to pass through the parish were lines serving local ironstone quarries. Population figures show this:

	1801	*1851*	*1911*
Kettering	3011	5198	29972
Burton Latimer	669	1007	3420
Desborough	831	1350	4092
Rothwell	1409	2278	4416

As will be seen when the growth of Northampton is considered, the non-arrival of the railway until much later did not hold back the expansion of the county town in the middle of the Victorian period. The case for Northampton to be included on the course of the London–Birmingham line was considered but rejected, not because the town opposed it, as legend had it, but for simple engineering reasons.[25] The great difference in level (at Blisworth it was about 315 feet above sea level) and the lower part of Northampton (about 195 feet) was far too formidable for the early steam engines to cope with. Stephenson is reported to have said that he could easily take his trains into the town but that it would be another matter to get them out again.

The actual route chosen also avoided Althorp and the likely opposition of great landowners. Its promoters were in any case more interested to begin with in a direct connection between the provincial capital, Birmingham, and the metropolis, than in catering for intermediate traffic. Consequently Northampton had to wait for its link with Birmingham until 1872 when the loop was built and it is noteworthy that even then, when locomotives were much

[25] V. A. Hatley, 'Northampton Vindicated', *Northants. Past and Present*, Vol. II, 6 (1959), pp. 305–9.

more powerful, the route made an almost right-angled turn south of Long Buckby to avoid high ground. The Spencers at Althorp were mollified by the provision of a private waiting room for the family, by plentiful supply of bridges over or archways under for their foxes, and by the right to stop any train at their convenience. The dining room at Althorp was rebuilt with the proceeds of the sale of land necessary to accommodate the line.[26]

Victorian townscapes

During the nineteenth century, in common with the rest of England, Northamptonshire experienced a great urban growth. The population of *Northampton* which was 7020 in 1801, had grown to 15,351 in 1831; by 1901 it was 87,021. It was connected with the expansion of the boot and shoe industry which had been stimulated by the demand for military and naval footwear during the Revolutionary and Napoleonic wars. The town had been linked with the Grand Union Canal by the railway from Gayton in 1805. Ten years later its own canal was opened and coal began to be brought in from the Midlands. Shoes went out all over England in return. By 1831 a third of the men living in the town were shoemakers; forty years later this proportion had risen to over two-fifths.

This growth obviously is reflected in the townscape today. Working-class housing grew up within the angles formed by the intersections of the main streets of the medieval borough. The ancient walls had been demolished in 1662 and after about 1835 new houses and streets went up among the suburban orchards, fields and market gardens. When one studies Law's map of 1847 (with its useful notes by V. A. Hatley) one is struck by the growth of working-class districts in the *west* and the *north* of the town; in the west part of the formerly walled area (e.g. Scarletwell),

[26] Information kindly given by Earl Spencer.

north of it (e.g. Bailiff Street) and to a small extent to the east (e.g. in New Town). This is quite unlike the development in other industrial towns of nineteenth-century Britain. The middle class 'genteel quarter' in Northampton sprang up along Billing Road and Cliftonville, towards the east. Geographical factors partly explain this, since the Nene valley, liable to flooding, restricted growth to the south and west. A more important reason was that building speculators realised that dwellings erected on Northampton's *extra-parochial* lands did not have to pay poor rates (at any rate until after 1857).[27]

Thomas Grundy, a local ironfounder, speculated in housing in a big way, establishing his own brickyard and promoting Northampton's first building society. He laid out six streets in an ambitious housing estate half a mile up the Wellingborough road; they were named Newton Road, East, South and West Streets, Melbourne and Bouverie Streets, the last two reflecting the liberal affinities of their projector. A third possible reason explaining the eastern spread of the middle-class district is that there was no problem in the town of smoke from a large number of industrial premises being carried eastwards by the prevailing winds because the shoe industry was still unmechanised during this period. This is opposed to the experience of most other industrial towns, including Bolton, Manchester and Birmingham where the middle-class areas spread south-west.

Consequently the eastern suburbs developed into the middle-class areas. Derngate and Albion Place still have a number of fine Regency and early Victorian houses. Victoria Place dates from 1837; Spencer Parade, in what might be called Pantomime Cinderella style—a castellated and

[27] V. A. Hatley and J. Rajczonek, *Shoe Makers* and V. A. Hatley, 'Some Aspects of Northampton's History, 1815–51', *Northants. Past and Present* (1965–6), pp. 243–53. V. A. Hatley, *Notes on Law's Map of Northampton of 1847* (1972). These extra-parochial lands had belonged to St Andrew's Priory, Northampton, during the Middle Ages and did not come under parochial jurisdiction. They numbered about 300 acres in all.

romantic building for a generation reading Sir Walter Scott, with laburnum dripping gold in the front garden, dates from about 1840; the houses in the south portion of Cheyne Walk from the early 1840s. The splendid Victorian mansions of the 1850s and 60s overlooking the Nene valley south of the Billing road have their origin in the Corporation's policy of selling land here with the stipulation that only high-class housing should be developed on the site. 'Springfield', the present Borough Education offices, figures on Law's map of 1847.

Nowadays the planners aim to segregate industrial premises from residential areas, but during the nineteenth century Northampton contained industrial and domestic buildings intermingled. The journeymen shoemakers performed their tasks at home, returning a week's work to the premises of their employers on Saturdays, collecting their wages and a fresh supply of work. It was not until the 1850s that the first machines were installed for closing the upper components of shoes. In 1857 Moses Philip Manfield erected a great warehouse in Florentine Renaissance style in Campbell Square and there were strong protests from the Luddite-minded shoemakers who feared that "the monster of the mounts" would ride roughshod over them. From 1850 onwards many industrial buildings went up all over the town. In 1875 the *Northampton Mercury* referred to new shoe factories being built in areas "where the homes of their workers would be for resting and not for work".[28]

The town was built by private enterprise and as one walks through the 'Victorian jungle' of red brick and blue-slated streets, it is interesting to note the improved standards of building enforced by successive improvement acts. The 1843 Act laid down paving, draining and building regulations and directed that party-walls in terraced housing had to be carried up to twelve inches beyond the roof level to

[28] Quoted in G. H. Starmer (ed.), *Industrial Archaeology in Northamptonshire*, catalogue to exhibition held in Central Museum (Northampton, 1970), p. 21.

diminish fire risk—Lawrence Street for instance was started in the 1830s and the eastern end had no party-walls protruding on the skyline. The western part, which followed the curving hedgeline of the eighteenth-century landscape, was added after the Act. It has recently been demolished, as has Bailiff Street, which shared the same feature. The junction between party-walls and no party-walls can, however, still be seen in Great Russell Street although this street is likely to be knocked down in a year or two. Improvements came too late for some inhabitants of the borough. When cholera struck again in 1849 it carried off 43 victims from the Bridge Street slums, 39 of whom had been living in one block of 103 continuous houses which occupied a space 150 yards long by 50 yards wide.

Nineteenth-century Northampton acquired other marks of urban civilisation. A gasworks by the river introduced piped gas in the 1820s. Bridge Street Station, on the Blisworth–Peterborough branch line, brought a late railway connection in 1845. The extended Castle Station which largely obliterated the mighty medieval fortification was built on the Roade–Rugby loop line of the London and North Western railway in 1881. Two reservoirs belonging to the Water Company appear on Law's engraved map of 1847 to the south-east of the New Borough Gaol on the Mounts which was erected in 1845. Two new churches, St Katherine's (1839) and St Andrew's (1842), were added; St Edmund's followed in 1852 and the medieval body of St Giles' church was doubled in size to accommodate the swollen churchgoing population between 1853 and 1855. In 1815 there had been six places of Nonconformist worship in the town; during the next thirty years at least eight new congregations were formed.

A similar explosion in bricks and mortar occurred in the other towns in the county. *Kettering* in the eighteenth century had been a centre of textile manufacture, specialising in the worsted trade. After 1793 it shifted from the

Plate 42 New England, Peterborough. 'The Barracks'—three streets built by the Great Northern railway parallel with the skein of railway lines a mile and a half to the north of the medieval city. Now in process of demolition.

Plate 43 Cromwell Road, Peterborough. The first edition of the twenty-five inch to one mile Ordnance Survey map (1889) confirms what is evident on the ground, that these cottages with their changing rooflines and numerous datestones were built singly or in groups of three and were eventually joined into terraces. Their names are a quaint mixture of the pastoral and the military: General Cottages 1865, Osman Villa 1878, Myrtle House 1898.

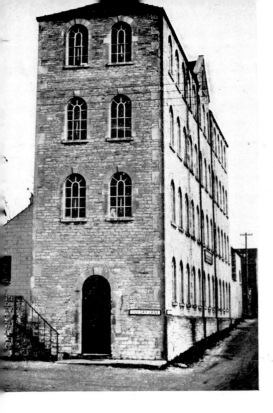

Plate 44 Brigstock. Factory (now of Wallis & Linnell) built in 1873-4 in the tradition of early-nineteenth-century Lancashire; four storeys with all windows arched. A bell under a pedimented gable summoned the operatives to work.

Plate 45 Long Buckby. Castle Factory, a small-scale industrial building in two phases, dating from the late 1860s and *c.* 1880. About this period machinery was introduced for all the basic processes of making shoes, and factory methods of control were adopted. 'Alfred Hare, Jun. Boot & Shoe manufacturer Castle Factory' is mentioned in the 1898 Kelly's Directory.

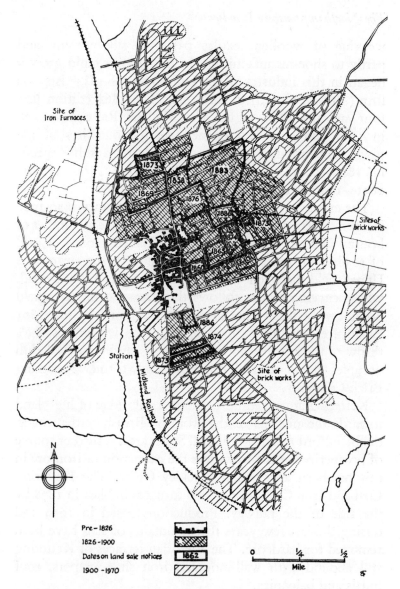

Fig. 19. The growth of Kettering in the nineteenth century

The base map was drawn by Peter Taylor and shows the early-nineteenth-century settlement (derived from R. Smith's map published in 1826), with the astonishing growth in Victoria's reign added. Superimposed are the details of the areas involved in land sales, 1860–6, provided by Ronald Greenall of the University of Leicester.

weaving of woollen textiles partly to silk-weaving and partly to shoe-manufacturing. In the 1860s a rapid growth began in this industry, Kelly's directory of 1854 lists one firm (Messrs. Gotch) in the town. The 1864 edition lists four and the 1869, eight. The Midland Railway arrived in 1857 and a station opened on the outskirts of the town. The population increased with remarkable speed: in 1801—3011; 1851—5198; 1871—7184; 1881—11,095; 1891—19,454; 1901—28,653.

The expansion of the town in the twenty years 1880-1900 is impressively documented by the extraordinary number of houses with dated (and frequently initialled) stones. A grid of roads with red brick terrace housing sprang up on the Upper field between Rockingham road and Bath road, whose curving course follows the stream acting as a field boundary between the allotments laid out in the 1803 Enclosure Act. Three brickworks arose within a stone's throw of the stream. Today the town's rugby football club occupies the yard and quarry of the former Kettering Brick Company.

Kettering advanced north along a dry ridge of high land towards the nucleus of the Romano-British settlement in the Blandford Avenue–Mitchell Street area. A further source of prosperity for the town was the extraction of iron ore in this northern area round Weekley Glebe. The Kettering Coal and Iron Co. Ltd. put two furnaces in blast in 1878 by the side of the railway. Production ceased in 1959 and during the last few years the mountains of slag have been removed for hardcore. The Victorian terraces of Kettering still abound with wall-mounted iron shoe-scrapers, roof finials and balconies.

The expansion of the Victorian working-class town to the north can be partly explained by the inhibiting effect of the railway, effectively blocking development to the west.[29]

[29] A fine series of maps by P. Taylor illustrating the growth of the town was published in *A Walk round Kettering*, Kettering Civic Society (1972).

More important is the clue afforded by the enclosure map. It is noteworthy that the areas of early development were on land occupied by smaller landowners interested in speculating in working-class housing. The big men, the Duke of Buccleuch and the Rector of Kettering, were not interested in quick profits, and they owned practically all the fields to the south and east of the town. The houses of the rich boot and shoe manufacturers are found sprinkled along Headlands and Queensberry Road. The great variety of design of these houses, while sharing common materials— red brick and Weldon freestone dressings, commands respect. Kettering owes much to the Gotch family which provided the organisation of the town's boot and shoe industry in the first half of the nineteenth century and engendered a fine architect, J. A. Gotch, with a national reputation, who is responsible for the distinctive design of many of the shops, public buildings and large houses put up at the end of the century.

During the same period the nearby town of *Rothwell* (which had been the head of a hundred and an important market town in the Middle Ages) and the large villages of Burton Latimer and Desborough also turned over to the shoe production on a large scale. Rothwell grew from 1409 in 1801 to 2278 in 1851 and had increased to 4416 by 1911. This increase in population fitted into the triangles and rectangles of the enclosure around. Hence Greening Road and Nunnery Avenue are squeezed into Jon Jontin's allotment of 17a 3r 7p to the west of the Nunnery while Gordon and Jubilee Streets were laid down in the triangular piece belonging to the same Mr Jontin. Behind the houses built for the Victorian shoe workers of Rothwell are backyard workshops where the shoes were made.

A similar feature is seen in the shoe towns of Raunds and Rushden. *Rushden* had a fantastic growth period between 1880 and 1900 when its population leapt from 3657 to

12,453. Irthlingborough, Finedon and Earls Barton were all
similarly bursting at the seams in these years. They are
unlovely towns and H. E. Bates, referring to Rushden, has
remarked on the "palpably dreadful mess of that mixture of
blue slate, factory, chapel and that harsh Midland red brick
which equally oppresses heart, soul, eye and senses".[30] He
goes on to add that the geography of Rushden might well
have been laid out by some shoemaking dictator who had
insisted that for every hundred yards of dwelling house there
should be thirty or forty of factory sandwiched between
them and had then added the humanitarian proviso that a
bakehouse and a chapel or two should somehow be tucked
among them. As someone who spent ten years in industrial
Lancashire, this strikes me as a little harsh to Rushden which
compares well, in townscape and amenities, to parts of
industrial Lancashire, Yorkshire, the Potteries and the South
Wales mining towns. Uneasily stitched on to Rushden by
a piece of inter-war ribbon development is the ancient
borough of *Higham Ferrers*. Here in a little group of streets
hedged in by small rectangular three-storey boot factories
there is a nice display of late Victorian social attitudes in
bricks and mortar. The foreman's house, double fronted
and separate, is at the top of the street; below are the two-
up, two-down dwellings of the operatives.

Another town which grew remarkably during this period
was *Wellingborough*. Originally a village, which happened to
be the centre of the congery of estates in the middle Nene
valley belonging to the abbey of Crowland, it grew to a small
market town by the beginning of the eighteenth century. It
is full of good houses of the Georgian period which indicate
a modest prosperity arising from serving a purely agricultural district. The only industries were lace-making, a small
amount of weaving, and later the manufacture of boots and
shoes. Its population was 3325 in 1801 but this had increased
to 4454 by 1821 owing "to the numerous families of

[30] H. E. Bates, *The Vanished World* (London, 1969), p. 33.

journeymen shoemakers who went to reside there during the war".[31]

The turning point of the town's history came with the railway connections. In 1845 Wellingborough Station on the Blisworth–Peterborough branch line (L.N.W.R.) was opened. In 1857 The Midland Railway's main line passed through the town and the company made it the first great mineral and goods station out of London, sixty-five miles from the metropolis. Enormous quantities of ironstone began to be mined in and around the town. Blast furnaces were set up for the production of pig iron. Messrs. Butlin's East End Ironworks provided employment for the rapidly rising population which rocketed from 6382 in 1861 to 18,412 in 1901.

All this brought startling changes to the townscape. Large locomotive sheds were erected, flanked by a mesh of sidings; a hostel or lodging house for engine drivers and firemen was built. Working-class terraces in red brick, soon soot-blackened, covered the east side of the town between Mill Road and Midland Road. Presiding over their blue slate roofs is the ironstone bulk of the tower of St Mary's church, which has the most startlingly beautiful interior of any church known to me in the county, all gold, cream and blue; a richly caparisoned baldachin, a rambling rood screen and fretted pendant fan-vaulting, the inspired creation of Sir Ninian Comper, given a free hand here between 1908 and 1930. Today the town is poised on a new phase of development as it prepares to take London overspill population. It is to be hoped that due regard will be paid to integrate the considerable character of the buildings of Wellingborough's past with the new.

We last saw *Peterborough* as a small medieval city dominated by the great monastery under whose walls it was founded. Five railway companies converged on the city between 1841–51: a branch from the London–Birmingham

[31] V. A. Hatley and J. Rajczonek, *Shoe Makers*, p. 5.

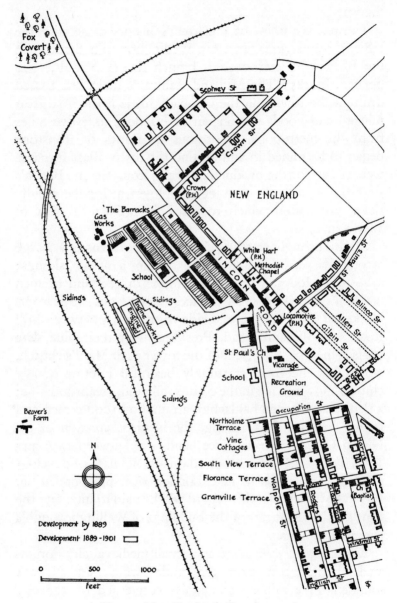

Fig. 20. New England, Peterborough

arrived in 1845; a Midland branch joined Peterborough to Stamford in 1846. The Eastern Counties joined Ely to Peterborough in the same year and the Great Northern came last in 1850.[32] In this tangle of line duplication was inevitable; seven separate yards and four locomotive depots were built. The railways encouraged the mushroom growth of the city but constrained its development in certain directions. Its extension was largely inhibited to the west. But north a grid of streets parallel with the railway was laid out in the 1860s. Two 'railway villages', peopled by company workers of the Great Northern and the Midland, grew up at New England (Fig. 20 and Plate 42) and Spittal (on the site of St Leonard's Hospital). The rows of identical yellow stock brick terraces lining unmade-up roads with wooden palings enclosing their gardens, symbolise the almost military discipline the G.N.R. imposed on its armies of employees; the village is known as 'The Barracks' and was equipped with everything necessary for education and salvation. A temporary iron school was erected here in 1856 and soon afterwards shareholders provided £700 for a permanent building, which was in turn replaced in 1891 by the school standing in Walpole Street. A new church (St Paul's), almost wholly financed by the directors, was built in Walpole Street in 1869. It was designed by James Teale and

[32] Peterborough's complex railway history is dealt with in D. I. Gordon, *A Regional History of the Railways of Great Britain*, Vol. 5, *The Eastern Counties* (Newton Abbot, 1968), pp. 225-31.

Fig. 20. New England, Peterborough

The Great Northern railway built as distinctive a railway town as Swindon, Wolverton or Crewe in this northern suburb of Peterborough in the 1860s. Parallel with the Lincoln road were laid out rows of brick terraces, and a full complement of schools, public houses, chapels and recreation ground was gradually added to the settlement. The barrack-like homes of the railway employees contrast with the haphazard and spasmodic development of private housing in the 1880s–90s. Compiled from the 1889–1901 six inches to one mile Ordnance Survey maps.

E. B. Denison, son of the chairman of the company. Damnation via drink was also at hand, for flanking the Wesleyan chapel and post office were three public houses, the Crown, White Hart and Locomotive. By the 1901 twenty-five-inch Ordnance Survey map a recreation ground had been added between the north end of Walpole Street and Lincoln Road and spare fields to the south-east between 'The Barracks'and the growing suburbs of the city had been laid out in allotments.

9. Modern landscapes

*Agricultural depression and the effects of two world wars.
Ironstone quarrying and restoration. Sand and gravel
extraction. Motorways. Disappearing hedgerows.
The expansion of towns. The future landscape*

Agricultural depression and the effects of two world wars

IT IS CLEAR that by the middle of the nineteenth century
the north and east of the county were predominantly under
arable and the south and the west mainly a pastoral landscape. Despite the great growth in the towns, Northamptonshire in 1850 was still a land of villages with most of the
population dependent on agriculture. Twenty years later,
except for the Harborough country and the riverside meadows of the Welland and the Nene, two-thirds of the county
was under arable crops, chiefly wheat, barley, pulses,
turnips, swedes and rotation grasses. High rents made it
possible for landowners to invest substantial amounts in
drainage and building schemes as we have seen, and a brief
golden period of prosperity lasting from 1840 to 1870
brought rich dividends.

This picture was shattered when the great depression
overcame agriculture in the late seventies and eighties of
the nineteenth century. The opening up of the middle west
of America encouraged the flow of cheap prairie-grown
corn into the country, no longer protected by corn laws.
Northamptonshire farmers, weakened as they were by bad
harvests and cattle plague, were hit particularly hard.
Most of their arable, except in the north-east, was only
marginally corn land. Money was now available only for the

maintenance of capital equipment. Agricultural depression led to the conversion of much land into permanent pasture, the arable acreage dropping from nearly 286,000 acres in 1872 to just over 206,000 acres in 1900; by 1912 it was as low as 188,622 acres, two-thirds of the acreage of 1872. Wheat, for instance, fell from 82,000 acres in 1872 to 45,919 in 1919.[1]

The effects of the depression on the rural landscape are familiar to anyone involved in farming whose memory goes back fifty years. Most of the buildings and much of the equipment still being used up to the outbreak of the Second World War dated from the mid-Victorian period of High Farming. Buildings became ramshackle; hedgerows were neglected; fields reverted to scrub. The 1914–18 War led to a short-lived prosperity in agriculture produced by the ploughing-up programme and high rents and prices which went with it. In the 1920s, however, depression fell once more on the industry and the county reverted to largely pastoral farming, dairying in the upland pastures of the western part and fatstock-rearing in the Nene valley. By 1929 the acreages of the three chief corn crops were: wheat 30,901, barley 20,982 and oats 19,817.

The impact of the Second World War on the landscape was more long-lived than the First. Ploughing-up started early on in the war and the traditional agricultural policies were overridden on the great and little estates. Braybrooke parish, for instance, had only thirty acres of arable at the outbreak of the 1939–45 War. Its cattle pastures were now quickly broken up by the plough. On the 10,000 acres of the estates of the Duke of Buccleuch, centred at Grafton Underwood, Geddington, Newton, Warkton and Weekley, the proportion devoted to arable before the war was twenty-five per cent; during the war this rocketed to seventy-five per cent. This changeover to arable has continued during

[1] S. H. Beaver, *The Land of Britain*, Land Utilisation Survey of Britain Part 58, 'Northamptonshire' (London, 1943), p. 391.

the twenty-five years after the Second World War and the trend shows no sign at present of reversing.

Until 1939 horses had been a regular part of the landscape, providing the main traction power. Their shoes lie scattered thickly in the ploughsoil now turned by giant diesel-engined crawler-tractors. They lasted longer in the Soke of Peterborough where there are many smallholdings, but the shortage of labour occasioned by the war led to a quickening mechanisation. Much machinery came from America; combines and balers which had been very rare were now used by the Agricultural Executive committees which controlled farming during the emergency. Many a Fordson tractor now rusting forlornly in farmyards was busily working during these years. The increase in mechanisation with a corresponding drop in the numbers of agricultural workers has gone on.

A more temporary but dramatic incursion of war on the landscape was the building of military airfields and other camps. Attracted by the gently undulating uplands which were out of range of most enemy counter-attacks, the RAF and USAF laid out aerodromes from which Wellingtons, Lancasters and the first Flying Fortresses set out to bomb Germany. During our first two or three years at Kettering in the early sixties we used to go blackberrying among the sinister decaying buildings of the former bombing aerodrome at Grafton Underwood. The 120 acres of runways are now being broken up by the Boughton estates for hardcore, which goes to build estate roads or is sold for motorways. This land will be cultivated again only with difficulty but so far £25,000 has been spent on reclamation and drainage. Tree-planting in strips is being tried on the site of old runways. The hangars have lately been re-roofed and the single-storey buildings, many of them disposed and hidden in the woods for safety, went on being used for temporary housing until the early 1960s. At Desborough, a British bombing airfield, the runways are still well preserved, and the perimeter track is now used as a rally-cross course. Five hangars survive as vehicle stores for the Post Office and local farms. The residential buildings, used until two years ago as Civil Defence stores, are also upstanding, but the isolated control tower, surrounded by fields of wheat, is crumbling into decay. The runways at Silverstone have been transformed into a race track.[2]

A further interesting hangover from these years are the concrete lay-bys, to be found on minor country lanes near former airfields. These are bomb-bays; some can be seen on Warkton common; others in the lanes leading to the aerodrome at Harrington. These roads were barricaded, with sentries posted during war time. P.O.W. camps were dotted all over the countryside and traces can still be seen twenty-five years later of hutted encampments as at Little Addington and Boughton Park. The park itself at Boughton was knocked about during the stationing of tanks and troops here. There was a tank training ground of a 1000 acres of 'Dog and Stick country' at Grafton in Burton Latimer parish. When this area was cleared in 1946 and returned to agriculture, Mr Grundy of Kettering was brought in to do the job, with his steam-tackle ploughing, the last occasion this was used in the county. Bombing ranges were at Pilton and at Preston Capes. Such scars are temporary, bulldozers soon erase them from the fields.

The impact of war on woodland was even more drastic. As one drives or walks through the county, Northamptonshire gives the impression of being quite a well-wooded county and it is only when one considers the total area occupied by woodland that one realises that this amounts only to a small and reducing fraction. In 1924 25,087 acres of woodland accounted for about four per cent of the total acreage of the county. It was located in roughly the same areas as at the time of Domesday Book, some forty genera-

[2] For these last two paragraphs I acknowledge useful information from P. Stamper of Boughton.

tions earlier; Rockingham forest in the north; and Salcey forest and Whittlewood on the southern boundary with Buckinghamshire. During the 1914–18 War government purchasers with compulsory felling orders arrived to doom trees for the war effort. The woods on Harlestone heath on the estate of Earl Spencer of Althorp were removed and replanted with conifers. These in turn had just about matured before being cut down in the 1939–45 War. Earl Spencer recalled that his grandfather had refused £50 offered for an oak to be used in the 'wooden walls' of England, at the time of the Crimean War; but when the demand arose in the Second World War for wooden keels for trawlers to resist German magnetic mines he himself allowed a dozen mighty oaks to be taken from Althorp Park.

Recent study of the Rockingham forest region, rising out of alarm among conservationists, has established that over the last three centuries there has been a substantial reduction in the extent of woodland. The rate of clearance was slow from the seventeenth century until *c.* 1820, rapid during the vast fellings of 1820–80. Between 1885 and 1950 the acreage of woodland actually increased, but the period 1950 to 1970 has produced the highest rate of primary woodland reduction. Primary woodland to a botanist means the tree cover on sites which have never been completely cleared in the last 2000 or more years; these have interestingly different flora from those which have been cleared. The situation is:

9665 acres of primary woodland in 1950.
1297 acres have been cleared, 1950–70.
3646 acres are mainly coniferous.
4626 acres are broad-leaved woodland.
96 acres are park woodland.

Of the 4626 acres only 1550 acres are considered to be semi-natural. The historian of the landscape and the botanist link forces at this point in maintaining that this small area is of crucial importance for conservation—more so than secondary woodland—that which at some time has been completely cleared of trees, for cultivation, pasture, mining or habitation.[3]

When woodland management is considered, a contrast is seen between treatment of the private estate and the policy adopted by the national body, the Forestry Commission. There are 2000 acres of woodland in the Boughton estates between Kettering and Corby. Some of this is primary woodland, never touched by the axe; an instance being Boltwood Coppice consisting of beech, sycamore, ash and mixed hardwoods. A good deal was planted up to 250 years ago and the planting records at Boughton go back to the 1840s. Geddington Chase was laid out on radial lines at this time. During the Second World War vast areas were laid bare and it was only in the 1950s that replanting began on any scale. A big effort has been made to improve the plantations by clearing land of undergrowth, especially blackthorn and brambles, which had taken over from the traditional coppice and standards. Coppice timber such as hazel can be sold comparatively easily for thatching, hedge stakes and binders, but it is hardly economic to replant.

Since 1950 around a 1000 acres of woodland have been replanted. By felling selectively instead of clearing whole areas completely it is planned always to have a 'top storey'— that is a considerable number of trees left. This process is visually highly advantageous. The view of the Geddington Chase from the A43 demonstrates this. It is, however, highly expensive, costing three times as much as the National Forestry Commission work because it is impossible to introduce mechanical methods of clearing, planting or spraying unless clear felling is undertaken. Also remarkable

---

[3] G. F. Peterken, *Changes in the general character of woodland in Rockingham Forest since the 17th century*, Monks Wood Experimental Station (The Nature Conservancy, 1971).

complexities of species are being planted—oak, red oak, sycamore, ash, beech, hornbeam, elm, Norway maple, lime, larch (European, Japanese, and hybrid), Scots pine, Corsican pine, Douglas fir, western red cedar and western hemlock.

The Forestry Commission, since its formation in 1919, has taken over the management of the Crown Woods and has obtained most of the remaining large blocks of woodland, either leasehold or outright. During the agricultural depression between the wars a significant area of marginal agricultural land was acquired. We noticed that during the seventeenth and eighteenth centuries oak was grown more intensely, interspersed with ash, lime and hazel and worked usually on a 'coppice with standards' system. Later in the nineteenth century the oaks were planted in mixture with conifers—Scots pine, European larch and Norway spruce being most widely used. Oak remained the major species until the 1930s when the advantages of oak/conifer mixtures became apparent. Oak/Norway spruce were planted alternately, two rows oak, four or six rows Norway spruce. Initially the spruce was removed as Christmas trees but latterly it was allowed to grow with the oak until mature (about sixty years), when it was felled to leave a pure oak crop. This system continued until the 1950s, but in more recent years the emphasis turned towards pure conifer crops with mixtures only on the better ground. One factor is that soft wood gave a three and half per cent return on capital investment, hardwood only half a per cent. During 1971, however, the Forestry Commission has undergone a change of policy. Environmental problems, arising out of rapid urban growth, have created a different climate of opinion, and the Midland forests are now seen more as amenity forests with picnic and touring areas rather than simply as a reservoir of cheap timber. Consequently the Commission has begun not only to plant hardwoods but to conserve the hardwood element in some conifer mixtures.

Ironstone quarrying and restoration. Sand and gravel extraction

It will be recalled that iron-smelting had taken place in widely dispersed forest areas during the medieval period, but John Morton, writing in 1712 and marvelling at the extent of the former industry, stated definitely that there was no ore in the county. The rediscovery of the ore took place in 1851 and it was quickly found that ironstone underlay a large part of Northamptonshire. A small cold blast furnace was erected at Wellingborough in 1853 on a site to be served by the Midland railway four years later. In the next ten years quarries sprang up all along the outcrop of the bed where it overlooked or lay alongside an existing line of railway, as at Blisworth, Gayton, Duston, Wellingborough, Desborough and Stamford. There was no coal in the county but excellent rail facilities enabled the ore to be transported out to South Staffordshire, Derbyshire and South Wales. Also coal was brought in from Durham to fire the first three blast furnaces erected in the fifties and sixties at Wellingborough, Heyford and Finedon. There was a rapid expansion of quarrying in the sixties and seventies along the three principal lines of railway (L.N.W. main line, Midland main line and Northampton and Peterborough line).[4] These quarries were hand-worked and there are still men in Kettering and Islip who recall the heroic period before mechanisation when the topsoil and overburden were stripped by pick and shovel and barrowed by workmen along planks teetering thirty feet above the quarry floor, to be carefully respread and the land restored for agriculture as it had been.

The introduction by Lloyds' Ironstone Company at Corby of the first 'steam navvy' for excavating iron ore, combined with a belt conveyor for the stripping of overburden in 1897, led to the first areas of 'hill and dale'. Great

[4] S. H. Beaver, 'The Development of the Northamptonshire Iron Industry 1851–1930', *London Essays in Geography* (Cambridge, 1951), pp. 33–58.

Plate 46 Newborough. Early-nineteenth-century reclamation of the fen has produced a landscape recalling the mid-west prairies. Colonial-type settlements of brick houses and farms are sprinkled along the rectilinear grid of causewayed roads, bounded by ditched fields of peaty soil where potatoes, wheat and beet are raised.

Plate 47 St Bartholomew's church, Newborough. It was ordered to be built by the enclosure commissioners when they carved up this part of the fen in 1812. A strange building of yellow brick, with thin walls and large lancets, dating from 1830.

Plate 48 The making of the M1 motorway. A broad swathe of mud, ruts and ice through Salcey forest in January 1959.

soil-less ridges of stone and clay rising and falling as much as thirty feet produced a lunar landscape which disfigured large parts of the northern half of the county particularly from the time between the two world wars. Attempts to cover these unsightly areas by planting trees were well-intentioned but misguided. Conifers were chosen for the rapid timber growth considered necessary for Britain in the bastion economy thinking fashionable after the First World War, but they were unsuited to the deciduous woodland naturally found in the Midland plain. The humus deposition supposed to make soil under the trees was poor, vermin proliferated and access roads for removing timber were difficult to drive through the huge furrows of the 'hill and dale'.

Effective measures for the restoration of land worked for ironstone have only been made since the Mineral Workings Act of 1951 which established the Ironstone Restoration fund. In the first twelve years producers restored progressively to agriculture over 4250 acres of their current working while the local authority had reclaimed 2000 acres left derelict prior to 1950.[5] The technique seen today around Corby, the sole remaining centre for iron-smelting, is that giant scrapers strip topsoil in advance of workings and move it back behind the quarry. The colossal walking draglines, their white gleaming booms, up to 303 feet long, looking like mobile bridge sections, remove the overburden in two lifts, 1600 tons an hour, to uncover the ironstone bed which may lie fifty feet below the surface. The material is temporarily deposited in a long ridge over the area already cleared of ironstone. A small mechanical shovel loads the ironstone, which has previously been loosened by blasting, on to the railway wagons. The ridge is then levelled and the topsoil replaced.

This moving scar of yellow, white and grey rock up to a mile in length is the temporary effect of ironstone-working

---

[5] *Ironstone and Agriculture.* Published by the National Council of Associated Iron Ore Producers. N.D.

on the landscape of the 1970s. The area cleared, levelled and resown has, of course, sunk two or three feet and a rather featureless countryside with larger, straight-edged fields, new access roads, cattle troughs, quickset hedges and farm buildings takes over. The rental of such restored land is never more than two-thirds its former value. The natural drainage is upset; it is very difficult to replace the exact contours, and subsoil boulders now on the surface shatter ploughshares; it takes years for the soil to settle sufficiently to make it worth while to embark on drainage schemes. Nevertheless, compared with the appalling problems of dereliction in other parts of Britain, Northamptonshire can furnish encouraging examples of what can be done.[6]

Archaeologists have long realised that one of the most momentous implications for their subject is the need of a modern industrial urban society for sand and gravel. As we saw in the first chapter, the gravel terraces of the rivers Nene and Welland were as thickly settled in prehistoric and Roman times as were the chalk downs of the South.[7] The effect on the modern landscape of these large-scale workings is radical. At Maxey on the Welland gravels, between the church and the village, irregular emerald-green, water-filled pits mirror conical mounds of sifted and graded gravel. Contrasting with these biscuit-coloured eroded pyramids are intricate stairways and railings leading up to rakish machinery which dredges and then spits out the proceeds. Green cylinders stand like giant bottles against huge cumulus-dominated skyscapes. At Billing, only three miles east of Northampton, we see what happens when battalions of caravans are marshalled by the side of flooded gravel pits to make a summer playground; lines of black poplars and scraggy willows drip rain on white caravan

---

[6] John Barr, *Derelict Britain* (London, 1969), pp. 164–7.

[7] The threat was outlined by A. E. Brown in *B.F.N.A.S.*, 2 (November 1967), pp. 41–43 and maps.

roofs. Shoals of boats pulled out of the 'lakes' for the winter like heaps of shellfish on a Danish midden. A constant roar of dumper trucks carrying out the weeping sand; a skeletal crane swivelling round; impermanent hut roofs; a convoy of black specks—coots sweeping across the gun-metal stretch of water. It is possible that eventually there will be a chain of lagoons stretching from Northampton through Thrapston to Oundle and that a comprehensive scheme of waterways, embracing a number of these worked-out areas, will form an overall recreational system for the future inhabitants of Northamptonshire.[8]

Motorways

The decision to construct a national motorway system was made in 1955; it had momentous implications for the Northamptonshire landscape because the county straddles the route adopted by the London–Yorkshire motorway.[9] Construction began in March 1958 and despite appalling difficulties arising out of the bad summer of that year the works were completed nineteen months later. The earth-works necessary to carry the dual thirty-six-foot carriageways of the main route, together with the twenty-six-foot counterparts of the Birmingham Spur, involved excavating about twelve million cubic yards (Plate 48). An attempt was made to fit the motorway into the countryside, thus avoiding a serious scar across the land. It must be admitted that twelve years later this had largely been accomplished. Breaks in the skyline by embankments or cuttings have been avoided; and where the motorway passes through a wood or crosses a ridge, it is usually on a curve to present an unbroken background. Great care has been taken to obtain

[8] *The Countryside Act, 1968. Report on Conservation and Recreation* (December 1968), Northamptonshire County Council Planning Department.
[9] *Proceedings of the Institution of Civil Engineers*, Vol. 15 (April 1960), pp. 317–400.

a flowing alignment. Horizontal and vertical curves are as long as possible, although these were high standard traffic considerations.

The profiles of road over-bridges form part of the easy-flowing alignment, but the designs of the bridges themselves, while admittedly cheap and efficient, are unpleasing to the eye. Designed by Sir Owen Williams and partners their long flat lintels and solid stubby columns with hefty abutments, are a brutal concrete addition to the landscape. The viaduct over the Nene valley and its flood plain is of flat slab construction with spans ranging from twenty-five to fifty-six feet supported on continuous walls perforated by arches. It is an extraordinary experience to stand under the motorway as it speeds over the river Avon at Lilbourne. The unceasing roar of traffic reverberates through the meadows swelling with the earthworks of the Norman motte-and-bailey castle. Yet underneath the viaduct all is quiet. The columns and aisles of the dimensions of the temples of Karnak form a huge covered implement shed and stockyard. The motorway cuts across farms, as did the railways, and cattle creeps or farm accesses of arch construction bore through its embankments at intervals.

One unexpected feature about the vegetation of motorway verges has recently been noticed as a result of surveys carried out in European Conservation Year. Despite the exhaust emissions of dirty dozens of lorries up and down the motorway, there are 384 species of plants happily colonising the slopes and verges of the M1. They include wild carrot, yellow vetchling, dark mullein, creeping Jenny, sun spurge, the cowslip and purging flax. Several species of butterflies, small mammals and birds, including kestrels are becoming a common sight and it is possible that foxes and badgers are establishing themselves along the banks of the motorway. The reason is that the hard shoulder acts as a kind of protective barrier against damage from poisonous exhaust fumes; also wildlife flourishes where protected from human trespass. Farmers with their herbicides and weedkillers, the public with their propensity for overpicking are likewise forbidden access.[10]

The corollary of improved roads and a motorway system has been the disappearance of much of the nineteenth-century transport system. The railways lasted just about 100 years and one of the most distinctive changes since the Second World War has been their rapid removal. At one point there was a total of 240 route miles of railways and as many as seventy-six stations in Northamptonshire. Since the closure of lines and stations began there have been 129 miles of railway line closed, including a mile and a quarter in tunnel and sixty-nine stations.

Mr Bevin of Welford recalled the disappearance of the branch line between Rugby, Market Harborough and Peterborough eight years ago. "We could tell the time, working in the fields, from the passenger trains; there were enough trains, we didn't need to have a watch." The track has now been taken up, the sleepers removed, the hard core lifted. The former line now is nothing more than an over-grown rough track running through the countryside. A neighbouring farmer has bought a stretch and uses it as an internal farm roadway.

These disused railways have many attractions. An abundance of wildlife, including rabbits, hares, foxes, badgers and wild birds are seen, especially on those lines abandoned some time ago. Wild flowers which are increasingly rare in fields sprayed by herbicides and denuded of hedgerow verges have also colonised railway lines. It is being realised that many stretches are ideal for walking, cycling, horse-riding and picnicking, and it is possible that some stretches may be purchased by the County Council and maintained for recreational uses.[11]

[10] The *Sunday Times*, 27th August, 1972.
[11] *Disused Railways of Northamptonshire*. A Report by the County Planning Officer (1971).

Disappearing hedgerows

We have noticed that some hedgerows originated in Anglo-Saxon territorial and parish boundaries. Others were planted by Tudor and Stuart enclosers. The greatest number were added to the landscape in the eighteenth- and nineteenth-century parliamentary enclosure period. The importance of these hedgerows as a habitat for wildlife is now being increasingly recognised by an ecologically-minded generation. It is realised that as the area of forest was reduced by cultivation, much of the wildlife of primitive natural woodland adapted itself to the environment of man-made hedges. In a typical mile of hedgerows, for instance, twenty birds nest, and four-fifths of our woodland bird species breed in hedges; two-thirds of our lowland mammals likewise. Hedgerows are moreover the pathway of animal and plant movement. Without them isolated colonies of wildlife in conserved areas would rapidly become vulnerable. They are then important biologically as well as interesting historically. It is a startling fact that they were being grubbed up and destroyed at the rate of 5000 miles a year over the whole country between 1945 and 1970.

The reasons for this destruction are economic. Hedgerows have no function in modern stock-farming and they simply get in the way of modern arable techniques. Farmers house all their stock indoors so they are no longer necessary as shelter belts. They have to be cut and laid periodically and seven to eight miles of hedges on a 300-acre farm may cost £350 to maintain per annum. Only on farms where game is an ancillary crop is there an economic reason for keeping hedges. For the arable farmer they are a bar to efficiency. The parliamentary enclosure commissioners laid out land in five-to-fifteen-acre fields. To use heavy machinery like combines economically, land must be in fifty-acre blocks. This, however, is sometimes disputed, as being unnecessarily large, creating boredom for farm workers.[12]

The roots of hedgerows hinder ploughing close to the margin of fields. Hedgerow trees catch on combines. Their shadow reduces crop acreage to the tune of an acre per mile of hedge. Hence the reversion to an open-field landscape in much of the area between Kettering and Huntingdon, Corby and Oundle.[13]

On the great estate of the Duke of Buccleuch between Kettering and Corby the traditional policy of trimming and maintaining the twenty-seven miles of roadside hedges on the 10,000 acres involved is tempered with the requirement of an average field size of thirty-five acres, which is considered compatible for modern machinery.

Not only is the move to larger field size apparently inexorable, the colouring of the landscape is changing under the dual pressures of herbicides and fertilisers. The very heavy use of nitrogenous fertilisers to aid plant growth is producing a bluer green landscape. A check may be made in the hues recorded in the landscape paintings of half a century ago. Moreover, selective weed killers are bringing about changes in the number of wild flowers. No longer are fields of poppies seen, although occasionally a brilliant red stripe across a field of young corn shows where the tractor driver has missed a small area or perhaps where an oil or gas pipe line has been driven through. Owing to the extension of cereal acreage there has been a tremendous increase in the wild oat. The use of combines which thrash wild oats and corn scatters the ripe seed of the weed over the land. It is immediately ploughed in since farmers now follow the combine with the plough. A further colour

[12] Fields of around thirty-five acres have been suggested as reasonable by the Farming and Wild Life Advisory Group, The Lodge, Sandy, Bedfordshire.

[13] M. D. Hooper, 'Hedges and History', *New Scientist* (31st December, 1970); 'The Botanical Importance of our Hedgerows', M. F. Perring (ed.), *The Flora of a Changing Britain* (London, 1970), pp. 58–62, and a lecture to the Kettering Civic Society, 1971 by M. D. Hooper.

change arises in large areas of the corn-growing part of the county when there is no longer any market for straw which is spewed out on to the fields by the combines and then burned. Crackling fires, blue plumes of smoke, scorched hedges and blackened fields result from this unpleasant technique.

In some places, however, as at Welford, wheat and rye is specially grown for thatching. A seed with long straw is used and the material is sold direct to the thatchers, a conservative breed of self-employed men. There are about twelve to fifteen thatchers still working in Northamptonshire. Some work in Norfolk reed but most cottages in the county are thatched in the traditional long straw. The old thatch is rarely completely stripped but is 'coated' with six to ten inches of thatching and it is reckoned that a new coating lasts two years per inch of thickness. Galvanised wire-netting has been used to protect the thatch from birds during the last twenty years.

The use of such traditional materials, while expensive (the total cost of thatching a two-bay cottage which may take six to eight weeks to complete is from £300 to £400), helps to preserve the rustic charm of many of the stone-built villages in the county. On the Boughton estates, no new building has been allowed for thirty years in the villages of Warkton, Weekley, Grafton, Newton and only limited development at Geddington. The result is that within a few miles of the developing new town of Corby and the more slowly expanding town of Kettering there is an area of villages of high visual amenity.

Radical changes in building materials for farms in other parts of the county are taking place. Asbestos, steel and concrete are now used instead of limestone, ironstone, Collyweston slate, brick and thatch. The design of farm buildings is also changing; on arable farms grain stores are now nearly always huge square or rectangular planned buildings; bins are rapidly being superseded by blowers which dry the grain on the floor by blasting warm air through it. This largely automated process is also noticeable in stock-farming; here dairy and meat production units are getting larger. Where two men in the early 1950s milked fifty cows, twenty years later one man can milk a hundred. To do this, silage towers, cylindrical structures of reinforced concrete or steel, make their appearance in the landscape. The silage or haylage is blown in very dry, and chopped fine, emptied automatically and fed mechanically to the mangers. A particularly noticeable instance are the double towers at Woodford which dominate several miles of the undulating country between Kettering and Thrapston. On the opposite side of the same valley is the pre-Roman Iron Age farm site of Twywell with its corn storage pits and ditched stock enclosures.

In the landscape of the future it is possible that stock will disappear altogether from the fields. The practice of 'zero grazing' involves the animals living out their lives in yards and grass is carted to them and fed them on the concrete. It is said to double the grass output but so far has only been used on several smaller holdings in the county. At present many farmers believe that grazing animals regenerate land that has been arable for several years by putting back organic matter and by getting rid of the arable weeds such as wild oat. Some also, it is pleasing to record, look on hedges as useful barriers for stock control and for shelter, and regard themselves as responsible for maintaining the visual beauties of the countryside, seeing the continuation of hedges and hedgerow trees as vital for that purpose.

The expansion of towns
Northampton

The decision was taken in 1965 to promote the expansion of Northampton as a regional capital and to increase its population from 130,000 to 230,000 by the 1980s. It was realised that the master plan would have to free the expanded town of its rigid hierarchy of radial roads which we have noticed was the legacy of its ancient position as a route centre in the East Midlands. Two high-speed motorway standard roads were to be built to link the expanded town more effectively with the national network by relieving present roads of traffic and by distributing traffic north and south of the existing town. Transverse roads were to connect the high-speed roads with local distributors which were to provide access into the residential areas. Most of the land set aside for new housing lies between these two high-speed roads and the historian of the landscape can already make some assessment of the changes being brought about in the eastern district beyond Weston Favell.

The land form in this area is gently undulating and falls gradually towards the Nene valley which in this area is flanked by watermeadows, belts of willow and poplar and lakes formed in worked-out gravel pits. Below Abington Mill the Nene valley is being used as a controlled flood plain and a scheme has been prepared by the development authorities for control of storm water flow (which will result from the development of roads and housing) into Billing Brook by means of a series of shallow balancing ponds. The district is dissected by the Billing and Ecton Brooks, both well wooded and, as well as making water features of the brooks by a series of stepped ponds, it is planned to use the woodland belts as backcloths to development and as recreation areas. Small spinney and hedgerow trees of elm, oak, beech and ash will be retained to relieve the dreariness of brick and concrete. Six villages, Great and Little Billing, Great Houghton, Wootton, Hardingstone and Collingtree, all fall within the area of expansion, but the planners claim that they do not intend to destroy their individual identity. It is difficult to comprehend how villages can go on existing as such when gobbled up by

urban expansion involving 100,000 people. The many substantial stone-built farms in the area will be bought for
communal use and their names have been used to identify
future residential areas. What mars the plan is the prodigious
area, 3034 acres, which is thus being taken from agriculture
and public amenity, owing to the determination on the part
of developers to provide 'what the public requires' rather
than what the nation needs—which is a radical re-education
in the undesirability of spreading subtopia, however well
planned, across the rapidly shrinking rural landscape.[14] The
traditional pattern of detached, semi-detached or terraced
houses each with their own patch of garden is desired by
many—but the sight of neglected gardens on new estates
is an indication that horticulture is not universally liked,
whereas Georgian-type squares with high-density accommodation are.

Corby New Town

Well within living memory Corby was a small stone-built
village of Scandinavian origin centred round its thirteenth-
century church with a population of under 1600, largely
dependent on agriculture. In forty years it has been transformed into one of the major iron and steel producing
towns of Great Britain—one of the most remarkable
developments in the Northamptonshire landscape of the
twentieth century. Stewarts and Lloyds came into the area
in 1934 and sited their steelworks in the middle of the ironstone field to the north-east of the village so that prevailing
winds would take the fallout away from the settlement.
They built some 2200 houses for their workers who were
mostly drawn from Scotland. The layout of these houses
shows the influence of Barry Parker and Hampstead Garden

[14] *Planning Proposals for the eastern district of Northampton,* Northampton
Development Corporation (January 1971). Also Gordon Redfern, Lecture
to Kettering Civic Society, February 1972.

Suburb. These company houses were financed by building societies and were cheap jobs put up to the west of the village. Another momentous decision was to put executive houses out in Carlton Park; this pattern of separating the managers from the shop floor has been continued. It has produced in effect a single-class town with unfortunate consequences for public leadership and public order. House-building virtually ceased between 1939 and 1945 when the steelworks' main contribution to the war effort was the flexible pipeline under the ocean. These were years of tremendous pressures on inadequate housing. The town stood still. There were no shopping facilities to speak of, a lack of schools and other amenities, and until the building restrictions lifted, no house building. By 1950 the population was ten times the size of the 1931 census. In this year Corby New Town was designated under the New Towns Act of 1946 and the Corby Development Corporation was established to plan for all the developments required to make a worth-while town of 60,000 persons. This involved first of all the construction of the town centre *ab initio*, some three-quarters of a mile west of the old village which was hemmed in by the steelworks and consequently not able to provide an adequate nucleus to the town. Lord Holford designed this with its neo-Festival of Britain architecture; a disappointing feature is that a dual carriageway, Corporation Street, ploughs its way through the main shopping area.[15] Secondly they have encouraged much light industrial development to diversify the town's economic base, dangerously dominated by one industry, and to provide jobs for women.

Most interesting to the historian of the twentieth-century landscape is the distinctive way the residential accommodation has been treated. The original decision to locate the steelworks in the middle rather than on the edge of the

[15] To be fair, it is planned to close Corporation Street to traffic in the future.

ironstone bed was realised to be a mistake, because the town is now encircled by areas of quarrying, either previously worked, or in course of excavation for which planning approval has been granted. This has forced the residential expansion in a south-westerly direction away from the steelworks and it has restricted building. Residential areas which have already been finished, such as Kingswood and Danesholme, are surrounded by perimeter loops linked to high-speed roads from which vehicular cul-de-sacs radiate like fingers towards the centre. In the centre is an open space containing a primary school and recreation facilities and it is linked by 'greenways', part of a strategic footpath network, to the other four quarters of the residential area. This open space preserves woodlands on two of its edges and on the other two a hard urban edge comprising a high-density spine on which the communal facilities are placed. The motor car is allowed to approach, cautiously, up cul-de-sacs to the back of the spine, but the front approaches to Lincoln Way, for instance, are monopolised by the pedestrian who penetrates through archways, up stairways, piazzas and courtyards (Plate 36). The silhouette of the central spine is ingeniously varied in height and the eight main types of dwellings, varying in size from one-person flats to six-person maisonettes are skilfully permutated and interlocked, ensuring maximum privacy. There is as much variation as the simple and cheap materials—brick, weatherboarding, concrete slabs, and a brown facing brick, chosen for its affinity with the local stone—allow. Trees have been retained from the ancient field pattern wherever possible, and hundreds of semi-mature trees brought in by tractor and planted by the corporation have softened the raw appearance of the new estates.

This mechanised townscape is far removed from the first tentative moves towards planning seen in early medieval Brackley. Economic circumstances inhibited Brackley's growth, preventing it from ever growing into a flourishing

town. National economic policy restricting industrial investment already casts a shadow over Corby's future.[16]

Peterborough

The future of Peterborough is tied up with the fact that it
will expand from 85,000 (1970) to 185,000 by 1985, with
the additional population coming mostly from London's
overspill. A plan prepared by the Peterborough Development Corporation proposes to retain the historic centre
dominated by the cathedral as the nucleus of the expanded
Greater Peterborough.[17] If they chose to build up this
centre in the usual way it would devalue the city's one big
asset, its monumental cathedral. They propose, fortunately,
to keep the urban scale around the market place as it is and
to put bigger buildings a little further out. These will have
the double advantage of containing the existing historic
core and defining it in a way not possible before. At the
northern end of the shopping spine of Bridge Street and
Long Causeway, there will be Landgate, a large square on
the dividing line between inner Peterborough and the
dreary twilight area of Victorian industrial suburbs. To the
south, blocking a newly pedestrianised Bridge Street,
Rivergate will provide a high piazza over the multi-storey
car park from which the south face of the cathedral will be
seen. To the south-west a wall of offices or shops will
contain the professional precinct, mostly historic buildings
around Priestgate. The south-eastern approach, open at
present, will give way to a broad stretch of wooded parkland extending to the Nene and the fens beyond. The original
market place, now a maelstrom of traffic, will have its
surface lowered and perhaps will revert to its original use.

[16] John Stedman, Lecture to Kettering Civic Society, 1971. H. G. W.
Hamilton, *General Manager's Notes on Corby* (October 1971). *The Architects
Journal Information Library*, 6th, 13th November, 1968, pp. 1069–84, 1133–46.
[17] *Greater Peterborough City Centre Plan*, Peterborough Development
Corporation (1971).

It will be in the centre of a traffic-free north–south axis thickly planted with trees designed to contrast with the hard stone townscape of the market place suitably cowering before the massive stone bulk of the cathedral. This plan, if it is carried through, will give Peterborough a worthy visual setting for a great regional centre.

Daventry

A fourth town for which substantial expansion is planned, is in the west of the county. Daventry, as we have seen, originated as a medieval market centre and grew to a coaching town in the eighteenth century. It was then by-passed by the Grand Union Canal which came within a mile and a half of the town and the main railway line which passed through Weedon Bec and Long Buckby. In the motoring age, however, Daventry is well placed to take advantage of its accessibility to two major routes, the M1 motorway, three miles away, with access points to north and south of the town, and the trunk road, A5. Its population in 1948 was just under 4000. This began to grow in the 1950s with the establishment of a tapered roller bearing factory by British Timken Ltd., but it was the decision taken in 1963 by the City of Birmingham and the Northamptonshire County Council to provide for the expansion of the town to a total population of about 36,000 people within the next ten years that produced the rapid urban growth we are witnessing now.

The older part of the town stands on a low, flat-topped spur between the valleys of two streams and these have been dammed to form two reservoirs for the Grand Union Canal. There are low hills to the south, east and west, enclosing the town visually and physically. Within this context, which incidentally is all first-class agricultural land, it is proposed to expand the town.

The old centre is well situated to serve the new town and

the idea is to keep groups of buildings of particular architectural or historic interest to attempt to preserve the existing character and scale of the town. The whole of the existing main shopping area in the High Street will be retained, and turned into a pedestrian precinct; its character is considerable and is enhanced by an excellent street-improvement scheme which is a shining example to the other towns in the county. Several important buildings like Holy Cross church, the Congregational and Catholic churches, moot hall and police station have a guaranteed continuing existence. It is this willingness to integrate old with new that is Daventry's strength. Imaginative surgery rather than insensitive demolition produces a town centre attuned to human needs and the quality of life.

The centre is linked by walkways to residential areas and by an internal vehicular circulation with convenient accesses to principal roads. These are designed to cope with twice-daily peak flows of home-work traffic. They take the towns-folk of Daventry back into the housing areas which, like those at Corby, are planned on a cellular basis, permitting large units of residential and industrial land to be developed without being cut up by major traffic roads. One feature of the Daventry townscape is perhaps unfortunate. Normally in new and expanding towns the proportion of service to manufacturing employment is a third to two-thirds. The purchase of a large area of industrial land by the Ford Motor Company for use as a distribution centre for spares has led to an adjustment of this to fifty-fifty by 1981. This means that more agricultural land is being used for indus-trial purposes, for service employment is calculated at a lower density of nineteen per acre; whereas for manufactur-ing employment, forty per acre.[18]

[18] *Daventry Town map, written analysis,* Northamptonshire County Council (January 1967). Daventry Master Plan: Daventry Supplement, *The Birmingham Post,* 21st October, 1969, 11th November, 1970.

Wellingborough

It is more difficult to envisage what will happen to this town in the next twenty years because I am writing this a month before a detailed report is due to be published, with only a copy of the revised Town Map (February 1972) in front of me. As we have seen, an agreement was made in 1962 between Wellingborough Urban District Council and the Greater London Council for the transfer of industry and population from the London area to Wellingborough. It is estimated that the town will grow from its present population of about 38,000 persons to some 60,000 by 1981 and 83,000 by 1991. The map shows the enlarged town spreading both to the east and west of the river Ise, swallowing up the small district centre of Finedon. It seems that the surrounding villages of Great Doddington, Wilby, Irchester and Great Harrowden will survive, however precariously, on the urban edge. The existing valley will be utilised for walkways, playing fields and general amenity but about 1000 acres, mostly good agricultural land, will be handed over to industry.

The pressures of this scale of development on the centre of the town will be enormous. We are told that around one million square feet of floor space for shops, offices and other town centre uses, together with car-parking for between 4000 and 5000 cars, will be required. It is envisaged ultimately to pedestrianise the town centre and "to retain groups of buildings of particular architectural and historic interest and as far as possible to preserve the existing character of the town". Wellingborough at present preserves a considerable number of buildings listed as of architectural and historic importance. Surely the splendid architectural talents at the beck and call of the Greater London Council, allied to strong local pride in the historical character of the town, will produce some really brilliant solutions to central town development. Experience,

Fig. 21. Landscape protection and conservation in Northamptonshire. Seven areas (A–G) are considered most vulnerable to new development and worthy of protection Place names are conservation areas.

A. *The Aynho area* Undulating countryside, extensive tree and hedge cover. The limit to the east is determined by a relatively featureless plain and to the west by the Cherwell valley. The church spire of King's Sutton and the villages of Charlton and Aynho enhance this area.

B. *The Hemplow Hills, Cottesbrooke and Brington area* Prominent features in the area north-west of the county town are the Hemplow Hills rising from the plain which extends into Warwickshire and Leicestershire. Extensive views can be obtained, especially from Honey

however, from the neighbouring towns of Northampton and Kettering shows that this will not be enough. Only determined groups of citizens, in touch with the grass roots of public opinion, articulate and well-informed about planning and architectural matters, organised in amenity societies and willing in the last resort to take up the cudgels with officialdom and pay for their own expert advice, can hope to afford historical buildings of character, some protection against the rampant commercial interests which flourish in the hot bed of central town developments.

The future landscape

The population of Northamptonshire and the County Borough will rise from 468,000 in 1971 to about 800,000 within the next twenty years. Development on such a scale demands planning of a high order if we are to avoid the

---

Hill. The Cottesbrooke and Creaton area has undulating countryside with good tree and hedgerow cover. Striking features are Ravensthorpe and Hollowell Reservoirs and Cottesbrooke Park. Further south the parklands of Brockhall and Althorp.

C. *The Catesby and Fawsley area* Well-treed rolling upland with a parkland quality. Fawsley Park and Badby Wood are the focal points. The Catesby area has strongly domed hills giving long views of low-relief countryside.

D. *The Eydon and Culworth area* Well-treed, attractive views across both Northamptonshire and neighbouring counties. Boddington canal reservoir and valley form a landscape attraction.

E. *Rockingham forest and lower Nene valley* Many areas of woodland and attractive villages. Scarcity of tree cover on flood plain. Church spires are visible from sides and floor of valley. Good views from Titchmarsh, Wadenhoe and Warmington.

F. *The Welland valley* Tree cover is extensive round Market Harborough but sparse in the Rockingham–Harringworth area, thus emphasising the striking topography of the valley. Villages in the area have retained their historic character and enhance the landscape.

G. *The Whittlewood and Hazelborough forest area* This area extends into Buckinghamshire where its woodland and parkland form a backdrop for one of the landscape priority areas of that county.

deplorable misuse of our natural resources which led to many of the ugly and wasteful features in Victorian and early-twentieth-century landscapes. Pressure upon the countryside for urbanisation and for the provision of utility services which population growth demands has led the County Council to mount a study to identify the more attractive areas of the countryside, in order to formulate a policy recommending protection and conservation for these special areas. The criteria used for determining which areas had the 'best' landscape included appreciable changes in contour levels, interesting land forms, good tree and hedgerow cover, areas with no visual intrusions such as electricity transmission lines or modern development not conforming to the historic characteristics of towns and villages, and well-maintained land, buildings or other features. Those considered worthy of special protection included rolling valley sides with continuous, or at least intermittent, good views and good tree cover, small ill-defined valleys and small strongly domed hills. A base grid of kilometre squares was selected to map these and by plotting the squares of highest landscape value several areas appeared as suitable for further consideration in terms of special protection and conservation (Fig. 21).[19]

One of the most significant effects of the virtual doubling of the population in the next twenty years will be the demand for recreational facilities and this, as much as urbanisation, will put added strains on the countryside. The County Council, under the provisions of the Countryside Act, 1968, have opened two country parks at Barnwell and Irchester. The Barnwell picnic park of thirty acres is in a former gravel quarry, while the Irchester country park is 200 acres of old ironstone workings, much of which are covered by established conifers on the hill and dale formation. Both claim to be centres for the study of wildlife but it is difficult

[19] *Landscape Protection and Conservation in Northamptonshire*, County Planning Office (1972) from which Fig. 21 is drawn.

to imagine that there will be much non-human wildlife left to study once they are well established in the public mind as a centre for recreation. Detailed studies of the canals, the Nene valley, lakes, reservoirs and gravel pits, woodlands, disused railways, are being undertaken so that further recreational proposals may be considered.

It will be clear from this book that most of the pleasure I derive from the landscape arises from the dimension that a study of local history gives to it. In the last resort, however, my judgment is a more subjective one—the distillation of a thousand days spent enjoyably in the open air in the company of family and good friends. What would I wish old George Clarke of Scaldwell to paint if he were vouchsafed a second term? What would still delight John Clare's all-seeing eye? Walking in the fog through sopping waist-high decayed grasses across Broughton Common on a December day, a route first fashioned by prehistoric men three millennia before. Climbing the steep slopes of Arbury Hill on an autumn afternoon, following the irregular line of hedgerow of an Anglo-Saxon estate boundary, spilling over with ripe blackberries, bilberries and crab apples; and at the top, a succession of green and blue valleys, criss-crossed with hedge lines and little blobs of trees as in a Flemish landscape. The shouts of the excavators over the golden wheat fields of Lyveden as they make a new find, grovelling in the earth that hides a village, deserted four hundred years ago. The warm orange glowing walls of the thatched cottages of the village of Rockingham which line the steeply falling street leading to the lush meadows of the Welland valley. One's headlamps picking up the arching trees while driving back from supper at Wadenhoe; mist rising from the damp meadows on either side of the causewayed road which leads across the Nene. Walking along the silent banks of the Nene between Cotterstock and Perio; a perfect reflection of the great trees of high summer in the brimming waters of the river. The pale fretwork chimneys and mullions of Tresham's great house at Rushton seen between the blue blur of skeletal trees and rising from snow-covered fields. The magical incandescence of the blast furnaces of Corby lighting the blackened landscape with an unearthly red glow. The long grey shape of Peterborough Cathedral seen from a distance, with the astonishing series of pinnacles, pediments, towers and turrets of its mighty west front etched against a lowering sky . . . Northamptonshire and the Soke means to me all these fragments of memory, and more.

Index

rivers *cont.*—
Thames, 26; Harpers Brook, 28, 124;
Ise, 28, 37, 55, 56, 61, 63, 68, 113, 305;
Willow Brook, 28; Tove, 29, 31, 48,
99
Roade, 217
roads; Roman, 41, 45; Watling Street,
41, 57, 255; Banbury Lane, 57; Port-
way, 57; green roads, 94; Anglo-
Saxon, 130; medieval, 131; enclosure,
235–6; turnpike, 236, 250; drove,
247–9; modern, 298
Robin Hood, 136
Robinson, Rev. William, 251
Rockingham, 29, 37, 59; Castle, 115,
181–2; Park, 177; enclosure, 231
Rockingham forest, 101, 226, 232, 285
Rollright Stones, 248
Rothersthorpe, 218, 263
Rothwell, place-name, 58; field, 104;
salters, 131; poaching at, 180; market
house, 205; open fields, 230; horse-
racing at, 243; Victorian, 275
Rous, John, 193
Royal Commission on Historical Monu-
ments, 32
Rugby, 293
Rushden, 133; Victorian, 275–6
Rushton, enclosure, 188–90; Win-
stanley's drawing, 204; Hall, 205;
triangular, lodge, 205

St Joseph, Dr J. K., 30, 69, 160*fn*, 163
Salcey forest, 196, 226, 285
Salisbury, Earl of, 197
salt roads, 83, 131, 137
Sanders Gorse, 245
Saxton, Christopher, 25, 208, 210
Scaldwell, 68, 218
schools, 219–21; Oundle, 158–9; Kettering, 221; Peterborough, 279
Seabourne, M. V. J., 216, 217
sheep, Roman, 50; Anglo-Saxon, 73;
medieval, 123, 170–1, 174, 179;
Tudor, 184–5, 186–7, 189, 190–1,
193, 197; eighteenth century, 229
shire, the origin of Northamptonshire,
85
shoe industry, 156, 267–8, 269, 275
Shutlanger, house, 214; name, 253*fn*
Sibbertoft, 69, 116; enclosure, 227–8
Silverstone, hunting lodge, 103, 132;
fishpond, 119; motor racing circuit,
120, 284
slates, Collyweston, 180–1, 296, 232
Slipton, 81
Smithfield Market, London, 249
Snapes Wood, 179
Southam, 247

Southwick, 64; hall, 117
Speed, John, 65, 209
Spencer family, 185, 187, 202–3, 211,
251, 269, 285
Spencer, Sir John, 187, 211
spires, medieval, 126–7
Spratton, Norman church, 125; cob
cottage, 218; farm at, 249
Stafford, Sir Humphrey, 201
Stamford, 25, 29, 32, 35, 38, 49, 55, 65,
71, 86, 103, 104, 135; pottery, 111, 139,
166; origins of, 138–9; mint, 139;
churches, 139–40; cloth market, 170;
cattle from, 251; iron ore quarry, 288
Stamford Hall, 246
staunches, 257–8
Steane, deserted medieval village, place-
name, 78; house, 202; chapel, 205
Stewarts & Lloyds, Corby, 299
Stephenson, George and Robert, 240,
264, 266, 268
Stony Stratford, 130
Stoke Bruerne, 264
Stowe Nine Churches, cross, 78; land
charter, 97
Strafford, 2nd Earl of, 246
Strixton, deserted medieval village, 92;
mill, 114
Stuckbury, deserted medieval village,
72, 95, 165, 248
Sudborough, cemeteries, 55; forest, 105
Sulby, deserted medieval village, 122,
163
Sulgrave, Saxon Hall, 79; ringwork,
115–16; field, 248
Syresham, 73; forest village, 98, 232,
235, 248
Sywell, 224; lodge farm, 240

Tallington, 38
Tansor, 64, 79
Tate, W., *Inclosure Movements in North-
amptonshire*, 230
Telford, Thomas, 255
temples, heathen, 56, 86
thatching, 296
Theodore of Tarsus, 76
Thornhaugh, 31
Thorpe Achurch, 78, 86
Thorpe Malsor, 55
Thorpe Mandeville, 248
Thorpe Waterville, 125
Thrapston, 33, 37; boundary stone, 47;
name, 56; site, 58; roads, 133, 253;
bridge, 135; Nene navigation at, 257;
lakes, 291
Thrupp, deserted medieval village, 174
Thurning, 72
Tillemans, Peter, 174, 222, 226

Wythemail, deserted medieval village,
64, 166–7, 168, 171

Yardley Gobion, 232
Yardley Hastings, 118
Yardley Wharf, 264
Yarwell, 232

Yaxley, 57
Yelvertoft, 131
York, 52
Young, Arthur, 223, 233

zero grazing, 297

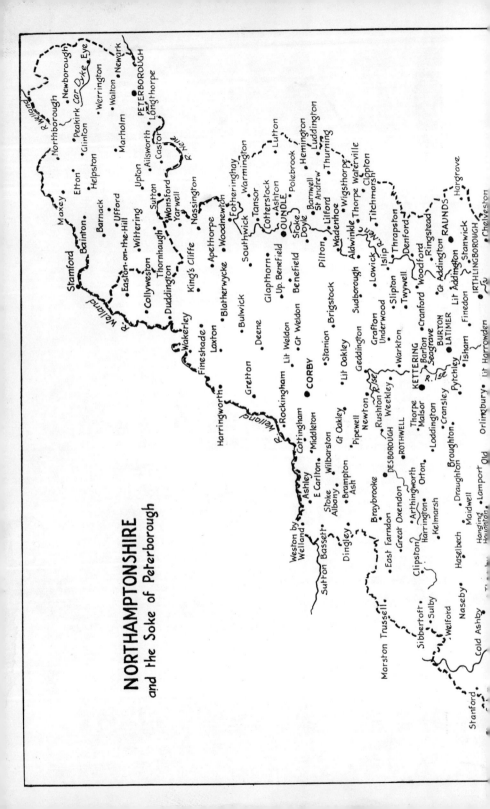

NORTHAMPTONSHIRE
and the Soke of Peterborough